ROCKING THE CRADLE

THOUGHTS ON FEMINISM, MOTHERHOOD AND THE POSSIBILITY OF EMPOWERED MOTHERING

2006

Published by:
Demeter Press
c/o Association for Research on Mothering
726 Atkinson College, York University
4700 Keele Street
Toronto, Ontario M3J 1P3
Telephone: (416) 736-2100 x 60366
Email: arm@yorku.ca Web site: www.yorku.ca/crm

Printed and Bound in Canada
by AGMV Printers

Interior Design: Luciana Ricciutelli
Cover Design: Renée Knapp
Photo of cradle: Courtesy of Gina and Iris Wong Wylie

Library and Archives Canada Cataloguing in Publication

O'Reilly, Andrea, 1961-

Rocking the cradle : thoughts on feminism, motherhood and the possibility of empowered mothering / by Andrea O'Reilly

Includes bibliographical references

ISBN 1-55014-449-9

1. Motherhood. 2. Feminism. I. Title.

HQ759.O65 2006   306.874'3
C2006-900884-1

ROCKING THE CRADLE

THOUGHTS ON FEMINISM, MOTHERHOOD AND THE POSSIBILITY OF EMPOWERED MOTHERING

Andrea O'Reilly

DEMETER PRESS
TORONTO, ONTARIO

CONTENTS

ACKNOWLEDGEMENTS

It is often said that "It takes a village to raise a child." I would suggest likewise "that it takes a village to write a book." An author, like mothers everywhere, soon comes to realize that she requires a caring community of othermothers to "raise" a book well. Fortunately, I have been blessed with such kin. Thank you to Randy Chase who, as always, proofed the manuscript with care and skill. My deepest appreciation to "my fairy godmother," Luciana Ricciutelli, who, once again, waved her wand and transformed my pumpkin manuscript into a book Special thanks to Renée Knapp for restoring my faith and keeping me from despair. I am deeply grateful to Sara Ruddick for giving us a vision of empowered mothering in her book, *Maternal Thinking*, and for championing me as I struggled to create my own. Thank you also to the members of the Association for Research on Mothering, in particular Marie Porter, Fiona Green, Judith Stadtman Tucker and Petra Büskens. My thinking on mothering was enriched and sustained by this splendid community of scholars. And, finally, my deepest appreciation to my children, Jesse, Erin and Casey, and, to my spouse Terry Conlin. Thank you, to paraphrase Erma Bombeck, "for loving me the most, when I deserved it the least."

PREFACE

GOOD QUESTION ... I'LL BE WRITING ON THIS

In *Rocking the Cradle* Andrea O'Reilly gathers together eleven essays written in a distinctive voice and organized by a dominant aim: to undermine, or less politely destroy or "smash," patriarchal motherhood while empowering in its stead women engaged in the practice of mothering. Motherhood is an identity or social role imposed on mothers. Motherhood—to take one of Andrea's examples —is defined in North America by the demand that a "good mother" be a heterosexual wife. Instead of motherhood, which is a social identity and role, Andrea imagines an activity or practice of mothering which can empower the women who engage in it.

Andrea often cites Adrienne Rich who, more than anyone else, is the mother that she "thinks back through."[1] "We know more about the air we breathe, the seas we travel, than about the nature and meaning of motherhood," Rich has taught her. The essays O'Reilly has selected from her writings represent her attempt made over fifteen years to remedy our ignorance. Astonishing energy flows from keyboard and classroom as she writes, then organizes, then writes again.

Andrea was 22 when she began her studies of women's literature. She had ahead of her an honors thesis to write, job to be acquired and kept, a "tenure track" to run on, a Ph.D. dissertation to begin, continue and finish, and then a tenured and promoted position to secure. After a tumultuous pregnancy, childbirth and labour, she also had an infant to care for. This infant was followed by a second and then a third. None were "planned." All had the same father, a spouse who is a somewhat obscure but responsible and benign presence between the lines of O'Reilly's story.

Each of Andrea's babies singly, and all of them collectively as "children," made it unnecessarily difficult for their mother to do her work as a graduate student, teacher or writer. Readers should now turn to Chapter Three on mothering in academe in order to get a sense of the scrappy fighting narrator who is speaking to them throughout this collection as well as getting some inkling of the outrageous treatment of mothers in graduate school only ten to fifteen years ago.

Andrea O'Reilly wrote her first article on mothering and taught her first course on motherhood in 1990 when she was 29. The youngest of her three children was then only ten months old; at least metaphorically Andrea was still rocking the cradle. From 1990 to 2005, from her first to her final essay in *Rocking the Cradle*, she speaks as a mother, a student of mothering, and an organizer on behalf of women who mother. As a teacher she invented a course on motherhood that feminists and mothers needed. She had to invent the course because, even in Women's Studies, there were no feminist courses that focused on mothering and motherhood.

When it seemed to Andrea that "maternal scholars" who studied motherhood did not have the intellectual community which lively scholarship requires, she founded an Association for Research on Mothering (ARM). When maternal scholars seemed to lack public spaces in which to write and talk with each other, she began to organize conferences and then to publish the *Journal of the Association for Research on Mothering*. She has now edited several collections of papers on topics that call for maternal, scholarly attention.

Today—the winter of 2006—Andrea O'Reilly continues to write, teach, organize and edit. Her account of her current life is sprinkled with future plans—calls for papers, conference invitations, forthcoming books, even tours. She now adds to these many activities a publishing venture: *Rocking the Cradle* will be the first book to be issued by Demeter Press, founded by O'Reilly and her colleagues to publish works on mothering and motherhood. *Rocking the Cradle* is their first book. It will be followed by a book on Aboriginal mothering and then by a book on mothering and poetry called *White Ink*.

ARM and its various public ventures are meant to be "inclusive" in at least two familiar senses of that term. ARM hopes to bring together "scholars, writers, activists, professionals, agencies, policy makers, parents and artists." Their association will include *all* mothers, First Nations, immigrant, refugee mothers, working class, lesbian, mothers with disabilities, mothers of colours.

We, feminists, know after several decades of many trials and even more errors that real connections between scholar and activist, policy maker and artist are slowly and imperfectly formed. Strong personal associations or political coalitions that do not wash out or assimilate difference are hard won. Nonetheless, the *ideal* of scholar-mothers connected in and to the world, respectful of differences among each other, informs the policies of ARM and the language of its self-evaluation.

A few weeks ago, when I felt nearly overwhelmed by O'Reilly's energy and puzzled by her ability to produce so widely conferences, books, journals, and interviews, I wrote asking her how she had made ARM and all it stood for happen.

> *In 1990 you wrote the first paper in your book. How did you move from an individual paper writer to someone who held a conference (1997), formed an organization (1998), started a journal and held numerous events? Did you have friends, connections? Are you extremely social? Who else was involved? Just anything that lets me know how it happened.*

In reply Andrea spoke of her passionate conviction and optimism:

> *Yes, I am social, but more than that, I am passionate about my beliefs … and have always gone by gut and vision. If something needs to be done, you go out and make it happen, and worry about the details later.*

Then she spoke with characteristic passion of "wonderful, wonderful other mothers" among her early mentors and then among women on her staff who made things happen.

The cover of *Rocking the Cradle*, with its block print and warm colour, invites participation. Newcomers can see where they might enter, question and participate. The ARM web site is strongly printed, its phone, fax, e-mail and address available. "Andrea O'Reilly" is in clear mid-size print, neither evasive nor overwhelming. Thoughts belong as much to the mobile-like title gently arched above as to the author named below. The back lit crib/cradle is still and empty, a dream place waiting for a mother's dreams, nightmares, and then as her relationship develops, a child . DEMETER PRESS spelled out across the top is a reminder that ARM is in public and determined to stay there, and we who hold the book in our hands are welcome to visit.

I am reminded of a line taken from a breathless note Andrea wrote in haste as she was getting ready to go to Denmark to meet her son.

> *"How it all happened? Good question … I will be writing on this."*

Good Question—she recognizes the questioner. Hears what is asked of her, then promises "I will write about this…."; the promise of women down the ages who use writing as a tool of combat against despair, against the brutalizing of vulnerable people, against those who brutalize them.

I have rarely played an active part in ARM yet I have become used to its presence. When I am preoccupied by an issue related to motherhood I scan the Calls for Papers, imagining a venue in which I can explore my preoccupying concern. Just now, for example, when poetry is my daily and necessary fare, I am tempted to ask about the forthcoming *White Ink*. Last summer I tried and failed to write for the grandmother issue. Now I will read it with special interest.

In the late '90s, as the decade of Rwanda and Sarajevo (to use two charged names) drew to a close, I needed to explain to myself more than to others, the connections I had once made between mothering and non-violence. I took advantage of ARM's journal issue on "Mothering, Fathering and a Culture of Peace" to try to recover (or abandon) the idea of a "feminist maternal peace politics." I slipped in and out of autobiography, abided by or ignored disciplinary customs, even did a bit of research. My research subjects were about a dozen children ranging from the ages of four months to eleven years and their parents. The group included my two children and four grandchildren. I proceeded by letting questions spin in my head, then hovered like a hawk over any hint of familial combat, re-read some literature of non-violence, especially Martin Luther King, and finally invented and recognized connections between "parenting and peace" and sent my article across the border to Canada.

A few days later the Trade Towers were attacked. About a week later the copy-edited typescript was returned looking entirely inappropriate, meager, and silly. I tried to pull back, to pull out, even made some nasty crack about the copy-editing. It was then that I met Luciana Ricciutelli who I believe had copy-edited my essay and was in any case assigned the job of calming me down and keeping my article, for which space was already allotted, in place. But I was caught in a knot. I had to write after an attack but before the bombing I was certain would follow; I had to recognize the terror and loss the U.S. had suffered and, so I feared, the terror and loss its government would soon be inflicting.

I believe Luciana and I spoke only once directly, then e-mailed many times. I later thanked her for patience, reassurance and editorial skill amidst computer failures, miscommunication and fears of war. With Luciana's help I wrote a "prescript" drawing together stricken children, passionate parents, and what we now recognize as "suicide missions." I remember Luciana saying, with no discernable impatience, "the paper is okay. Let it go." These were words strong enough to remind me that in every crisis I become obsessed with my own sentences; and that, south of the Canadian border, I was still an American of the bombing classes, whose world was always contracting to my doorstep. Together we searched for an ending, and settled with lines from Neruda: "Now I'll count up to twelve/and you keep quiet and I will go."

In working with Luciana I had in effect taken up the invitation implicit in the cover of *Rocking the Cradle*. I called, e-mailed, phoned, and then, by accepting the help I was given, made my way to words rather than settling for silence.

Now, five years later, I am writing this preface because I told Andrea that I was troubled by the way she and other feminists talked about "intensive mothering" as a form of patriarchal motherhood. Where she saw feminist critique I saw a new kind of mother blaming. I worried too about just whose mother or whose customs she would indict as patriarchal. Andrea, too, has been troubled; she is revising her remarks on feminism; attending particularly, as is her wont, to customs and politics of women of colour, especially African-American mothers. She said, "Let's talk"—and followed with a proposal for arranging a conversation online.

This morning, in speaking with friends, I twice referred to this preface as something I must finish "for the kids in Toronto." Why, one friend asked, do I speak of "the kids" when referring to a woman now turning 45? I am an "old woman" as one grandchild frankly remarked. I am conscious of age and like to believe that I respectfully respond to the age consciousness of others.

Andrea speaks at the beginning of her book about her age and the age of her children. The "children"— 21, 19, 16—are now adults who can "drive, drink, vote, quit school and have sex." As she writes her youngest child plays a guitar below her, strumming a lyric of lament for the frustrations of being a virgin. Her oldest child is traveling in Denmark where Andrea will visit him for a brief trip together. Andrea is poignantly aware of her distance from mothers who mark their children's age in months rather than years, and who are kept awake by the wail of a teething infant, while she is alerted to the sound of a clock that reminds her of the hours passing with her children still not home.

Andrea usually speaks in the cadences of "linear time"—"time as project, teleology, departure, progression and arrival." Now she is speaking in the voice of "Mother Time"[2] which is marked by a "double focus" on the passing particular—a child not yet home, a lunch box to prepare— and on the moment where time stands still, revealing a precious singular life that seems eternal even as it arises through the passing of generations and is subject to the permanent possibility of loss. I picture this Andrea on the deck of a ship with her son and her mother embracing each other and the beauty they travel in.

I met Andrea only once in a packed classroom at her first conference on mother-daughter relationships. She was then 35, a bit older than my first child. She was cool, poised, and in no way invited "motherly" feelings toward herself and her projects. As Andrea approaches 45, I have turned 71. Reading this book has given me far more pleasure, more life, than I anticipated. When I speak fondly of Andrea and her staff at ARM as the "kids from Toronto," I recognize a gift that has traveled across boundaries of age and nation.

We attend often to what women need from "mothers" and "mentors"; attend too little perhaps to what we who are old need from "daughters" who create and preserve what we care for and care about, whose energy and sheer determination carry us on.

I have chosen to end by alluding to a story of crude male violence; you can read it more fully at the end of Andrea's preface. Andrea is a fighter; I want to remember the world that she fights. The target of violence, like so many abused and violated women, had occupied male space, in particular a pit tacitly reserved for males at an all age punk concert. The protagonist of this particular story is Andrea's older daughter who was beat up, along with her younger sister who was trying to protect her. When they return home they find over a hundred messages on the punk web site cheering on the violence that they have just suffered.

How did it happen? Good question. I'll be writing on this.

—*Sara Ruddick*, March 15, 2006

Sara Ruddick lives in New York City where for many years she taught at New School University, especially at Eugene Lang College. She is the author of Maternal Thinking: Toward a Politics of Peace *and co-editor, with Julia Hanigsberg, of* Mother Troubles: Reflections on Contemporary Maternal Dilemmas. *She is currently co-editing with Joan Callahan and Bonnie Mann a special issue of* Hypatia *entitled "Against Heterosexualism." She hopes soon to complete a monograph now entitled, "The Terror of Terrorism."*

[1]Virginia Woolf: "We think back through our mothers if we are women" from *A Room of One's Own*. In addition to Adrienne Rich, especially *Of Woman Born*, Andrea draws on women of colour, especially African-American literature and especially of Toni Morrison, to discover new ideas of mothering and to test her own. But her bibliography is extensive and extending and knows no bounds.

[2]I am drawing upon Julia Kristeva's well-known contrast in "Women's Time." I substitute the Margaret Urban Walker's *Mother Time* to suggest that certain conceptions of time might arise from practices of mothering for women and men. "Double focus" (from *Maternal Thinking*) would be such a conception.

FOREWORD

ROCKING THE CRADLE TO CHANGE THE WORLD

Last year we celebrated a milestone birthday for all three of our children—Jesse, our son, turned 21, the age of adulthood; Erin, our eldest daughter, turned 19, the age you can legally drink in our province; and our youngest, Casey, turned 16, the age in which children are no longer regarded as minors and are able to drive. This month I turn 45, and while not a momentous birthday as 40 and 50 are, it does decisively define me as middle-age. That I am this age and that my children can now drive, drink, vote, quit school, and have sex (to mention only a few of the markers of adulthood) astounds and astonishes me. It *was* just yesterday that our eldest strong-willed daughter, after crawling well past her first year, did finally agree to the whole business of walking, and our timid son, after changing schools in grade three, was able to finally settle in and meet friends. Today that same shy son is thousands of miles away, taking his third year of university in Denmark, and that headstrong daughter has decided against university so she can travel west and join a punk band. And my baby, as I write this foreword, sits downstairs strumming her guitar listening to Guns-N-Roses and Courtney Love, writing lyrics on, and I quote, "the frustrations about being a virgin." That I am an older mother of adult children was made painfully evident to me two weeks ago as I sat waiting in an obstetrician's office (whom I was seeing for my quite debilitating perimenopause—itself a marker of waning fertility). Two women began talking—one holding a newborn and the other looking to be about seven months pregnant. A third woman joined in the conversation and inquired on the age of the newborn and the expected due date of the pregnant woman. After asking her questions, she said that she too was a mother of a 21-month-old son. In the fleeting moment between the word 21 and the word month, I felt I was, or could be, a part of this age-old motherhood conversation. But at the word month I suffered an acute sensation of disconnection or disengagement, or what sociologists would term cognitive dissonance. My son, after all, is 21 *years* old and the last time I saw him was five months ago when he turned back for one last wave as he passed through the security gates at the airport. What do I have in common with these women who have only just begun the journey of motherhood while mine is nearing its completion? What could I have said that would have enabled me to join in on a conversation about the sleepless nights of early motherhood when what keeps me awake is not the cry of a teething infant but the sound of a clock marking the hours my daughter has not yet returned home? And while I know that I will always be a mother and that my mothering will continue well into my children's adult years replete with many more motherhood challenges, I did feel, in that moment, more allied with the older professional woman in the waiting room who was busy consulting with clients on her cell phone than I did with those new mothers who seemed unabashedly hopeful in the promise of new motherhood.

I tell this story because it serves as an appropriate way to open this volume *Rocking the Cradle*: a collection of essays on motherhood and mothering written over the last 15 years. In *Of Woman Born*, Adrienne Rich writes, "I could not begin to think of writing a book on motherhood until I began to feel strong enough, and unambivalent enough in my love for my children, so that I could dare to return to a ground which seemed to me the most painful, incomprehensible, and ambiguous I ever travelled" (15). With my children nearly grown, and having fully emerged from what Marni Jackson calls the mother zone—"the hole in culture where mothers go" (3) I feel, as did Rich, that the time is right for a collection of my essays on motherhood to be published, particularly as this volume is the first book published by Demeter Press, a press I founded to publish works on motherhood. The articles republished for this collection were written between 1990 and 2005. The first essay was written in 1990 when my children were ten months, three and five years of age, while the last was written in 2005 when my children were 21, 18 and 16. I began writing on motherhood in a serious and sustained way when my youngest was not yet one and I completed the last essay in this collection the week of that child's sixteenth birthday. During this time, 1990-2005, I completed my Ph.D., secured a tenure-track job and acquired tenure and promotion. In those 15 years, as I raised my children and advanced in my career, I thought of little else. From my first graduate paper to my most recent book, I was consumed and absorbed by the topic of motherhood.

The collection, while it does not contain all of my work on motherhood, does, I think, provide a useful overview of the salient and compelling motherhood issues as I saw them over the last 15 years. To be sure, this volume does not purport to be representative of all that has been said or could be said on the subject matter. Rather, this collection is to be read simply as an individual account of the subject matter by someone who has spent a great deal of time thinking about motherhood as a writer, scholar, researcher, teacher, director, publisher, and mother over these last 15 years. More specifically, the aim of this volume is to introduce readers to, what most agree, is the central issue in motherhood studies today: namely the study of the oppressive and the empowering aspects of maternity, and the complex relationship between the two. While feminist research on motherhood has focused on many topics over the last 15 years—work, family, sexuality, cultural differences, public policy, images of motherhood, to name but a few—these studies and reflections have been informed and shaped by larger questions: namely, how do we challenge patriarchal motherhood? How do we create feminist mothering? And finally, how are the two aims interconnected?[1] This volume will explore these central questions by way of a section on motherhood and another on mothering. The first section is concerned with identifying, interrupting, and deconstructing the patriarchal discourse of motherhood while the second examines the formulation and articulation of a counter maternal narrative, one that redefines mothering as an empowered and empowering practice.

These 15 years were book-ended and punctuated by three noteworthy events. The year I wrote my first article on motherhood, 1990, was also the year I began designing Canada's first university course on motherhood, described in the second chapter of this volume. When I became a mother unexpectedly at the age of 23, I reflected back on all the courses I'd taken and realized I'd never had a single course in which motherhood was discussed in a thorough way—and this was in coursework leading to a degree in Women's Studies. To fill the gap, I developed a course on motherhood—the first course on motherhood and mothering in Canada. I opened this article with Adrienne Rich's oft-cited quote: "We know more about the air we breathe, the seas we travel, than about the nature and meaning of motherhood" (11). I designed this course as a correction to the silencing of motherhood in academe. As I note in this chapter, as late as 1991, York University, with two large and successful Women's Studies programs and a student population of more than 40,000, did not offer a single course on the subject of motherhood. This course on motherhood designed in 1990, at the inception of my career as a feminist scholar on motherhood, anticipates the third significant event, namely the launching of Demeter Press in 2005, the year I began working on this collection of essays. *Rocking the Cradle* is being published to celebrate and commemorate the launch of Demeter Press by the *Association for Research on Mothering*, the research centre on Motherhood I founded and now direct. Demeter Press will publish books on and about motherhood, the first and only scholarly press to do so. Demeter Press serves as an appropriate bookend for my intellectual journey through motherhood over these last 15 years. Both the course and the press, established at the beginning and end, respectively, of this intellectual journey, share the same mission and mandate: to make feminist scholarship on motherhood more visible and accessible inside and outside the academe.

As my inquiry is framed by these two incidents, it is likewise demarcated by another significant event that occurred exactly at the midway point of these fifteen years. In 1998, I established the *Association for Research on Mothering* and in early 1999, its journal, the *Journal of the Association for Research on Mothering*. ARM is the first and still only research association on the topic of Motherhood-Mothering. Now in its eighth year ARM has 500-plus members from more than a dozen countries and its journal will see the publication of its sixteenth issue this year. Similar to my reasons for designing a university course on motherhood and later launching a press on Motherhood, I established ARM because, as recent as 1998, the topic of motherhood remained, in many academic disciplines, at the margins of scholarly inquiry. Discussions with professors across Canada and the United States revealed to me that scant attention has been paid to motherhood in Women's Studies classrooms or at feminist conferences. Motherhood, compared to topics such as work, sexuality, violence or images of women, remained marginal to the feminist inquiry. Many maternal scholars can recall and recount an instance where their motherhood research was viewed with suspicion, if not outright dismissal. Real academics don't do motherhood (either in research or in life); at least not ones who seek a "real" tenured job. ARM was formed to promote, showcase, and make visible maternal scholarship and to accord legitimacy to this academic field. Most importantly, ARM was established to provide a community for like-minded scholars who research and work in the area of motherhood. Scholarship, both at the university and community level, as we all know, is enriched by dialogue and debate, broadened through knowledge/resources sharing and sustained by a sense of belonging. ARM's mandate is to simultaneously build a community of maternal scholars—academic and grassroots—and to promote maternal scholarship. ARM was formed in the hope of creating a maternal community that Sara Ruddick, among others, has argued is essential, in this instance, for the well-being of maternal scholarship. As Virginia Wolfe recognized the need for women writers to have "a room of one's own," I believe that feminist scholars of motherhood, likewise, need an association to call our own. To this end, ARM and its journal were instituted.

My thinking on motherhood over the last 15 years simultaneously initiated these three events and was influenced by them. The organization of the volume likewise reflects the trajectory of these events. The first section on "Motherhood" is composed of essays written between 1990-98; while the articles in section two on "Mothering" were written between 1998 and 2005. It was not until I was working on the volume did I realize that my thinking on motherhood falls neatly under these two distinct themes and that such are not only ordered chronologically but also demarcated by the year 1998; the year I established ARM. Whether or not this shift in focus was deliberate, it remains telling because central to ARM is a challenge to the institution of motherhood to make possible considerations of empowered or feminist mothering.

Motherhood and Mothering

In *Of Woman Born*, Rich distinguishes "between two meanings of mother-hood, one superimposed on the other: the *potential* relationship of any woman to her powers of reproduction—and to children; and the *institution*—which aims at ensuring that that potential—and all women—shall remain under male control" (13, emphasis in original). *Of Woman Born*, Rich emphasizes, "is not an attack on the family or on mothering *except as defined and restricted under patriarchy*" (14, emphasis in original). The term motherhood refers to the patriarchal institution of motherhood which is male-defined and controlled and is deeply oppressive to women, while the word mothering refers to women's experiences of mothering which are female-defined and centred and potentially empowering to women. The reality of patriarchal motherhood thus must be distinguished from the possibility or potentiality of gynocentric or feminist mothering. In other words, while motherhood, as an institution, is a male-defined site of oppression, women's own experiences of mothering can nonetheless be a source of power.

Patriarchal motherhood, however, as Rich argued and I discuss in the introduction to this volume, must be differentiated from the possibility or potentiality of mothering. "To destroy the institution is not to abolish motherhood," Rich writes, "It is to release the creation and sustenance of life into the same realm of decision, struggle, surprise, imagination and conscious intelligence, as any difficult, but freely chosen work" (280). It has long been recognized among scholars of motherhood that Rich's distinction between mothering and motherhood was what enabled feminists to recognize that motherhood is not naturally, necessarily or inevitably oppressive, a view held by some Second Wave feminists. Rather, mothering, freed from motherhood, could be experienced as a site of empowerment, a location of social change if, to use Rich's words, women became "outlaws from the institution of motherhood." However, in *Of Woman Born*, there is little discussion of mothering or how its potentiality may be realized. The notable exception is the brief reference Rich made to her summer holiday in Vermont when her husband was away and she and her sons lived "as conspirators, outlaws from the institution of motherhood" (195). However, while mothering is not described or theorized in *Of Woman Born*, the text, in distinguishing moth-ering from motherhood and in identifying the potential empowerment of mothering, made possible later feminist work on mothering, particularly those that analyzed mothering as a site of power and resistance for women. As well, in interrupting and deconstructing the patriarchal narrative of motherhood, Rich destabilized the hold this discourse has on the meaning and practice of mothering and cleared the space for the articulation of counter narratives of mothering, in particular woman-centred and feminist meanings and experiences of mothering.

The oppressive and the empowering dimensions of maternity, as well as the complex relationship between the two, first identified by Rich in *Of Woman Born*, have been the focus of feminist research on motherhood over the last three decades. Umansky, in her study of feminism between 1968 and 1982, ascertained two competing feminist views on motherhood: the "negative" discourse that "focusse[s] on motherhood as a social mandate, an oppressive institution, a compromise of woman's independence," and the "positive" discourse which "argue[s] that motherhood minus 'patriarchy' ... holds the truly spectacular potential to bond women to each other and to nature, to foster a liberating knowledge of self, to release the very creativity and generativity that the institution of motherhood denies to women" (2-3). Lauri Umansky's classification is drawn from the distinction Rich made between the patriarchal institution of motherhood and a nonpatriarchal experience of mothering, and provides a useful backdrop for a reading of this volume. More specifically, the chapters build upon Rich and later Unmansky's distinction between mothering and motherhood to develop a transgressive/transformative theory and practice of maternity, what I term "a mothering against motherhood."

Mothering Against Motherhood

Motherhood

The central argument of this collection is that patriarchal motherhood is oppressive to women and that it must be dismantled so as to make possible other more empowered practices of mothering. We must, in other words, move from motherhood to mothering. This movement is achieved by actively and consciously mothering against motherhood. Patriarchal motherhood is dismantled, or more accurately destablized, by critiquing and correcting its oppressive systems as they are manifested in both ideology and practice. An example of such would be that as the patriarchal ideology of motherhood defines mothers as nonsexual subjects in accordance with the age-old whore-madonna dichotomy, the mother would claim and celebrate a robust and vibrant sexuality. Likewise, as the patriarchal motherhood mandates maternal selflessness, a mothering against motherhood practice would insist upon a life outside and beyond motherhood. And while motherhood regards motherwork as privatized labour undertaken in the domestic sphere, mothering regards such as an explicitly and profoundly political-social practice. Mothering against motherhood is thus a transgressive and transformative practice; it seeks to both challenge and change. A transgressive/transformative maternal practice originates from and depends upon the realization that patriarchal motherhood is indeed oppressive.

"[F]or most of what we know as the 'mainstream' of recorded history," Rich writes, "motherhood as institution has ghettoized and degraded female potentialities" (13). However, as Rich argues, this meaning of motherhood is neither natural nor inevitable. "The patriarchal institution of motherhood," Rich explains, "is not the 'human condition' any more than rape, prostitution, and slavery are" (33). Rather motherhood, in Rich's words, "has a history, it has an ideology" (33). Mothering seeks to undermine patriarchal motherhood by exposing, tracking, and eventually countering the ways that patriarchal motherhood, as both institution and ideology, normalizes and naturalizes oppressive motherhood as the best and *only* way to mother. In this way, patriarchal motherhood functions as a master discourse or hegemonic narrative that defines how women *must* mother. In this manner, motherhood operates as a patriarchal institution to constrain, regulate and dominate women and their mothering. The dominant discourse, as Erika Horwitz explains, "promotes an ideal that is impossible to achieve and often leaves mothers feeling inadequate, deficient, and guilty"(2004: 45) Alongside the idealized mother we find the "bad" mother, women who, by choice or circumstance, are not the selfless and tireless nurturers of idealized motherhood. "Over the past century," as Molly Ladd-Taylor and Lauri Umansky note, "women classed as 'bad' mothers have fallen into three general groups: those who did not live in a 'traditional' nuclear family; those who would not or could not protect their children from harm, and those whose children went wrong" (1998: 3). Since most, if not all, mothers have, at one time or another, fallen into one of the above categories—from single moms to mothers of "troubled teens"—we are all, as Ladd-Taylor and Umansky remind us, "bad" mothers (1998: 3). Mother-blame thus, like the idealization of motherhood, causes mothers to feel anxious and ashamed about what they perceive to be their inadequate mothering. The patriarchal ideology of "good" motherhood cause women to feel bad about their mothering; many mothers, as a result, strive to change and correct their mothering to more closely conform to the idealized mother and so avoid mother-blame. However, since no mother can achieve idealized motherhood, women bring to their lived experiences of mothering self-recrimination, anxiety and guilt. In turn, mothers who do not seek to achieve, either by choice or circumstance, idealized motherhood, become "unfit" mothers who find themselves and their mothering under public scrutiny and surveillance. In each, the normative discourse informs, if not defines, the manner in which women practice mothering.

The chapters in section one explore the history and ideology of patriarchal motherhood. In particular they discuss and detail the workings of the current patriarchal discourse of good motherhood; namely intensive (Hays) or sensitive mothering (Wakerdine and Lucy). As well they consider how patriarchal motherhood manifests itself in other regulatory maternal discourses, specifically childbirth, mothers in academe, and mothers and daughters. (The description of section chapters begin on page 23.) In rereading the chapters for this collection I recognize that, at times, my use of patriarchal motherhood seems crude and cumbersome; simplistic and naive. I seem to suggest that there is a stable, essential, and fixed ideology/institution of motherhood that oppresses women similarly and equally regardless of differences in class, race, culture, sexual orientation. That motherhood is bad and mothers are good. Emily Jeremiah's recent critique of Rich's *Of Woman Born* could be said of my work: "Rich's concept of mothering, as corrupted by patriarchal constructions of femininity," Jeremiah writes, "occasionally suggests that there is an authentic type of mothering behaviour that lies outside of patriarchy; Rich thus falls into an essential trap common in radical feminist thought, which frequently takes refuge in ideas of a fixed female or maternal self" (2004: 60). If I were to revise these chapters I would be more nuanced in my use of patriarchal motherhood. In particular, more attention would be given to how women are oppressed *differently* in and through patriarchal motherhood. As well, while I remain convinced that patriarchal motherhood is oppressive to mothers, I do not think, as my writing at times suggests, that mother's oppression can be solely and only reduced to the institution/ideology of motherhood. Aspects of mother-love and mother-work remain arduous, if not oppressive, regardless whether they take place within, outside, or against patriarchal motherhood. Empowered mothering may ameliorate many/most of the adversities of patriarchal motherhood; it can not, however, eliminate all of them. "To posit a utopian space outside of patriarchy, and thereby suggest a potential untarnished maternal subjectivity, is," Jeremiah explains, "to ignore the complex psychological interaction between subject and ideology" (60). Indeed, while the comforting of a coliky infant is evidently made easier with an involved partner, rest for the mother and so forth, the baby will, of course, still cry.

Mothering

As the first section examines the various ways patriarchal motherhood functions as a hegemonic ideology to disempower mothers, section two considers how this may be resisted through a feminist practice/theory of mothering. A feminist practice/theory of mothering functions as counter narrative of motherhood. It seeks to interrupt the master narrative of motherhood to imagine and implement a view of mothering that is *empowering* to women. This mode of mothering positions mothers, in Rich's words, as "outlaws from the institution of motherhood." The chapters in section one on motherhood are concerned with uncovering and challenging oppressive normative scripts of motherhood, while the focus of the chapters in section two is upon the formulation and articulation of a counter discourse of mothering; one that redefines patriarchal motherhood as a feminist enterprise. The primary objective of feminist mothering is to make mothering less oppressive to women. In so doing, the feminist standpoint on mothering, as discussed in the introduction, emphasizes maternal power and ascribes agency to mothers and value to motherwork. In so doing, mothering in feminist theory and practice becomes reconfigured as a social act. While patriarchal motherhood defines motherwork as solely privatized care undertaken in the domestic sphere, feminist mothering regards such as explicitly and profoundly political and public. This political-social dimension of mothering is manifested in two ways. The first occurs in the home wherein these mothers bring about social change through the anti-sexist childrearing of children, or, in the instance of African- American mothering, through a motherwork that has as its explicit aim the empowerment of black children. Whether such be called "A Politics of the Heart" as I do, or "Home is where the Revolution is" as Cecelie Berry does, this perspective regards the motherwork undertaken in the private sphere as having social consequence and political significance. The second way that mothering, in feminist practice, becomes a public act is through maternal activism. Motherhood, in Western culture, is most often seen as a private, and more specifically, an apolitical enterprise. In contrast, feminist mothers understand motherwork to have social and political import. For many feminist mothers, their commitment to both feminism and to children becomes expressed as maternal activism. Mothers, through maternal activism, use their position as mothers to lobby for social and political change. Central to the feminist challenge to patriarchal motherhood is this redefinition of mothework as a political act, undertaken at home and in the world at large.

In writing the chapters for the section, I struggled with what word to use to describe a theory and practice of mothering that is non-patriarchal. Rich uses the word courageous to define a non-patriarchal practice of mothering while Baba Cooper calls such a practice radical mothering. Susan Douglas and Meredith Michaels, more recently in *The Mommy Myth*, use the word rebellious to describe outlaw mothering. Hip is Ariel Gore's term for transgressive mothering. However, as Marrit Ingman notes in her recent memoir, *Inconsol-*

able: How I Threw My Mental Health Out with the Diapers, the notion of hip often becomes associated more with a style of mothering than a politic of one.[2] In the chapters that follow I use feminist and empowered interchangeably to signify a mothering theory and practice that challenges, resists, and dismantles the patriarchal institution/ideology of motherhood. However, I do not define what I mean by empowered or feminist or how the two may differ. Reading through the chapters for this volume I realize that my discussion of non-patriarchal mothering would benefit from a fuller discussion of the meaning of feminist and empowered mothering. To this discussion, I now turn.

Feminist Mothering

Feminist mothering, as noted above, functions as a counter narrative or oppositional discourse: its meaning is constructed as a *negation* of patriarchal motherhood. In other words, our understanding of feminist mothering is determined more by what it is not (i.e., patriarchal motherhood) rather than by what it is. However, as we recognize that feminist mothering, in its origins and function, is a counter narrative, I believe we need to define more directly, more specifically, this mode of mothering, in both theory and practice. In her book *Feminist Mothers*, the first and still only book length study of the subject matter, Tuula Gordon in her concluding chapter "What is a Feminist Mother?" observes, "[I]t seems impossible to conclude by explaining what a feminist mother is, or to answer the underlying question of how people conduct their lives according to alternative ideologies, in this case feminism" (148). However, Gordon does say that her study of feminist mothers reveals some 'particular factors"; they are:

> The way in which [mothers] challenge and criticise myths of motherhood; the way in which they consider it their right to work: the anti-sexist (and anti-racist) way in which they try to bring up their children; the way in which they expect the fathers of the children to participate in joint everyday lives; and the way in which many of them are politically active. (149)

Gordon goes on to conclude:

> Feminism emphasizes that women are strong, that women have rights as women, and they can support each other as women. Thus "feminist mothers" have been able to develop critical orientations towards societal structures and cultures, stereotypical expectations and myths of motherhood. They do that in the context of exploring how the

personal is political, and with the support of the networks of women which place them beyond collective isolation. (150)

Rose L. Glickman in her book, *Daughters of Feminists*, likewise emphasizes that feminist mothering must be understood as lived resistance to the norma-tive—stereotypical—expectations of both motherhood and womanhood. She writes:

[For these feminist mothers] there is no "apart from their feminism" and no matter how ordinary their lives seem from the outside to the casual observer, *their feminism was a profound defiance of convention....* Flying in the face of tradition, feminist mothers expected their daughters to do the same. (22, emphasis added)

"The mothers' struggle," Glickman continues, "to shake off the dust of tradition was the basic dynamic of the daughters' formative years" (21).

Whether it manifested itself in combining motherhood with paid employ-ment, insisting that fathers be involved in childcare, engaging in activism, creating a life outside of motherhood, these studies reveal that feminist mothering developed in response to the mother's dissatisfaction with, dislike of, traditional motherhood. Commenting upon Gordon's study, Erika Horwitz in her thesis, "Mothers' Resistance to the Western Dominant Discourse on Mothering," observes: "Her findings suggest that mothers can hold beliefs that are not in agreement with those promoted by the dominant discourses on motherhood. Gordon alerts us to the possibility that *the process of resistance entails making different choices about how one wants to practice mothering*" (58, emphasis added). Both Gordon and Glickman look specifically at mothers who identify as feminist while Horwitz in the above thesis and her later chapter, "Resistance as a Site of Empowerment: The Journey Away from Maternal Sacrifice," is interested in "the experiences of women who believe they were resisting the dominant discourse of mothering [but] who may or may not see themselves as feminist" (44, 45). Empowered mothering thus signifies a general resistance to patriarchal motherhood while feminist mothering refers to a particular style of empowered mothering in which this resistance is developed from and expressed through a feminist identification or conscious-ness. While the two seem similar, there are significant differences that warrant further elaboration.

In her chapter, "Resistance as Empowerment," noted above, Erika Horwitz argues that while resistant, empowered mothering is characterized by many themes, they all centre upon a challenge to patriarchal motherhood. These themes include: the importance of mothers meeting their own needs; being a

Mother does not fulfill all of women's needs; involving others in their children's upbringing; actively questioning the expectations that are placed on mothers by society; challenging mainstream parenting practices; not believing that mothers are solely responsible for how children turn out; and challenging the idea that the only emotion a mother ever feels toward their children is love. In the introduction to this volume, I explore how empowered mothering begins with the recognition that both mothers and children benefit when the mother lives her life and practices mothering from a position of agency, authority, authenticity, and autonomy. Empowered mothering thus, as I discuss at length, calls into question the dictates of patriarchal motherhood. Feminist mothering differs from empowered mothering insofar as the mother identifies as a feminist and practices mothering from a feminist perspective or consciousness. A feminist mother, in other words, is a woman whose mothering, in theory and practice, is shaped and influenced by feminism. Thus, while there is much overlap between empowered and feminist mothering, the later is informed by a particular philosophy and politic, namely Feminism. The women's demands that their husbands be more involved or that they need time off from motherhood in the Horwitz study did not derive from a larger challenge to gender inequity. For example, one woman in the study remarked that "If I was going to love that baby, have any quality of time with that baby, I had to get away from that baby. I had to meet my own needs" (Horwitz 48); and another mother "chose to paint her nails while her baby cried in her crib because 'she has needs and wants'" (47). These women resisted patriarchal motherhood, in one woman's words "to have a higher quality of life", or in the words of another "to make me a better mother for my children" (52). The reasons for their resistance are more personal than political and as a consequence are not developed from an awareness of how motherhood functions as cultural/ideological institution to oppress women in patriarchal society. These mothers resist patriarchal motherhood simply to make the experience of mothering more rewarding for themselves and their children. Insofar as this aim challenges the patriarchal mandate of maternal selflessness, sacrifice, and martyrdom, these mothers are resistant in their insistence upon more time for themselves and support from others. However, these demands do not originate from a feminist desire to dismantle a patriarchal institution. In contrast, feminist mothers resist because they recognize that gender inequity, in particular male privilege and power, is produced, maintained, and perpetuated (i.e., though sexist childrearing) in patriarchal motherhood. As feminists, feminist mothers reject an institution founded upon gender inequity, and as mothers, they refuse to raise children in such a sexist environment. Thus, while in practice the two seem similar—i.e., demanding more involvement from fathers, insisting upon a life outside of motherhood—only with feminist mothering does this involve a larger awareness of, and challenge to, the gender (among other) inequities of patriarchal culture.

Feminist mothering seeks the eradication of the institution of motherhood as it understands it to be a patriarchal institution in which gender inequality, or more specifically the oppression of women, is enforced, maintained, and perpetuated Thus feminist mothering, as examined in section two, becomes concerned specifically with feminist practices of gender socialization and models of mother–child relations so as to raise a new generation of empowered daughters and empathetic sons. However, and as I examine fully in chapter ten, the latter—anti-sexist childrearing—depends on the former—the eradication of patriarchal motherhood. We cannot affect changes in childrearing without first changing the conditions of motherhood. A review of feminist thought on motherhood, however, reveals that a critique of the institution of motherhood and a concern with new modes of childrearing have developed independently of each other, and that feminists committed to the abolition of motherhood and the achievement of mothering have seldom considered what this means for the mother *herself*, apart from the issue of childrearing.

Fiona Green, in her research on feminist mothering, interviews feminist mothers who, in Green's words, "live Rich's emancipatory vision of motherhood" (130). "Driven by their feminist consciousness, their intense love for their children and the need to be true to themselves, their families, and their parenting, [these] feminist mothers," Green writes, "choose to parent in a way that challenges the status quo" (130). They do so, according to Green, by way of two different approaches: "overt strategies of resistance" and "subversive strategies of resistance" (130). To illustrate the first strategy, Green gives the example of a lesbian lone parent who births and raises a child without any connection to man. "No man ever called the shots in my home," the woman explains, "nor did a man ever support me in any way. So that is really breaking the rules in the patriarchy" (131). According to Green, this is "a deliberate act of resistance to dominant conceptions and practices of mothering" (131).

The second strategy is less overt; with this approach, mothers "under the cover of the institution of motherhood effectively challenge patriarchy, and their subversive activity often goes unnoticed" (132). Green provides examples of two heterosexual married mothers to illustrate this strategy, one who raises a son to make him consciously aware of social injustices, while the second mother "actively encourages the nurturing and non-competitive tendencies of her son, while supporting her daughter in her pursuits of maths and science" (133). The second subversive strategy thus seems to focus on childrearing undertaken by women in the institution of motherhood, while the former, the overt strategy, involves a challenge to the institution itself and is concerned with the empowerment of the mother. In the example of overt resistance, when discussing the mother's choice to rear her daughter with an othermother during a difficult time in her daughter's adolescence, Green comments that this mother "enjoy[ed] a level of freedom and strength that she would not have experienced had she conformed to patriarchal [motherhood]" (132).

I refer to Green's research here because it illustrates well the way the two demands of feminist mothering both interface and underpin one another. Feminist mothering seeks to dismantle motherhood *for mothers themselves*, so that they may achieve empowerment in mothering. That is reason enough to abolish motherhood. However, in so doing we also invest mothers with the needed agency, authenticity, and authority to affect the feminist childrearing they desire. In Chapter Six of this volume, "Home is Where the Revolution Is," I discuss how African-American mothering is a site of empowerment for women because it accords mothers power alongside responsibility; as well it eschews the patriarchal dictates of intensive mothering. In contrast, in Anglo-American feminist thought there is little written on mothering as site of empowerment *for mothers themselves*. Instead, feminist mothers seek to practice anti-sexist childrearing within the institution of motherhood. Again, and as I examine in the chapters that follow, this is not enough. Feminist mothers, I argue, must recognize that the changes we pursue in childrearing are made possible only through changes in mothering. Only then does feminist mothering become a truly transgressive/transformative practice.

While the above discussion helps to distinguish between empowered and feminist mothering, it begs the larger question of how to define Feminism itself. Feminism, as scholars of Women's Studies are well aware, is composed of many, 'perspectives and positions'': Socialist, Liberal, Radical, Third Wave to name but a few. For the purpose of this collection, I rely upon a very open-ended definition of feminism: the recognition that most (all?) cultures are patriarchal and that such cultures give prominence, power, and privilege to men and the masculine and depend upon the oppression, if not disparagement, of women and the feminine. Feminists are committed to challenging and transforming this gender inequity in all of its manifestations: cultural, economic, political, philosophical, social, ideological, sexual and so forth. As well, most feminisms (including my own) seek to dismantle other hierarchical binary systems such as race (racism), sexuality (heterosexism), economics (classism), and ability (abilism). A feminist mother, therefore, in the context of this definition of feminism, challenges male privilege and power in her own life and that of her children. In her own life, this would mean the mother insisting upon gender equality in the home and a life and identity outside of motherhood. As well, it would mean that the important work of mothering would be culturally valued and supported and that mothers, likewise, would perform this motherwork from a place of agency and authority. In the context of children, feminist mothering means dismantling traditional gender socialization practices that privilege boys as preferable and superior to girls and in which boys are socialized to be masculine and girls feminine. Feminist mothering thus seeks to transform both the patriarchal role of motherhood and that of childrearing.

The word feminism, however, remains troubled. In her book on feminist daughters, Glickman wrote: "I ruled out daughters whose mothers' lives can surely be described as feminist, but who reject the label. Once, in my search for Latina daughters, I spoke with the head of a Latino women's health collective. She said she couldn't help me because "although we have the consciousness, in our culture we don't' use the word [feminist]." The consciousness without the word is not what I'm looking for" (xv-xvi). However, in insisting upon the word feminist, you will inevitably, as the above incidence demonstrates, exclude the mothering experiences of women of colour. The term feminism, as African American scholars Patricia Hill Collins and bell hooks among others have argued, is understood to be a white term for many black women. As a daughter, a woman of colour, in Glickman's study commented: '[Feminism] has overwhelmingly, statistically, benefited white women disproportionately to women of colour" (168). And another daughter remarked: "Here you are reading all these feminist writers who are telling you to bust out of the kitchen and get into work force. What does that have to do with the majority of women of colour who have always been in the kitchen *and* the work force at the same time?" (emphasis in original, 169). Indeed as the mothers of colour in Gordon's study emphasized, "black women are critical of feminism dominated by white women for ideological, political and strategic reasons" (140). The question thus remains: How do you develop a specific study of feminist mothering without excluding the many women—women of colour and working class women—who eschew or disavow the word feminism? While, I do not believe there are easy answers to such questions, I see a broader understanding of feminism, to include womanist, anti-racist, global feminist perspectives, as a way to begin talking about women of colour and their specific theory and practice of feminist mothering.

In the introduction of this volume, I argue that feminist mothering or empowered mothering more generally are characterized by agency, authority, autonomy, and authenticity. In a recent conference paper, "Mothering Under Duress: Examining the Inclusiveness of Feminist Theory," Amy Middleton argues that such a definition is problematic because it limits feminist mothering to, in her words, "educated, middle to upper class women with access to financial and human resources." She writes: "These criteria and the way in which they are realized in these women's lives are extremely difficult, and in some cases impossible, for women who do not have access to recourse such as substantial finances and good childcare and/or women who are in other situations of duress such as being in an abusive relationship, having a mental illness or being addicted to drugs or alcohol." This criticism suggests that I have been less than clear in my use of these terms. The terms agency, authority, autonomy, authenticity, are not to be read as restricted to economic and educational resources. Rather, these terms are to be read in the context of a resistance to patriarchal motherhood. The concept of authenticity, for example, refers to the refusal to wear, what Susan Maushart terms, the "mask of motherhood." The mask of motherhood, Maushart explains, is an "assemblage of fronts –mostly brave, serene, and all knowing—that we use to disguise the chaos and complexity of or lived experience" (2) To be masked, Maushart continues, is "to deny and repress what we experience, to misrepresent it, even to ourselves" (1-2). "The mask of motherhood," Maushart continues, "keeps women from speaking clearly what they know and from hearing truths too threatening to face" (7). "Authentic" mothers, in contrast, seek to unmask motherhood and refuse to partake in, what Mary Kay Blakely has termed, "the national game of Let's Pretend—the fantasy in which we are all supposed to pass for perfect mothers, living in perfect families" (12). To be authentic is to be truthful and true to oneself in motherhood.

Similarly, authority refers to confidence and conviction in oneself as a mother. Authority means, in this instance, the refusal to, in Sara Ruddick's words, "relinquish authority and repudiate one's own perceptions and values" (112). As well, agency means not power but, in Rich's words " to refuse to be a victim and then go on from there" (246). From this perspective, agency, authority, authenticity, and autonomy are as available to 'marginalized' women as they are to women of privilege. In fact, I would argue that such agency, authority, and autonomy of empowered mothering are *more* evident in the maternal practices/theories of mothers who are poor, lesbian, young, or women of colour as evidenced in the collection *Breeder: Real-Life Stories from the New Generation of Mothers* (Gore and Lavender). Privileged women, I would suggest, with more resources and status in motherhood, are often less able or likely to perceive and oppose their oppression. Furthermore, when I speak of agency and the like I do not mean to say that mothers necessarily have these things, but rather that empowered mothers understand that they *should* have them and seek to attain them. Patriarchal mothers, in contrast, do not believe that mothers need or want agency, authority, autonomy, or authority. Or put another way: patriarchal motherhood depends on the very denial of maternal agency and so forth. When I use such terms I mean to signify struggle, not necessarily success. Again to quote from Rich: "The quality of the mother's life—however, embattled and unprotected—is her primary bequest to her daughter, because a woman who can believe in herself, who is a fighter, and who continues to struggle to create livable space around her, is demonstrating to her daughter that these possibilities exist" (247).This is what a mothering of agency, authority, autonomy, and authenticity seeks to demonstrate and achieve and, as such, it is certainly not restricted to women of privilege.

In *Of Woman Born*, Rich writes: "We do not think of the power stolen from us and the power withheld from us in the name of the institution of motherhood" (275). The chapters of section two examine how mothers can and do reclaim that power in and through feminist mothering. However, what should have been emphasized more in the chapters that follow is that feminist mothering, as a counter narrative, is formed and performed in opposition to the hegemonic discourse of patriarchal motherhood. Therefore, while we may seek to mother against, outside, or beyond motherhood, mothering can never fully free itself from motherhood. In other words, even as we resist motherhood, it contains mothering. Despite our struggle to be otherwise, even the most resistant mothers find themselves, at times, restrained in and by the institution of motherhood. Indeed, even to imagine a mothering apart from motherhood may be impossible. This was made glaringly apparent to me last year when the publisher of my edited volume *Mother Outlaws: Theories and Practices of Empowered Mothering* commissioned the book to artists for possible cover designs. Despite having read the introduction to the book, the artists were not able to imagine empowered mothering in a cover design. Instead, artist after artist submitted image after image of pregnant bodies, usually in a decapitated form. That these artists could only perceive maternal power in the embodiment of a pregnant body reveals how unimaginable and unrepresentational empowered mothering is in our patriarchal culture. The chapters of section two thus may be read as my attempt to envision and theorize upon what is deemed unimaginable in patriarchal culture.

This volume opens with an introduction entitled "From Patriarchal Motherhood to Feminist Mothering." The introduction explores at length the emergence of a contemporary manifestation of patriarchal motherhood, namely intensive mothering. I consider reasons for its emergence at this particular historical moment; as well I examine how it operates as a hegemonic discourse to regulate and restrain women and their mothering. Finally, the introduction considers how patriarchal motherhood may be challenged through feminist mothering.

Section 1: Motherhood

Chapter One, "Labour Signs: The Semiotics of Birthing" examines how the medical model of birth emerged as the official meaning of childbirth. Mapping a Foucauldian analysis of how definitions of childbirth come to be constructed, codified, mobilized on Barthes' semiotic theory of myth as a process of signification, I trace the steps by which this particular definition of birth is normalized as the only—i.e., universal and real—meaning of birth and how this normative discourse, in turn, determines the material conditions of women's birthing. Drawing upon my own experiences of childbirth, I go on to consider how the medical definition interprets birth as a mode of production. Finally, I explore whether woman-centred discourses of birth offer an empowered birthing experience for women. I conclude that the political liberation of birth promised by the counter-discourse is ultimately contaminated by the medical model's militarism; as well as compromised by its discursive inscription of birth as a "natural" experience. The chapter concludes reflecting upon how to achieve a truly empowering, liberating experience of childbirth.

Chapter Two, "Talking Back in Mother Tongue: A Feminist Course on Mothering-Motherhood," is an essay on my experience of teaching and designing a feminist course on motherhood. In this chapter I present this Mothering course as site of resistance against the patriarchal institution of motherhood. The first section of the course explores how the patriarchal discourse of motherhood works as ideology to normalize women's oppression in motherhood. Section two of the course seeks to interrupt this discourse by giving voice to women's own experiences of mothering, experiences that are marginalized, masked, and demonized by the master narrative of motherhood.

Chapter Three, "What's a Girl Like You Doing in a Nice Place Like This? Mothering in the Academe," reflects upon my experience of being a mother and a graduate student in the late 1980s and recounts the various forms of discrimination—institutional and attitudinal—I encountered as a mother-student. When I wrote this piece I sensed that the discrimination I experienced was attributable to a larger and systemic bias against mothers in the academe. However, at the time I wrote the narrative, the research on being a mother in the academe was only just becoming available, so I could not locate my story within this larger framework. With that information now available, I would like to relay, briefly, some of the findings of this research to establish a context for reading this chapter.

A 1988 Canadian Association of University Teachers report stated that: "of all the professions, that of university teaching is the one in which women have the least number of children" (cited in Dagg and Thompson 84). Likewise surprising, is the scarcity of research on mothers in the academe. "The inclusion of women in academia as subjects of research on work and family/parenting," as Alice Fothergill and Kathryn Felty note, "has occurred only recently—and only in a limited way" (9). A review of the literature reveals that becoming and being a mother in academia has a deleterious impact on women's career advancement. The American Association of University

Professors confirmed in their *Statement of Principles on Family Responsibility and Academic Work*, that "although increasing numbers of women have entered academia, their academic status has been slow to improve: women remain disproportionately represented within instructor, lecturer, unranked positions; more than 57 percent of those holding such positions are women while among full professors only 26 percent are women; likewise among full-time faculty women, only 48 percent are tenured whereas 68 percent of men are." Mason and Goulden's study (cited in Hile-Bassett), that examined the effect of early babies on women's academic career, reveals that "women with early babies are less likely to achieve tenure than women with late babies or no children."[3] While more women are earning their doctorates, as Alice Fothergill and Kathryn Felty note, "the structure of tenure-track jobs has not changed in any real way to accommodate them" (17). Perhaps this is why, they continue, "the number of women in tenure track jobs has *declined*: from 46 percent in 1977 to 32 percent in 1995" (17). This research on motherhood in academia shows, as noted by Angela Simeone, that "marriage and family, while having a positive effect on the [academic] careers of men, has a negative effect on the progress of women's careers. Married women, particularly with children are more likely to have dropped out of graduate school, have interrupted or abandoned their careers, be unemployed or employed in a job unrelated to their training, or to hold lower academic rank" (12). Indeed, "university settings have been found to be so hostile to women, as Fothergill and Felty observe, "that the 'Ivory Tower' has been called the 'Toxic Tower' by some in academia" (9).[4] Indeed, as my chapter will show, that was how I experienced academia as a mother-student.

"'Ain't that Love?' Antiracism and Racial Constructions of Motherhood," the fourth chapter, explores how the development and dissemination of one normative discourse of motherhood—that of so-called sensitive mothering—causes other experiences of mothering—working-class, ethnic—to be marginalized and delegitimized. I use my students' responses to Toni Morrison's *Sula* to examine the effects of codifying white, middle-class women's experiences of motherhood as the official and only meaning of motherhood. The struggle against racism, as I explore in this chapter, requires a challenge to this codification. Likewise, the formation of feminist mothering must begin with the recognition that as normative discourses of motherhood are sexist, they are likewise racist.

The section concludes with "Across the Divide: Contemporary Anglo-American Feminist Theory on the Mother-Daughter Relationship." This chapter describes the course I designed and taught on "Mothers and Daughters: From Estrangement to Empowerment" at York University in the early 1990s. The course aims to identify and expose the cultural practices that underpin the patriarchal narrative of mother-daughter estrangement—sanction against mother-daughter closeness, daughter-centricity, mother-blame, cultural devaluation of motherhood, matrophobia, inauthentic mothering, fear of maternal power and normative maternal discourses. The chapter concludes by examining various strategies—motherline, maternal narratives and feminist mothering—by which mothers and daughters may deconstruct the patriarchal narrative so as to write their own stories of motherhood and daughterhood, ones scripted from relationships of empowerment as opposed to connection. In this, the chapter serves as a bridge between the first section on patriarchal motherhood and the following one on feminist mothering.

Section Two: Mothering

The section opens with two articles on African-American mothering. The first examines how African-American mothering may be read as a counter narrative of empowered mothering, while the next chapter explores Toni Morrison's theory of motherwork as political praxis. I include these two chapters because they demonstrate how motherwork, in the counter narrative of mothering, assumes political import and social significance, as contrasted to the dominant discourse which defines motherhood as an apolitical and private undertaking. Chapter Six, "'Home is Where the Revolution Is':[5] Womanist Thought on African-American Mothering," draws upon the writings of many Black feminist writers including Patricia Hill Collins, Patricia Bell-Scott, Carol Stack, bell hooks, Gloria Wade-Gayles, Alice Walker, Wanda Thomas Bernard and Joyce Ladner, to explore how mothering functions as a site of power in African-American culture. I explore five themes in this redefinition that serve to dismantle patriarchal motherhood and position mothering as an identity and role of power-empowerment. The African-American tradition of motherhood centres upon the recognition that mothering, in its concern with the physical and psychological well-being of children and its focus upon the empowerment of children, has cultural and political import, value, and prominence and that motherhood, as a consequence, is a site of power for Black women. The chapter will examine this tradition of African-American mothering under five interrelated topics: "Othermothering and Community Mothering," "Motherhood as Social Activism and a Site of Power," "Matrifocality," "Nurturance as Resistance: Providing a Homeplace," and "The Motherline: Mothers as Cultural Bearers." Next it will examine this tradition in the context of mothers' relationships with their children. Specifically, the chapter will consider how daughters seek identification or connection with their mothers due to the cultural centrality and significance of the mother role and how this connection gives rise to the daughters' empowerment in African-American culture.

Chapter Seven, "'A Politics of the Heart': Toni Morrison's Theory of Motherwork," explores how motherwork, in Morrison's view, assumes as its central aim the empowerment of black children. The central question of Morrison's writing, I argue, is how mothers, raising black children in a racist and sexist world, can best protect their children and instruct them in how to protect themselves from the racism and sexism that seeks to harm them. In particular, the chapter examines how Morrison defines the responsibilities of motherwork in terms of four distinct yet interrelated tasks; namely, preservation, nurturance, cultural bearing and healing. The above discussion is developed from Sara Ruddick's theory of maternal practice. Together these four tasks enable mothers to 1) protect their children, physically and psychologically, 2) teach children how to protect themselves, and 3) heal adults who were unprotected as children and hence harmed. This, I conclude, is Morrison's theory of motherwork: a "Politics of the Heart."

Chapter Eight, "In Black and White: African-American and Anglo-American Feminist Perspectives on Mothers and Sons," examines three schools of feminist thought with respect to mothers and sons to determine how women's maternal role/identity and the mother-son relationship are represented in each. The chapter opens referencing the ancient myths of Jocasta/Oedipus and Clytemnestra/Orestes. These patriarchal narratives both in their ancient forms and in their modern renditions enact maternal erasure and enforce mother-son separation. The chapter goes on to argue that maternal erasure and disconnection are central as well to early Anglo-American feminist thought on mothers and sons, which tended to downplay and devalue women's role and identity as mothers. The chapter considers how recent Anglo-American feminist writings on mothers and sons call into question the patriarchal and early feminist perspective on maternal displacement to emphasize mother and son connection. Finally, the chapter reviews recent African-American feminist thought on mothers and sons to explore both its emphasis on maternal presence and involvement and its specific, racially determined mode of rearing sons. These new feminist perspectives—Anglo-American and African-Americanl—the chapter concludes, by highlighting maternal agency and authority and in foregrounding mother-son connection, have imagined and made possible a truly feminist narrative of mothers and sons.

"A Mom and Her Son: Thoughts on Feminist Mothering," Chapter Nine, reflects upon how feminism shaped the mothering of my son and how being a mother of a son redefined my feminism. When raising my son Jesse I did not overtly or consciously set out to impart feminist teachings. However, and as I examine in this piece, I did practice what I term radical mothering, or more specifically, resistance to the traditional practices of male socialization that mandates both mother-son disconnection and "macho" masculinity in boys. In nurturing a connected and close relationship with my son and in allowing and affirming the very strong feminine dimensions of his personality, my son grew up with the knowledge that it was alright to be a sensitive boy and indeed quite normal to need your mother. The chapter also considers how my feminism was rethought, reworked, and redefined in and through the mothering of my son, most significantly in terms of the way I understood gender difference. Being the mother of a "good" son I came to realize that the masculine is not inherently evil, as I had believed in my pre-mother of son, Radical feminist days. As well, I explore how, through this realization, I was able to discover and honour the so-called masculine dimensions of my self that were before unacknowledged or unaffirmed.

The final chapter, "'This is What Feminism Is: The Acting and Living ... Not Just the Told': Mentoring and Modeling Feminism," argues that feminist mothering must first and primarily be concerned with the empowerment of mothers. In contrast, much of current literature on feminist mothering is concerned with anti-sexist childrearing, or more specifically, raising empowered daughters and relational sons with little attention paid to the mother herself or the condition under which she mothers. A challenge to traditional gender socialization is, of course, integral to any theory and practice of feminist mothering. However, I argue, that the empowerment of mother must be the primary aim of feminist mothering if it is to function as a truly transformative theory and practice. To fully and completely liberate children from traditional childrearing, mothers must first seek to liberate themselves from traditional motherhood; they must, to use Rich's terminology, mother against motherhood. By way of a conversation with my two daughters—Erin (18) and Casey (15)—this chapter will explore the interface between the empowerment of mothers and anti-sexist childrearing and the argument that the later depends on the former. More specifically I will argue that, in order for mothers to mentor feminism for their daughters, they must seek to model it in themselves.

Conclusion

The evening before I began writing this foreword I was in a car accident: the man behind me lost control of his car when he dropped his water bottle and sideswiped my car as I was turning right onto my concession. A few days later as I was writing the foreword in earnest, I fell on ice on my back deck when calling the dogs in and hit my head hard, face forward, on the cement. I spent the next day in the emergency ward. While neither the car accident nor the head injury ended up being serious, I wondered upon the significance of these events, particularly as this was my first car accident and the first time I had a head injury requiring medical attention. Moreover, as someone with a Ph.D. in English, I tend to look for symbolism in uncanny happenings such as these. Perhaps these events could be read as signifying, figuratively if not literally, the distraction of my writing state. However, at the time, I read them metaphorically, to symbolize what we, as feminist mothers, must do to patriarchal motherhood, namely sideswipe and smash it. I thought this until a third and far more shocking and serious event occurred in this peculiar week. My two daughters, now 19 and 16, were badly beat up at an all-age punk show at a legion hall, (in, I may add, a very conservative, "whitebread" area). My eldest was dancing in the pit, an area generally designated and demarcated as male space at punk shows. The singer in the band pointed to my daughter and yelled "that girl in the red hair needs to shave her fucking armpits." My daughter, never one to walk away from such an attack, gave the guy the finger and lifted her armpits in defiance. The crowd turned hostile and, out of nowhere, a man punched my five-foot, 105-pound daughter directly in the face and broke her glasses and bruised her badly. Things worsened: they ended up holding her down so others could punch her and dragged her by the hair across the floor. My other daughter was also hit trying to defend her. That evening when she got home, she posted what happened on the web board of the local punk scene. Less than ten hours later she received 105 responses, most of them negative, a.k.a.,"the bitch had it coming." One man, who calls himself "I am a cunt," posted an image of a hairy armpit and wrote in caps: "SELF EXPLANATORY. THE BITCH GOT PWNED."[6]

I share this story because it has relevance to this topic of feminist mothering. What happened to my daughters is an appalling incident of what a friend appropriately termed feminist bashing.[7] This violence reveals the consequences, and I would add dangers, of raising our daughters to be feminists in a world hostile to empowered women. Adrienne Rich, as I explore in the chapter "A Mom and Her Son: Thoughts on Feminist Mothering," has argued that "the fear of alienating a male child from his culture seems to go deep, even among women who reject that culture for themselves everyday of their lives" (205). We worry that, as feminist mothers, we may, again in Rich's words, turn our sons "into misfits and outsiders" (205). I would argue that we also need to be concerned about our daughters. As we raise them feminist, we must prepare and ready them for survival in a patriarchal world. And, as the above story has made painfully clear to me, resistance to patriarchy is indeed dangerous for our feminist daughters, so we must teach them well.

The above story has also brought home to me the difficulties and dangers of feminist mothering for ourselves as mothers and feminists. Rereading these chapters for this collection, it appears, at times, that feminist mothering is easy and effortless, that it comes without perils and penalties. More needs to be said on how truly arduous it is to challenge patriarchy as feminist mothers and how very much we need community to do so. This observation leads me to what I see as two other omissions in the volume. In several of the chapters I make reference to how motherwork may be expressed as maternal activism; however, there is little reference to how such functions in either my theory or practice of mothering. Raising three children, while finishing a Ph.D. and securing tenure and promotion, left me little time for maternal activism. However, I do see my teaching on motherhood, establishment of the Association for Research on Mothering, and creation of Demeter Press as a type of maternal activism. As well, my current work, at least in research, looks at maternal activism.[8] As this collection needs to be more outward looking to consider maternal activism, it likewise needs to look more inward to theorize maternal subjectivity and my own experience of mothering, more specifically. In this collection, I speak at length about how patriarchal motherhood is oppressive to mothers and how it must be changed, not only to effect feminist childrearing but, as importantly, to make mothering a more empowered experience *for mothers themselves*. As well I emphasize the need for women to speak truthfully about motherhood to achieve authentic mothering and to build the feminist-maternal community that is necessary for the empowerment of mothers. Interestingly, most of my discussions on feminist mothering focus upon anti-sexist childrearing with little mention of my subjectivity as a mother or reflection upon my lived resistance to patriarchal motherhood. With this collection of essays published and my children all but grown, I feel prepared to finally tell my (m)other side of the story.[9]

When I became a mother to my three children in the 1980s, many of my feminist friends and colleagues made me feel as if I had in some irrevocable and fundamental way failed feminism—sold out, been duped, gone over to the other side—or in the language of current feminist discourse, fallen prey to the false consciousness of patriarchal ideology. To them, becoming a mother meant loss: a loss of opportunity, power, freedom, and the ability to determine and define one's life. And as such, motherhood was understood to be inherently and profoundly oppressive to women. However, as the following chapters seek to show, motherhood is not necessarily or inevitably oppressive to women. Rather, feminist mothering affords women power and enables them to affect the societal changes they seek for themselves, their children, and the world at large. Thus, as we critique motherhood, we must be very clear that it is the patriarchal institution we condemn and not mothering itself. We must be ever vigilant in this so we, as feminists, are not misunderstood or misrepresented as being complicit in the patriarchal devaluation of motherhood. Or in the title of my forthcoming essay, we must find a place "between the baby and the bathwater" where we may assail patriarchal motherhood, while at the same time affirming and confirming the value and power of feminist mothering.[10] Thus, while I do not believe that the hand the rocks the cradle rules the world, I do think, in conclusion, that by rocking the cradle—i.e., undermining patriarchal motherhood—we may indeed *change* the world.

[1]Please visit the Association for Research on Mothering (ARM) website www.yorku.ca/crm for a listing of the various topics explored by maternal scholars. ARM, founded in 1998 and now with more than 500 members worldwide, is the first international feminist organization devoted specifically to the topic of mothering-motherhood. ARM hosts two international conferences a year, and publishes the *Journal of the Association for Research on Mothering* bi-annually. For more information please visit the ARM website.
[2]In *Inconsolable*, Ingman writes: "I became pregnant during the groundswell— to my knowledge anyway—of 'hip' parenting as a zeitgeist. You could be a mother and still be yourself. You could still play pedal steel in a punkability band; you could still wear Fluevogs and color your hair purple" (187). However, upon becoming a mother, she learned that "hip" parenting, while still "a great idea—in theory" was woefully inapplicable to her life (187). She writes: "Cut to me, at home with a newborn. I'd envisioned myself tucked contentedly in my nursing station: The IKEA rocker, nutrition bars and water at my side, my sweet pacific baby in my arms while I listened to *All Things Considered* and pondered the evils I would vanquish for my son and all children (the flat tax, standardized testing in our schools, mercury in our ground water). But that wasn't quite the reality. Instead, I was eating a microwave burrito and watching *Montel* with the captions on. And I was a long way from gallivanting around in my snakeskin-print leather flares. I wasn't even sure where they were" (188-89).
[3]As quoted in the introduction to *Parenting and Professing* by Rachel Hile-Bassett (2).
[4]To date, only two book-length studies have been published on the topic of being a mother in academe: Vol. 5.2 (Fall/Winter 2003) of the *Journal of the Association on Mothering* issue on "Mothering in the Academy," and the recent collection, *Parenting and Professing: Balancing Family Work with an Academic Career*, edited by Rachel Hile-Basset (2005). The first is composed of scholarly articles on the subject matter while the second is a collection of 24 essays by women and two men on their experiences of being a parent in academe. Several themes may be identified in the current literature on motherhood and academia. Fothergill and Felty's study, based on a survey of 24 mothers (with two follow-up interviews) from a mid-size university in the Midwestern United

States, identified three salient themes: "Productivity in career, concern with perceptions of colleagues; and the paradox of academic work as stressful and demanding at the same that it provides flexibility and autonomy" (12). A central finding of Hile-Bassett's collection "is that the obstacles to successfully combining parenting and work result almost entirely from attitudes entrenched in the academic culture, not from the exigencies of the work itself" (1). As seen in the narratives from *Parenting and Professing*, family-friendly policies have not been widely adopted and utilization rates are low, often because parents fear professional repercussions for using them. The prevailing ethos of academic culture is that the career is to be prioritized above all else. To do otherwise, is to risk being perceived as not committed to your profession, or worse, not being taken seriously as a "real" scholar. Mothers on the tenure track thus often practice what is termed "discrimination avoidance"; "behaviors intended to minimize any apparent or actual intrusions of family life on academic commitments. Such behaviors," as Hile-Bassett, explains, "can include opting out of partnering and children altogether, delaying childbearing or limiting the number of children, attempting to hide one's caregiver status by not taking advantage of family-friendly policies" (5). Women, unable or unwilling to stay in the mother closet, often find themselves marginalized in part-time and non-tenure track positions. Indeed, as these stories show, women who "choose" marginalized academic work often do so because of family commitments. Another central issue noted by the literature is what may be termed the scheduling of motherhood. Lesley D. Harman and Petra Remy's 1993 research on the academic and family lives of faculty in Ontario, and published in their 2002 article, found that women seek to manage the conflict between the biological clock and academic clock in four different ways: "1) delay of childbearing, 2) delay of degree or career, 3) combining both career and family, 4) decision of career over children" (108). For a further discussion on this please see the above two collections and my "Foreword" to *Parenting and Professing* (O'Reilly 2005).

[5]I am thankful to Heather Hewett for drawing my attention to this quote by Cecelie Berry. Please see Hewett's forthcoming article, "Third-Wave Era Feminism and the Emerging Mothers Movement," *Journal of the Association for Research on Mothering* 8 (1,2) (forthcoming, Summer 2006), and Cecelie Berry's article, "Home is Where the Revolution Is," (available online: www.Salon.com).

[6]In the Urban dictionary "PWNED" is defined as: "A corruption of the word "Owned." This originated in an online game called Warcraft, where a map designer misspelled "owned." When the computer beat a player, it was supposed to say, so-and-so "has been owned." Instead, it said, so-and-so "has been pwned." It basically means "to own" or to be dominated by an opponent

or situation, especially by some god-like or computer-like force. My daughter, with the man writing "pwned" in his email, has been put "back" in her place by a "god-like" opponent aka patriarchy. Truly frightening! I am immensely grateful to Renée Knapp for researching the meaning of this word.

[7]I am indebted to Renée Knapp for identifying the violence done to my daughter as an act of feminist bashing. My daughter was attacked because she was perceived and identified as a feminist. She was dancing in the male pit, did not shave her armpits, and did not sit back and take it when she was assaulted for such.

[8]Please see my forthcoming edited book on *Feminist Mothering*, as well as *Mothering a Movement: Activist Mothers Speak Out on Why We Need to Change the World and How To Do It*, co-edited with Judith Stadtman Tucker (forthcoming).

[9]Maternal subjectivity is the topic of my next edited volume. Please *see MotherSelf: Theorizing and Representing Maternal Subjectivities*, edited with Silvia Caporale-Bizzini. My forthcoming essay, "Between the Baby and the Bathwater: Towards a Mother-Centred Feminist Theory of Mothering," (2006) focuses upon my lived experiences of feminist mothering and appears in the *Journal of the Association for Research on Mothering's* special double-issue on "Motherhood and Feminism" (Summer 2006). As well, in the next year I hope to finally complete my book-length memoir of motherhood.

[10]See my article, "Between the Baby and the Bathwater: Towards a Mother-Centred Feminist Theory of Mothering," *Journal of the Association for Research on Mothering* 8 (1,2) (Summer 2006).

INTRODUCTION

FROM PATRIARCHAL MOTHERHOOD TO
FEMINIST MOTHERING

In *Of Woman Born*, Adrienne Rich, when discussing a vacation without her husband one summer, describes herself and her sons as "conspirators, outlaws from the institution of motherhood" (195). She writes:

> I remember one summer, living in a friend's house in Vermont. My husband was working abroad for several weeks and my three sons— nine, seven, and five years old—and I dwelt for most of that time by ourselves. Without a male adult in the house, without any reason for schedules, naps, regular mealtimes, or early bedtimes so the two parents could talk, we fell into what I felt to be a delicious and sinful rhythm.... [W]e lived like castaways on some island of mothers and children. At night they fell asleep without murmur and I stayed up reading and writing as I had when a student, till the early morning hours. I remember thinking: This is what living with children could be—without school hours, fixed routines, naps, the conflict of being both mother and wife with no room for being simply, myself. Driving home once after midnight from a late drive-in movie ... with three sleeping children in the back of the car, I felt wide awake, elated; we had broken together all the rules of bedtime, the night rules, rules I myself thought I had to observe in the city or become a "bad mother." We were conspirators, outlaws from the institution of motherhood; I felt enormously in charge of my life. (194-195)

However, upon Rich's return to the city, the institution, in her words, "closed down on us again, and my own mistrust of myself as a 'good mother' returned, along with my resentment of the archetype" (195).

Rich's reflections on being an outlaw from the institution of motherhood and the references she makes to being a "good" and "bad" mother are drawn from the distinction she develops at the beginning of *Of Woman Born* between motherhood and mothering. Central to *Of Woman Born* and developed by subsequent motherhood scholars is the key distinction Rich makes between two meanings of motherhood, one superimposed on the other: "the *potential* relationship of any woman to her powers of reproduction and to children"; and "the *institution*—which aims at ensuring that that potential—and all women— shall remain under male control" (13, emphasis in original). The term motherhood refers to the patriarchal institution of motherhood which is male-defined and controlled and is deeply oppressive to women, while the word mothering refers to women's experiences of mothering which are female-defined and centred and potentially empowering to women. The reality of patriarchal motherhood thus must be distinguished from the possibility or potentiality of gynocentric or feminist mothering. To critique the institution of motherhood therefore "is not an attack on the family or on mothering *except as defined and restricted under patriarchy*" (Rich 14). In other words, while motherhood, as an institution, is a male-defined site of oppression, women's own experiences of mothering can nonetheless be a source of power.

In patriarchal culture women who mother in the institution of motherhood are regarded as good mothers while women who mother outside or against the institution of motherhood are viewed as "bad" mothers. In contrast, Rich argues that mothers, in order to resist patriarchal motherhood and achieve empowered mothering must be "bad" mothers, or more precisely, "mother outlaws." Therefore, and in opposition to the dominant and accepted view on motherhood, Rich defines empowered mothers as good mothers and patriar-chal mothers as bad mothers. It has long been recognized among scholars of motherhood that Rich's distinction between mothering and motherhood was what enabled feminists to recognize that motherhood is not naturally, neces-sarily or inevitably oppressive, a view held by many early Second Wave feminists. Rather, mothering, freed from the institution of motherhood, could be experienced as a site of empowerment, a location of social change. However, and as I examine in my edited collection *From Motherhood to Mothering: The Legacy of Adrienne Rich's Of Woman Born*, there is no discussion of empowered mothering or how its potentiality may be realized in Rich's book with the notable exception noted above. While this absence has puzzled scholars, most agree that, as mothering is not described or theorized in *Of Woman Born*, the text, in distinguishing mothering from motherhood and in identifying the potential empowerment of motherhood, enabled feminists to envision empowered mothering for women. And for many scholars, this is the true legacy of Rich's work.

This collection of essays may be read as a response to Rich's call for a theory and practice of feminist mothering, for as it seeks to dismantle patriarchal motherhood it opens a space for the possibility of empowered or feminist mothering. While most feminist scholars now distinguish mothering from motherhood and recognize that the former is not inherently oppressive, mothering has not been theorized in feminist literature. Numerous publications document why and how patriarchal motherhood is harmful, indeed unnatural, to mothers and children alike. However, only a handful of books examine feminist mothering, most notably the edited collection *Mother Journeys: Feminists Write About Mothering* (Reddy, Roth and Sheldon), Tuula Gordon's book, *Feminist Mothers*, and my forthcoming edited volume *Feminist Mothering*. However, much more needs to be written on the potentiality or possibility of empowered mothering first imagined by Rich 30 years ago. My work on feminist mothering, presented in section two of this volume, may be read as my effort, both personally and scholarly, to imagine and implement feminist mothering. In reflecting upon the need for more scholarship on feminist mothering, I am reminded of a comment made by Toni Morrison: "I wrote the books ... I wanted to read" (qtd. in Russell 43).

Feminist mothering, or what may be termed mothering against motherhood, has yet to be fully defined, documented or dramatized in feminist scholarship on motherhood. Rather, we know what feminist mothering is by what it is not, namely patriarchal motherhood. A central aim of my research is to develop, by way of theory and practice, a definition of feminist mothering. However, since feminist mothering is formulated and practiced in resistance to patriarchal motherhood, patriarchal motherhood itself must be studied.

Patriarchal Motherhood

I open my Women's Studies course on "Mothering-Motherhood" asking students to define "good" motherhood in contemporary culture: What does a good mother look like? What does she do or not do? Students commented that good mothers, as portrayed in the media or popular culture more generally, are white, heterosexual, able-bodied, married, and in a nuclear family with usually one to two children. Words such as altruistic, patient, loving, selfless, devoted, nurturing, cheerful were frequently mentioned. Good mothers put the needs of their children before their own, are available to their children whenever needed, and should the mother work outside the home, her children rather than her career should be at the centre of her life. Good mothers are the primary caregivers of their children: care other than that provided by the mother (i.e. daycare) is viewed as inferior and deficient. Children and culture at large do not see mothers as having a life before or outside of motherhood. As well, while students agreed that our culture regards mothering as natural to mothers, it simultaneously requires mothers to be well-versed in theories of childrearing. Several students remarked that good mothers today are concerned with their children's educational or more general psychological devel-opment: thus good mothers ensure that their children have many and varied opportunities for enrichment, learning, self-growth, and so forth. And, of course, mothers are not sexual!

"We all know the ideal of the good mother," Susan E. Chase and Mary Rogers argue in their book *Mothers and Children: Feminist Analyses and Personal Narratives*:

> Above all, she is selfless. Her children come before herself and any other need or person or commitment, no matter what. She loves her children unconditionally yet she is careful not to smother them with love and her own needs. She follows the advice of doctors and other experts and she educates herself about child development. She is ever present in her children's lives when they are young, and when they get older she is home everyday to greet them as they return from school. If she works outside the home, she arranges her job around her children so she can be there for them as much as possible, certainly whenever they are sick or unhappy. The good mother's success is reflected in her children's behaviour—they are well mannered and respectful to others; at the same time they have a strong sense of independence and self esteem. They grow up to be productive citizens. (30)

The above description refers to mothering as it practiced in the patriarchal institution of motherhood. Moreover, patriarchal motherhood, as the domi-nant ideology, becomes the mode of motherhood by which all mothers are regulated and judged.

This mode of mothering, what I term "sacrificial motherhood," however, is not a natural condition; rather it a style of mothering that emerged in the middle of the twentieth century. "The patriarchal institution of motherhood," Rich explains, "is not the 'human condition' any more than rape, prostitution, and slavery are" (33). Rather motherhood, "has a history, it has an ideology" (33). Motherhood operates as a patriarchal institution to constrain, regulate and dominate women and their mothering. "[F]or most of what we know as the 'mainstream' of recorded history," Rich writes, "motherhood as institution has ghettoized and degraded female potentialities" (13).

Feminist historians agree that motherhood is primarily *not* a natural or biological function; rather, it is specifically and fundamentally a cultural practice that is continuously redesigned in response to changing economic and societal factors. As a cultural construction, its meaning varies with time and place; there is no essential or universal experience of motherhood. Patriarchal motherhood, as described by students and in the quotation above, is neither natural nor inevitable. In this volume, I develop this concept further to argue that the institution and ideology of good motherhood are rewritten whenever a social reorganization is desired, particularly in the realm of gender roles and behaviour. Numerous works detail how the modern image—"full-time stay-at-home" mother, isolated in the private sphere and financially dependent on her husband—came about as result of industrialization. Industrialization took work out of the home and repositioned the domestic space, at least among the middle-class, as an exclusively nonproductive and private realm, separate from the public sphere of work. In this century, at the end of World War Two, the discourse of the "happy homemaker" made the "stay-at-home" mom and "apple pie" mode of mothering the normal and natural motherhood experience. The view that "stay-at-home" motherhood is what constitutes good motherhood emerged only in the post-war period to effect a social reorganization and, more particularly, to redesign feminine gender behaviour and roles. During World War Two we witnessed an unprecedented increase in women's employment to include white, middle-class mothers who had previously not been engaged in full-time employment. Thus in the war period, mothers were encouraged to work and celebrated for doing so, particularly in the propaganda films and literature. With the end of the war and the return of the soldiers, women were forced give up their wartime employment. This was orchestrated and facilitated by an ideological redesign of what constitutes good motherhood. Buttressed by the new psychological teachings, notably Bowlby's attachment theory, two beliefs emerged: 1) children require full-time "stay-at-home" mothering, and 2) children, without full-time mothering, would suffer from what was termed "maternal deprivation." According to Bowlby, as noted by Shari Thurer in *The Myths of Motherhood: How Culture Reinvents the Good Mother*, "maternal deprivation was as damaging in the first three years of life as German measles in the first three months of pregnancy: 'mother love in infancy is as important for mental health as proteins and vitamins for physical health'" (276).

Sacrificial motherhood, as described by my students, thus emerged as the dominant view of good mothering in the post-war period, or approximately 60 years ago. Sacrificial motherhood is characterized by three central themes. The first defines mothering as *natural* to women and essential to their being conveyed in the belief, as noted by Pamela Courtenay Hall, that "women are *naturally* mothers, they are born with a built-in set of capacities, dispositions, and desires to nurture children [... and that this] engagement of love and instinct is utterly distant from the world of paid work..." (59). Secondly, the mother is to be central caregiver of her biological children; and third, children require full-time mothering, or in the instance where the mother must work outside the home, the children must always come before the job. This model of mothering, as Sharon Hays explains in *The Cultural Contradictions of Motherhood*, "tells us that children are innocent and priceless, that their rearing should be carried out primarily by individual mothers and that it should be centered on children's needs, with methods that are informed by experts, labor intensive, and costly" (21). Hays calls this style of motherhood intensive mothering and argues that is has been the dominant mode of mothering since the Second World War. She emphasizes that intensive mothering is "a historically constructed *cultural model* for appropriate child care" (21, emphasis in original). "Conceptions of appropriate child rearing," she continues,

> are not simply a random conglomeration of disconnected ideas; they form a fully elaborated, logically cohesive framework for thinking about and acting toward children.... [W]e are told that [intensive mothering] is the best model, largely because it is what children need and deserve. This model was not developed overnight, however, nor is intensive mothering the only model available to mothers. (21)

Sharon Hays argues that intensive mothering emerged in the post-war period. I contend, in contrast, that while the origins of intensive mothering may be traced back to this time, intensive mothering, in its fully developed form, came about in the mid- to late-1980s. Hays argues, as noted above, that intensive mothering is characterized by three themes: "first, the mother is the central caregiver"; "mothering is regarded as more important than paid employment," and that such mothering requires "lavishing copious amounts of time, energy, and material resources on the child" (8). I would suggest that while the first two characterize mothering from post-war to present day, only mothering of the last 15 years can be characterized by the third theme: namely, children require copious amounts of time, energy, and material resources. The post-war discourse of good motherhood demanded that mothers be at home full-time with their children, however such did not necessitate the intensive mothering expected of mothers today. I see the post-war discourse of mother-hood covering the period between 1946 to the mid-'70s, the time when children of the baby boom generation were being raised and before they themselves were mothers. I term the post-war discourse on motherhood "custodial mothering" or the "flower pot" approach and see it as different from intensive mothering. Intensive mothering, in contrast, emerged in the 1980s and is practiced by the daughters born in the late baby boom years—1950 to 1968—who become mothers in the mid-'80s and '90s. While intensive mothering emerges from custodial mothering, I emphasize that it is a distinct motherhood discourse specific to its historical period. Most research on

Introduction

motherhood does not distinguish between the two; rather both are characterized as post-war mothering or more generally twentieth century mothering. To
fully understand how patriarchal ideologies of "good" motherhood function as
culturally constructed practices, ones that are continuously redesigned in
response to changing economic and societal factors, we must, I suggest,
distinguish between custodial and intensive mothering because these two
discourses emerged in response to two very different cultural transformations.

custodial
    The ideology of "good" motherhood in the post-war era required full-time
mothering but the emphasis was on the physical proximity of mother and
child—i.e., the mother was to be "at home" with the children, with little said
on the mother needing to be continually attuned to the psychological,
emotional or cognitive needs of her children. My mother, for example,
remembering the early 1960s, recalls "airing" my sister and me on the front
porch each morning while she tended to the housework. Domesticity—
keeping a clean house and serving well-prepared dinners—was, more than
children, what occupied the post-war mother's time and attention. In the
1950s and '60s, as well, there was a clearer division between the adult world and
the world of children. Children would spend their time out in the neighbourhood playing with other children; seldom would children look to their parents
for entertainment or amusement. And rarely were children enrolled in
programs with the exception of the occasional Brownies or Cub Scout meeting
in the school-age years.

intensive
    Today, the ideology of good motherhood demands more than mere physical
proximity of mother-child: contemporary mothers are expected to spend, to
use the discourse of the experts, "quality time" with their children. Mothers are
told to play with their children, read to them, and take classes with them. As
the children in the '50s and '60s would jump rope or play hide-and-seek with
the neighbourhood children or their siblings, today's children dance, swim,
and "cut and paste" with their mothers in one of many "moms and tots"
programs. And today, children as young as three months old are enrolled in a
multitude of classes from water-play for infants, French immersion for toddlers,
karate for pre-schoolers, and competitive skiing, skating or sailing for elementary school children. (An article I read recently also recommended reading and
singing to your child in utero.) Today, though they have fewer children and
more labour saving devices—from microwaves to take-out food—mothers
spend more time, energy (and I might add money) on their children than their
mothers did in the 1960s. And the majority of mothers today, unlike 40 years
ago, practice intensive mothering while engaged in full-time employment.
Mothering today, as in the post-war era, is "expert driven." However, mothering today is also, under the ideology of intensive mothering, more child-
centred than the "children should be seen but not heard" style of mothering

the characterized the post-war period. Finally, contemporary mothering demands of mothers far more time, energy, and money than was asked of mothers in the '50s and '60s. Toni Morrison's recently published novel, *Love*, delineates well the differences in these two styles of mothering. Vida, a mother and grandmother in the story, reflects:

> [Her grandson's generation] made her nervous. Nothing learned from her own childhood or from raising [her own daughter] Dolly worked with them, and everywhere parents were flummoxed. These days the first thought at Christmas was the children, in her own generation it was the last. Now, children wept if their birthdays weren't banquets; then the day was barely acknowledged. (148-149)

The ideology of intensive mothering, as Hays notes, "advise[s] mothers to expend a tremendous amount of time, energy and money in raising children" (x). However, as Hays continues, "In a society where over half of all mothers with young children are now working outside the home, one might wonder why our culture pressures women to dedicate so much of themselves to child rearing" (x).

> Today ... when well over half of all mothers are in the paid labor force, when the image of a career women is that of a competitive go-getter, and when the image of the family is one of disintegrating values and relationships, one would expect a de-emphasis on the ideology of child rearing as labor-intensive, emotionally absorbing work. (Hays 3)

Indeed, one would expect to locate the ideology of intensive mothering in the post-war period when middle-class mothers, engaged in full-time motherhood, had more time and energy to devote to child rearing. Instead, the emergence of intensive mothering parallels the increase in mothers' paid labour force participation.

Theorists of motherhood and mothers alike, offer various explanations to account for the emergence of intensive mothering over the last 20 years. Hays, for example, argues that

> the ideology of intensive child rearing practices persists, in part, because it serves the interests of men but also capitalism, the state, the middle class and Whites. Further, and on a deeper level ... the ideology of intensive mothering is protected and promoted because it holds a fragile but nonetheless, powerful cultural position as the

last best defense against what many people see as the impoverish-
ment of social ties, communal obligations, and unremunerated commitments. (xiii)

Elsewhere I have explored how the ideology of intensive mothering emerged
in the 1980s in response to changing demographics of motherhood. Today, for
the majority of middle-class women, motherhood is embarked upon only after
a career is established, when the woman is in her 30s. For these mothers the
hurriedness of intensive mothering is a continuation of their busy lives as
professional women; where once their daybooks were filled with business
lunches, office meetings, and the like, as intensive mothers, home with their
children, gymboree classes and "moms and tots" library visits schedule their
daytimers. Often these professional, highly educated women, unfamiliar and
perhaps uncomfortable with the everyday, devalued, invisible work of mothering and domesticity, fill up their days with public activities that can be
documented as productive and visible work. With fewer children, labour
saving devices and household help, child rearing, or more accurately the
enrichment and amusement of the one beloved child, becomes the focus of the
mother's time and attention; as opposed to cooking and cleaning as it was in
my mother's generation. And when these professional women return to their
careers, intensive mothering, as practiced in the evenings and weekends, is the
way a working mother, consciously or otherwise, compensates for her time
away from her children; it bespeaks the ambivalence and guilt contemporary
working mothers may feel about working and enjoying the work they do. As
well, intensive mothering, in its emphasis upon enrichment—toys, books,
games, activities, programs, camps, holidays, theatre, and so forth for children—emerged in response to mothers earning an income of their own and
having a say on how household money is to be spent. Mothers, more so than
fathers, are the consumers of items children need and want; thus as a mother's
earnings and economic independence increases, more money is spent on
children.

Finally, some argue that just as custodial mothering emerged in the post–war
period in response to new psychological theories that stressed the need for
mother-child attachment, intensive mothering in our time came about in
response to the new scientific research that emphasizes the importance of the
first five years of life in the intellectual, behavioural, emotional, and social
development of the child. Whatever the economic or social explanation may
be, the ideology of intensive mothering measures good mothering in accordance with the amount of time, money, and energy a mother expends on
childrearing. Raising one child today, as my mother frequently remarks,
demands more time, energy, and money than the raising of four in the post-war

period. Indeed, the demands made on mothers today are unparalled in our history.

Today's intensive mothering is also, as was custodial mothering in the post-war era, an ideological construction that functions as a backlash discourse, and, like all backlash discourses, it functions to regulate women, or more specifically in this instance, mothers. Drawing upon Naomi Wolf's theory of the "Beauty Myth," I believe the current discourse of intensive mothering emerged in response to women's increased social and economic independence: increased labour participation, entry into traditionally male areas of work, rise in female-initiated divorces, growth in female headed-households, and improved education. It seems that just as women were making inroads, feeling confident, a new discourse of motherhood emerged which made two things inevitable: that women would forever feel inadequate as mothers and that work and motherhood would be forever seen as in conflict and incompatible. I believe that the guilt and shame women experience in failing to live up to what is in fact an impossible ideal is neither accidental nor inconsequential. Rather it is deliberately manufactured and monitored. Just as the self-hate produced by the beauty myth undercuts and undermines women's sense of achievement in education or a career, the current discourse of intensive mothering gives rise to self-doubt, or more specifically guilt, that immobilizes women and robs them of their confidence as both workers and mothers. "The image of [perfect] motherhood," as Sheila Kitzinger notes, is a false one. "A woman who catches site of herself (unmasked as it were) sees a very different picture. And the message is clear she is a failure" (qtd. in Maushart 8). Given that no one can achieve intensive mothering, all mothers see themselves as failures. This is how the discourse works psychologically to regulate—i.e. paralyze—mothers, via guilt and shame. And, some mothers, believing that perfect motherhood could be achieved if they "just quit work," leave paid employment. This is how the discourse regulates on the level of the social and the economic.

The ideology of intensive mothering dictates that: 1) children can only be properly cared for by the biological mother; 2) this mothering must be provided 24/7; 3) the mother must always put children's needs before her own; 4) mothers must turn to the experts for instruction; 5) the mother is fully satisfied, fulfilled, completed, and composed in motherhood; and finally, 6) mothers must lavish excessive amounts of time, energy, and money in the rearing of their children. Each demand is predicated on the eradication, or at very least, sublimation of a mother's own selfhood and in particular her agency, autonomy, authenticity, and authority. The discourse of intensive mothering becomes oppressive not because children have needs, but because we, as a culture, dictate that only the biological mother is capable of fulfilling them, that children's needs must always come before those of the mother, and that children's needs must be responded to around the clock and with extensive time, money, and energy. "Infancy and early childhood *are* periods of high emotional and physical dependency and, moreover this is not a pure invention of patriarchal science...." However, as Petra Büskens continues, "*The problem is not the fact of this requirement but rather that meeting this need has come to rest exclusively, and in isolation, on the shoulders of biological mothers*" (81, emphasis in original). Indeed, as author Toni Morrison comments: "If you listen to your children and look at them, they make demands that you can live up to. They don't need all that overwhelming love either. I mean, that's just you being vain about it" (qtd. in Taylor-Guthrie 270-71). While sacrificial motherhood, and in particular intensive mothering, requires the denial of the mother's own selfhood in positioning the children's needs as always before her own, there are other ways to mother, ways that do not deny a mother her agency, autonomy, authenticity, and authority, and allow her both her selfhood and power. This is the subject of my research.

The patriarchal ideology of motherhood makes mothering deeply oppressive to women because sacrificial motherhood, both custodial and intensive, requires the repression or denial of the mother's own selfhood; as well it assigns mothers all the responsibility for mothering but gives them no real power from which to mother. Such "powerless responsibility," to use Rich's term, denies a mother the authority and agency to determine her own experiences of mothering. Mothering, in other words, is defined and controlled by the larger patriarchal society in which they live. Mothers do not make the rules, as Rich reminds us, they simply enforce them. Whether it is in the form of parenting books, a physician's advice or the father's rules, a mother raises her children in accordance with the values and expectations of the dominant culture. Mothers are policed by what Sara Ruddick calls the "gaze of others." Under the gaze of others, mothers "relinquish authority to others, [and] lose confidence in their own values" (111). "Teachers, grandparents, mates, friends, employers, even an anonymous passerby," continues Ruddick, "can judge a mother and find her wanting" (111-112). Ruddick calls this an abdication of maternal authority. "Fear of the gaze of others," she continues, "can be expressed intellectually as inauthenticity, a repudiation of one's own perceptions and values" (112). In *Of Woman Born*, Rich remembers her mother locking her in the closest at the age of four, for "childish behaviour—[her] father's order, but [her] mother carried them out—and being kept too long at piano lessons when she was six—again, at [her father's] insistence, but is was [her mother] who gave the lessons" (224). The "powerless responsibility" of patriarchal motherhood is predicated upon such abdication of maternal authority and inauthentic mothering. However, the denial of authority and authenticity demanded in both the mandate of powerless responsibility and in the discourse of sacrificial mother-hood, in particular intensive mothering, are neither natural nor inevitable. There are other discourses and modes of mothering, ones that afford mothers agency, autonomy, authenticity, and authority. To this discussion I now turn.

Empowered Mothering

"The institution of motherhood," Rich writes, "is not identical with bearing and caring for children, any more than the institution of heterosexuality is identical with intimacy and sexual love. Both create the prescriptions and the conditions in which choices are made or blocked; they are not 'reality' but they have shaped the circumstances of our lives" (42). "To destroy the institution is not to abolish motherhood." Rich continues, "It is to release the creation and sustenance of life into the same realm of decision, struggle, surprise, imagina-tion and conscious intelligence, as any difficult, but freely chosen work" (280). And while we may not yet know completely what empowered mothering looks like, we, in interrupting and deconstructing the patriarchal narrative of motherhood, have destabilized the hold this discourse has on the meaning and practice of mothering and have cleared the space for the articulation of counter narratives of mothering.

A counter narrative of empowered mothering is concerned with imagining and implementing a view of mothering that is *empowering* to women as opposed to oppressive as it is with the patriarchal institution of motherhood. Alterna-tively called authentic, radical, feminist or gynocentric mothering, this mode of mothering positions mothers, in Rich's words, as "outlaws from the institu-tion of motherhood." The theory and practice of empowered mothering recognizes that both mothers and children benefit when the mother lives her life and practices mothering from a position of agency, authority, authenticity, and autonomy. Secondly, this new perspective, in emphasizing maternal authority and ascribing agency to mothers and value to motherwork, defines motherhood as a political site wherein mother can affect social change through the socialization of children, in terms of challenging traditional patterns of gender acculturation through feminist child rearing and the world at large through political-social activism.

In *Of Woman Born* Rich writes: "We do not think of the power stolen from us and the power withheld from us in the name of the institution of mother-hood" (275). "The idea of maternal power has been domesticated." Rich continues, "In transfiguring and enslaving woman, the womb—the ultimate source of the power—has historically been turned against us and itself made into a source of powerlessness" (68). My research examines how mothers can and do reclaim that power, or more specifically the empowerment denied to them in the institution of motherhood. My examination of motherhood as a potential site of power, in which mothers have agency, authority, autonomy, and authenticity is developed in two parts. In the first, I am concerned with the mother role in terms of the mother herself—her experiences of it, the meanings she attaches to it—while with the second I focus upon the mother's role in relation to her children and the manner in which she raises them. In other words, the first aim of my research is to explore how feminist mothering affords mothers' agency, while the second aim is to examine how feminist mothering, in emphasizing maternal power and ascribing agency to mothers and value to motherwork, enables mothers to affect social change through the socialization of children, particularly in terms of challenging traditional patterns of gender acculturation. While my research distinguishes between the mother and child rearing for the point of discussion, the two are, of course, interconnected and overlapping. As well, and as I note in the foreword, the two are interdependent: we cannot effect changes in child rearing without first changing the conditions of motherhood. To paraphrase Adrienne Rich: what children need are mothers who want their own freedom and ours (247). In other words: only an empowered mother can empower children and children can only be empowered by an empowered mother.

In the above section on the patriarchal institution of motherhood I argued that patriarchal motherhood, particularly as it is expressed in the ideology of intensive mothering, oppresses women because: 1) children can only be properly cared for by the biological mother; 2) this mothering must be provided 24/7; 3) The mother must always put children's needs before her own; 4) mothers must turn to the experts for instruction; 5) the mother is fully satisfied, fulfilled, completed and composed in motherhood; and finally, 6) mothers must lavish excessive amounts of time, energy and money in the rearing of their children. The patriarchal ideology of motherhood makes mothering deeply oppressive to women because, in filling the above six demands, the mother must repress her own selfhood. As well, patriarchal motherhood, as noted in the above section, assigns mothers all the responsibility for mothering but gives them no real power from which to mother. Such "powerless responsibility," along with the six demands of "good" motherhood, denies a mother the authority, autonomy, authenticity, and agency to determine her own experiences of mothering.

Feminist mothers challenge the six attributes of good—i.e., intensive—motherhood and the mandate of powerless responsibility. Empowered mothering does not assign full responsibility of childcare to the biological mother, nor does it regard 24/7 mothering as necessary for children. Feminist mothers look to friends, family and their partners to assist with childcare, while lesbian mothers often raise their children with an involved co-mother. Likewise, as evidenced in Chapter Six, African-American mothers practice empowered mothering through the practice of othermothering. As well, in most instances, feminist and African-American women combine mothering with paid employment and/or activism, and so the full-time intensive mothering demanded in patriarchal motherhood is not practiced by these mothers. As well, many of these mothers call into question the belief that mothering requires excessive time, money, and energy, and thus practice a mode of mothering that is more compatible with paid employment. As well, empowered mothers see the development of a mother's selfhood as beneficial to mothering and not antithetical to it as is assumed in patriarchal motherhood. Consequently, empowered mothers do not always put their children's needs before their own nor did they only look to motherhood to define and realize their identity. Rather, their selfhood is fulfilled and expressed in various ways: work, activism, friendships, relationships, hobbies, and motherhood. Empowered mothers insist upon their own authority as mothers and refuse the relinquishment of their power as mandated in the patriarchal institution of motherhood and seen in the practice of inauthentic mothering described above.

Finally, for many feminist mothers, motherhood is understood to be a location or site of power wherein mothers can affect social change, both in the home through feminist child rearing and outside the home through maternal activism. Motherhood, in the dominant patriarchal ideology, is seen simply as a private, and more specifically, an apolitical enterprise. In contrast, empowered mothering for many feminist mothers and African-American mothers is understood to have cultural significance and political purpose. Building upon the work of Sara Ruddick, these mothers redefine motherwork as a socially engaged enterprise that seeks to effect cultural change through new feminist modes of gender socialization and interactions with daughters and sons.

The above themes of empowered mothers and empowered mothering may be found in the chapters of section two. However, not every empowered mother practices each theme of empowered mothering. The overall aim of empowered mothering is the redefinition of patriarchal motherhood to make mothering less oppressive and more empowering for mothers. Or more specifically, empowered mothers seek to fashion a mode of mothering that affords and affirms maternal agency, authority, autonomy, and authenticity and which confers and confirms power to and for mothers. However, such mothering, it must be emphasized, is practiced in a culture wherein patriarchal motherhood is the norm. In other words, empowered mothering, as it seeks to challenge patriarchal motherhood, remains defined by it. Consequently, while empowered mothering, in theory, may be fully and clearly defined and realized empowered mothering, in practice, it is far more contested and elusive, achieved and expressed in negotiation with the institution of patriarchal motherhood that it resists. Many of the chapters in the collection examine this theme of negotiation.

Conclusion

A central theme of my research, introduced above and explored at length in the chapters that follow, is that feminist mothering, in affirming maternal agency, authority, autonomy, and authenticity, makes motherhood more rewarding, fulfilling, and satisfying for women. Such mothering allows woman selfhood outside of motherhood and affords her power within motherhood. As well, the practice of othermothering or co-mothering, the ability to combine motherhood with work (paid employment and/or activism), and limiting the time, energy, and money spent on children relieves women of much of the isolation, dependency, boredom, and exhaustion experienced in patriarchal motherhood. It is evident that empowered mothering is better for mothers. Such mothering is also better for children. We understand that mothers content with and fulfilled by their lives make better mothers. Likewise, we recognize that children raised by depressed mothers are at risk. I want to suggest as well that empowered mothers are more effective mothers. Anyone who has been in an airplane knows the routine if oxygen masks are required: put on your mask and then assist children with theirs. This instruction initially seems to defy common sense; children should be helped first. However, the instruction recognizes that parents must be masked first because only then are they able to provide real and continued assistance to the child: unmasked they run they risk of becoming disoriented, ill or unconscious due to lack of oxygen and then of course would be of no use to the child. I see this instruction as a suitable metaphor for empowered mothering; mothers, empowered, are able to better care for and protect their children.

In her recent book *A Potent Spell: Mother Love and the Power of Fear*, Janna Malamud Smith references the myth of Demeter and Persephone to illustrate this theme: children are better served by empowered mothers. Demeter, Smith argues "is able to save her daughter because she is a powerful goddess who can make winter permanent and destroy humankind" (59). "Demeter," she continues, "possesses the very qualities that Mothers so often have lacked— adequate resources and strength to protect their children, particularly daughters" (59). Therefore, and contrary to patriarchal, or more generally accepted, wisdom, what a child needs most in the world, Smith argues, "is a *free and happy* mother" (167, emphasis added). Smith explains:

> [W]hat a child needs most is a free mother, one who feels that she is
> in fact living *her* life, and has adequate food, sleep, wages, education,

safety, opportunity, institutional support, health care, child care, and loving relationships. "Adequate" means enough to allow her to participate in the world—and in mothering.... A child needs a mother who has resources to enable her to make real choices, but also to create a feeling of adequate control—a state of mind that encourages a sense of agency, thus a good basis of maternal well-being, and a good foundation on which to stand while raising a child. Surely, child care prospers in this soil as well as, if not better than in any other. What is more, such a mother can imagine a life of possibility and hope, and can so offer this perspective to a child.... [Finally] a child needs a mother who lives and works within a context that respects her labour, and that realistically supports it without rationalizing oppression in the name of safety, or substituting idealization or sentimentality for resources. (167)

Ann Crittenden, cited by Smith, elaborates further: "Studies conducted on five continents have found that children are distinctly better off when the mother possess enough income and authority in the family to make investing in children a priority" (120). "The emergence of women as independent economic actors," Crittenden continues, "is not depriving children of vital support; it is giving them more powerful defenders. Depriving mothers of an income and influence of their own is harmful to children and a recipe for economic backwardness" (130). To return to the story of Demeter: "It is only because Demeter has autonomy and independent resources, as Smith explains, "that she can protect Persephone" (241). Conversely, "when a culture devalues and enslaves the mother, she can [not] be like Demeter and protect her daughter" (244). Therefore, and as Smith concludes: "If we are really interested in improving the lot of children, our best method would be laws and policy that supports mothers and mothering" (187). It is indeed remarkable, as Smith notes, that "[n]o society has ever voluntarily turned its laws and riches toward liberating mothers" (168).

The free mother valued by Smith and recognized as essential for the well-being of children however will be not found in the patriarchal institution of motherhood or in the practice of intensive mothering. Patriarchal motherhood, as explored above, robs women of their selfhood and power, and intensive mothering, in its emphasis on excessive time, attention, and energy, makes it difficult, if not impossible, for mothers to be autonomous and independent. Empowered, or to use Smith's term, free mothering thus only becomes possible in and through the destruction of patriarchal motherhood. Such mothers can better protect and defend their children as Smith observes. As well, and as noted above and explored in the chapters that follow, empowered mothers can make real and lasting changes in society through social-political activism and in the way they raise their children. More specifically, empowered mothers challenge and change, in the home and in the world at large, the gender roles that straightjacket our children and the harm of sexism, racism, classism, and heterosexism more generally. I want to suggest, as I conclude this introduction, that patriarchy resists empowered mothering precisely because it understands its real power to bring about a true and enduring cultural revolution. Indeed, it will be mothers, empowered and united, who will create the just and caring society, that "feminist new world," we seek for ourselves and all our children

I. MOTHERHOOD

CHAPTER ONE

LABOUR SIGNS

THE SEMIOTICS OF BIRTHING

Ten years ago when my three children were very young and while I was working toward my Ph.D., my spouse and I lived for seven years in a very tiny two-bedroom apartment on campus wherein our eight-by-ten bedroom served as both study and sleeping room for my spouse, myself, and the baby. In that cramped and crowded room, where books were stacked alongside the laundry pile, there used to hang from my bookshelf above the computer, and amidst the disorder of crumpled lecture notes, unpaid bills, and children's odd socks, a small picture of the Great Goddess Venus of Willendorf. Years ago when I was pregnant with my first child, I cut this picture from Merlin Stone's book, *When God Was A Woman*, with the intention of having it framed one day. Well, Venus never got her frame. Instead, in a rare moment of organization, I hung the picture with a piece of scotch tape in front of my books and beside my daughter's discarded barrettes and my son's broken watch band where she stayed until we moved several years later. But, I think that Venus, the Goddess of Birth, Life, and Nature, preferred to sit amongst the relics of my chaotic life rather than be entombed in a picture frame and isolated on a distant wall. She belonged with the dirt and disorder of my life. To confine Venus within a frame and to keep her clean behind glass would have been, I think, disrespectful to the life-force She embodies and represents. I used to like to watch my dusty Venus dance in the breeze alongside my books and my children's memorabilia while I worked. My dusty and dancing Venus was both earth and spirit: beside my children's junk and my books this Great Goddess signified wisdom, as well as life. Wise and nurturing, strong and caring, free yet responsible, my Venus sustained, inspired, and empowered me.

I begin this article on the semiotics of birthing with this memory of my dusty and dancing Venus because She, ten years after She danced in my student apartment, remains, in this culture of "high-tech" birth, a sign without a referent. The birthing woman today is the Venus behind glass within a frame, displayed as spectacle on a barren and distant wall. The sterilized, confined, and alienated Venus behind glass signifies the dominant discourse of birth as a medical event.

In her article, "Feminism, Medicine and the Meaning of Childbirth," Paula A. Treichler argues that while the term childbirth signifies multiple and diverse meanings, both discursively and socially, the medical meaning of birth has, "through a complex cultural process ... come to constitute [the] official 'definition' [of childbirth]" (122, 123). Similar to the frame that confines Venus, a definition, like the medical definition of birth, "sets limits, determines boundaries, distinguishes" (Treichler 123). "Definitions," Treichler continues, "claim to state what is" (123). The multiplicity of meanings which birth may signify are impoverished through the construction of an official—i.e., medical—definition of birth. Through the complex process of intersecting forces, economics, politics, cultural structures, medicine, or what de Lauretis (1987) would call "social technologies," the medical definition of birth is codified as the official and only meaning of childbirth. A definition, as Treichler explains, "represents the *outcome* of [political, economic and ideological] struggle" (133). In turn, the definition through its inscription in laws and social policies determines the material conditions of birthing.

The majority of women give birth in hospital because childbirth is defined as a medical event requiring technological intervention, "scientific expertise" and professional supervision. The medicalization of birth is the result of the medical meaning of birth accruing, in Treichler's words, "linguistic capital—the power to establish and enforce a particular definition of childbirth" (116). It is because the "medical establishment" holds a monopoly on the social technologies that it is able to define the meaning of childbirth and determine its material conditions. To rephrase de Lauretis: the construction of birth is both the product and process of its official medical definition.

The dominant definition of childbirth as medical event empties birth as signifier of its multiple and diverse meanings. The birthing woman is the Venus behind glass within a frame. Childbirth is stirrups, internal and external monitors, oxytocin drip, epidurals, episiotomies, and last, but not least, forceps. Through the codification and mobilization of the official-medical-definition of childbirth the sign birth is emptied of its diversity of meanings and thus becomes, in Barthes' process of signification, a signifier. The sign is appropriated by the official definition of birth, or what we may call the dominant ideology/mythology of childbirth. Through such appropriation the diverse meanings of birth are impoverished and the sign becomes an empty form that may be filled with a new medical definition/ideology of childbirth. Mapping Treichler's Foucauldian analysis of how definitions of childbirth come to be constructed, codified, and mobilized on Barthes' semiotic theory of myth as a process of signification allows us to trace the steps by which the particular definition of birth is naturalized as the only—i.e., universal and real—meaning of birth.

At the first level of signification, language, the relationship between the signifier and the signified, is born from linguistic convention. When we hear the word book, the image of standard-sized paper bound in cloth or paper comes to mind. Parents with young children experience daily how such associations are learned. At a restaurant once, a waiter served my two-year old daughter her coleslaw at the same time he said to my spouse "Here is your lobster." During the meal my daughter pointed to the few strands of coleslaw on her plate and said that she had eaten all of her lobster and wanted more. Because she heard the word lobster at the same time as she was given her coleslaw she thought that the word lobster signified coleslaw. For many years, whenever my daughter heard the word lobster, an image of green cabbage and not a red hard-shelled fish would come to mind. Such a mixed up association became all the more amusing when this same daughter at the age of six decided to become a vegetarian.

At the second level of signification, however, the relationship between the signifier, the first level sign emptied of meaning, and the signified is not defined by linguistic convention, but is rather ideologically overdetermined. Moreover, though the relationship of signifier and signified in language is dictated by linguistic convention, the relationship is not stable or fixed: slippage occurs because the signifier may signify diverse conceptualizations. The word birth for some may signify "natural" birth at home while for others the word brings to mind caesarean delivery or a "high-tech" hospital birth. At the level of myth, however, the relationship between the signifier and the signified is not conventional yet fluid but is rather arbitrary and rigid. There is no connection, linguistic, logical, or otherwise, between the signifier birth and the concept medicalized "high-tech" in hospital childbirth. The two merge, become one as a sign, through the process of signification which is myth. This signification, like the frame which confines Venus, contain the slippage of signifieds by constructing boundaries that restrict and control meaning. Birth, at the second level of myth, now signifies only one of the many conceptualizations of birth, that being childbirth as a medical event. The particular ideologically overdetermined definition or re-presentation of childbirth as a medical event, however, inscribes itself as the normal and the real. Through the process of signification the official definition of childbirth is able to suppress its own construction as an ideology and therefore can naturalize its specific medical treatment of childbirth as the universal "natural" birthing experience.

By overlapping Treichler's Foucauldian argument and Barthes' semiotic approach, we can better understand how one meaning of childbirth enters discourse as a constructed definition and how this definition enforces and reinforces its monopoly on meaning through signifying practices. The interplay of social technologies both produces and reproduces an official definition or dominant ideology. Again to rephrase de Lauretis (1987): the official definition/dominant ideology of birth is both the product and the process of its social technologies. Thus we must ask not only how the official definition of childbirth as medical event comes into being but also how this definition operates as a sign to enforce its meaning of birth and erase all others. In other words, we must track both the cultural process of the definitions' construction and the signifying practices of its re-presentation.

The official definition/dominant ideology of birth as the product of cultural (trans)formations and in the process of its signifying practices inscribes the birthing woman as object, rather than subject, her labour as an automated procedure rather than a natural process. In her book, *The Woman in the Body: A Cultural Analysis of Reproduction*, Emily Martin persuasively documents how, in her words, "reproduction is treated as a form of production" (57). Obstetrical literature, Martin describes, views the birthing woman as a machine, her labour as a form of factory production that must be supervised, managed, and controlled. The scientific and mechanical metaphors which pervade medical discourse result in the discursive erasure of the birthing woman as an active subject and facilitate her objectification in actual obstetrical policies and procedures. The uterus is defined as a machine which produces "efficient or inefficient contractions." Labour, as any mother can tell you, is divided into many stages and substages. The first stage includes the latent phase, the active phase, and transition. The second stage, commonly referred to as the "pushing" stage, involves the birth of the baby. The third stage involves the separation and delivery of the placenta. Each stage and substage, as Martin (1987) notes, is assigned a rate of progression: the latent stage should progress at 0.6 cm/hr; the active phase at 1.6 cm/hr for a first labour. If the woman's labour does not meet the medical rate of "normal" progression, the doctor, as supervisor, manager, or foreman, must intervene and "speed up production" through the implementation of "time-saving" equipment and "short cut" methods: breaking the amniotic sac, applying an oxytocin drip, using forceps, performing an episiotomy, or delivering the baby by cesarean. The mechanistic metaphors of medical discourse suggest that the achievement of technological intervention is not so much improved safety as increased productivity. Thus, as Martin concludes, "[the] complex process[of birth] that interrelates physical, emotional, and mental experience [is] treated as if it could be broken down and managed like other forms of production" (66).

The mechanistic metaphors which inscribe labour as a mode of production are often, as I discovered with my third pregnancy, deployed in the language of militarism. Into the forty-second week of pregnancy the doctor, during a prenatal "check-up" (a term which also requires unpacking in its inscription of the body as machine), outlined to my spouse and I the procedure to be taken now that I was "overdue." After drawing up the itinerary for the week—today a visit to the antenatal clinic for a NST (Non-Stress Test), tomorrow, the booking of the induction, Wednesday, an appointment with an obstetrician, ("overdue" I became a "high-risk" patient that required the supervision of an obstetrician), and Friday the seven o'clock arrival at hospital for the birth—my doctor sat back and announced that *the situation demands that we take action and become aggressive.* The word aggressive jolted me from my wandering thoughts: "late" with my two earlier pregnancies I had sat only half-listening, bored rather than shocked, by the week's agenda. But the word aggressive horrified and stunned me. The word conjured up images of the militarism of the corporate world and battlefields and not the emotions of joy, pride, and triumph I would experience in the birthing of my child. The word also signifies competition, hostility, hate, and even death and not the cooperation and harmony of spirit and body, the intimacy of mother and father, and the parent-child love which birthing creates in its giving of life. But, for my physician, such language is accurate and appropriate because of the medical discourse's inscription of the female body as an unreliable machine and labour as a mode of production which needs to be organized, controlled, and conquered. Through its signifying practices medical discourse empties the sign birth of its plurality of referents and erases, in the process, my meaning of childbirth. My stunned response is more than just an instance of linguistic incomprehension: his speech and my silence is a moment of ideological collision between the dominant enforced "legitimate" definition of birth and one marginal, erased "illegitimate" meaning of it.

Medical discourse, like all language, is never innocent, neutral, or second-ary. "The word childbirth," as Treichler explains, "is not merely a label, provided us by language, for a clear-cut event that already exists in the world: rather than describe, it inscribes, and makes the event intelligible to us. We cannot look through discourse to determine what childbirth 'really' is, for discourse itself is the site where such determination is inscribed" (132). The militaristic language of my physician and the mechanistic metaphors of his medical discourse do not describe my birthing experience but rather determine it as a condition of submission and a mode of production. Medical discourse defines rather than reflects the "reality" of birth: language is the opaque rather than transparent glass that frames my dusty and dancing Venus.

The fight against the medicalization of childbirth must, therefore, be waged in language. "[T]he best weapon against myth," Barthes writes, "is perhaps to mythify it in its turn, and to produce an *artificial* myth: and this reconstituted myth will in fact be a mythology" (135). Since the late '60s, various "alterna-tive" movements—feminism, midwifery, lay health-care organizations—have challenged the official definition/dominant ideology of childbirth as a medical procedure through contesting definitions, alternative mythologies of birth as a "natural" process. The discourses of feminism, midwifery, and the lay health-care movement appropriate the dominant myth of birth and, in Barthes' words, "use it as the departure point for a third semiological chain, to take its signification as the first term of a second myth" (135). At this third level of signification childbirth is re-presented as a natural experience rather than a medical event in which the birthing woman controls, rather than is controlled by, the material conditions of her labour.

Those of us who have read the literature of the home-birth movement or attended a Lamaze class realize how ideologically subversive and politically liberating this counter discourse of childbirth can be. It frees Venus from her frame and lets her dance on the earth once again. Choreographed by the labouring woman in rhythm with the natural motion of her own body, birth becomes a dance of joy and triumph which exhilarates and empowers the birthing woman.

The counter-discourse of birth is indeed subversive in its de-stabilization of the official definition/dominant ideology and liberating in its inscription of childbirth as an empowering female defined and controlled experience. However, this is alternative mythology because it is constituted from the form of the dominant mythology contaminated and contained by the hegemonic sign which creates it. As the alternative mythology is conceived by and in "sleeping with the enemy," the deviant definition of birth, as Treichler explains, "lives a double life... it has grown out of a struggle with a dominant structure which continues to shape it, even cannibalize it" (132). Counter discourses such as deviant definitions and alternative mythologies do not, as Treichler explains, "arise as a pure autonomous radical language embodying the purity of a new politics. Rather it arises from within the dominant discourse and learns to inhabit it from the outside" (132). Because counter discourses are born from the form of a dominant mythology in signifying practices or grow out of a struggle with a dominant structure, they, like Kristeva's semiotic language, must always exist within the dominant discourse, resisting, but never replacing it. The natural mode of childbirth as a product of cultural struggle and in the process of its mythic signifying practices is thus always framed by the discourse it seeks to dismantle.

The political liberation of birth promised by the counter-discourse is also compromised by its discursive inscription of birth as "natural" experience. The "natural" mode of childbirth, as Treichler observes, "[is] as tyrannical and prescriptive as the medical model—perhaps more so, because it pretends to be ideologically free and supportive of individuality" (130). If the labouring woman chooses an epidural for the relief of pain or must deliver her baby by caesarean, is the birth, therefore, "unnatural?" In its inscription of birth as "natural," the counter-discourse constructs an impasse between the discursive ideal and the "real" circumstances of birth.

With my first pregnancy I "prepared" for "natural" childbirth, (an oxymoron that foregrounds the ideological contradictions of the counter-discourse—preparing for something that is constituted as natural), by attending Lamaze classes. Drilled in breathing exercises, disciplined in "coping strategies," I, along with my spouse—now a trained coach—entered the hospital armed with all the required equipment—a paper bag for possible hyperventilation, a picture to focus upon during contractions—determined "to beat the odds" and succeed in "natural" childbirth. We were not prepared for "hemorrhaging during labour" which sabotaged our plans for a "natural" birth by necessitating technological intervention. After many hours of "managing" my labour, I, overwhelmed by fear and exhausted by the pain, "broke down," conceded "defeat" and asked for an epidural. (This militaristic language of "natural" childbirth—coping strategies, trained coach, beat the odds, etc. signals a discursive contamination and an ideological contradiction.)

Because birth is natural in the counter-discourse, I saw my medicalized technological birth as unnatural and illegitimate. I felt not joy and pride in birthing my child but shame, guilt, sorrow, and loss: I had failed, let my spouse down, deprived my child of a "gentle" birth and denied myself the promised exhilarating empowerment of a self-determined "natural" labour. All the women I spoke to after the birth of my son expressed similar emotions: our conversations always returned to our feeling of disappointment, guilt, grief, and anger. Because the counter-discourse of "natural" childbirth grounds the reality of birth in what is often an impossible to attain labour experience, it becomes a tyrannical and prescriptive master discourse which belittles and oppresses the very women it claims to empower and liberate. Between the discursive ideal and the "real" circumstances of birth is inscribed the shame, guilt, and sorrow of the labouring woman.

As an alternative mythology that is constituted from a dominant mythology, and as a deviant definition which comes from the struggle with an official definition, the counter-discourse of birth will, perhaps, never cleanse itself of its inevitable contamination. The counter-discourse of birth is polluted with the medical discourses' language of militarism. Birth is inscribed as a competitive sport or battle in which the birthing woman, drilled and disciplined in self-control, conquers her pain and proves she can take it (like a man). It is a testing-ground or rite of initiation which separates the women from the girls. The "natural" mode of childbirth also, as discussed above, positions itself, like the medical model of birth, as a tyrannical and prescriptive master discourse.

If alternative mythologies and deviant definitions ultimately result in the containment, contamination, and cannibalization of feminism, how do we displace the official definition/dominant ideology of birth, and define a truly liberating discourse of childbirth? For Treichler, discursive omnipotence is possible only in and through political power. She writes: "[W]e need to strengthen *feminist political aims*: Women's right to economic resources, information, self-determination, strategic alliances across race and class, access to appropriate resources, and participation in decision-making about the reproductive process" (133). With equal access to the social technologies, feminists may be able to codify and signify their own discourse of childbirth. Perhaps in a fair "contest of meanings" (equal access to the social technologies), we could construct an official definition of birth which could, in turn, as a dominant ideology, re-present itself as the first sign in the mythological process of signification.

Is such a discourse possible? Not in my lifetime, but perhaps in the lifetime of my children. But since official definitions of birth and their re-presentations as mythologies are constituted, codified, and mobilized on political terrain, it is on this turn that we must fight. Challenging, changing, and someday claiming, political power, we are empowered to discursively inscribe and, in turn, socially determine a truly feminist mode of reproduction. Then and only then will Venus truly dance to her own self-composed song of birth.

CHAPTER TWO

TALKING BACK IN MOTHER TONGUE

A FEMINIST COURSE ON MOTHERING-MOTHERHOOD

We know more about the air we breathe, the seas we travel, than about the nature and meaning of motherhood (Rich 11).

Maternal voices have been drowned by professional theory, ideologies of motherhood, sexist arrogance, and childhood fantasy. Voices that have been distorted and censored can only be *developing* voices. Alternately silenced and edging toward speech, mothers' voices are not voices of mothers as they are, but as they are becoming. (Ruddick 40)

Could it be that maternal discourse can exist in the text only on the condition that it remain fragmentary, incomplete...? (Hirsch 185)

In the spring and summer of 1991 I designed a third year university course on mothering and motherhood for the Women's Studies Program at Atkinson College, York University. When colleagues asked why I was designing a course on motherhood, I reflected upon a comment made by Toni Morrison: "I wrote the books ... I wanted to read" (qtd. in Russell 42). My course on mothering-motherhood was the course I had always wanted—and needed—to take.

I am the mother of three young children: my first child, a son, born in the final year of my Honours B.A. (1984), my second, a daughter, born three months into the first year of my doctoral studies (1986), and my third, a daughter, born mid-way through my Ph.D. program (1989). As well, I have been a student of Women's Studies for 12 years and have taught in the field for five. In the backlash of the late 1980s the subject of motherhood became increasingly central to the feminist inquiry. The 1980s, in particular the year 1989, marked an unprecedented proliferation of theoretical works, from across the disciplines, on mothering and motherhood. These included: Mary O'Brien's *The Politics of Reproduction*; Joyce Trebilcot's edited collection *Mothering: Essays in Feminist Theory*; the tenth anniversary edition of Adrienne Rich's

classic *Of Woman Born: Motherhood as Experience and Institution*; Sandra
Pollack and Jeanne Vaughn's *Politics of the Heart: A Lesbian Parenting Anthology*; Miriam Johnson's *Strong Mothers, Weak Wives*; Sara Ruddick's *Maternal Thinking*; Paula Caplan's *Don't Blame Mother*; Barbara Katz Rothman's *Recreating Motherhood: Ideology and Technology in a Patriarchal Society*; Marianne Hirsch's *The Mother/Daughter Plot: Narrative, Psychoanalysis, Feminism*; Valerie Walkerdine and Helen Lucey's *Democracy in the Kitchen: Regulating Mothers and Socializing Daughters*.

This feminist renaissance in mothering-motherhood did not, however, generate a conceptual rethinking of the university undergraduate Women Studies curriculum. The subject of motherhood remained secondary to more popular feminist topics of sexuality and work. And when motherhood was considered in the classroom the frame of reference for theoretical discussion was, more often than not, the "prison of domesticity" theme of late nineteenth-century literature or the "motherhood-as-patriarchal-trap" paradigm of early 1970s feminist thought. Indeed, as late as 1991, York, a university with two large and successful Women's Studies programs and a student population of over 40,000, did not offer a single course on the subject of mothering-motherhood.

The course I designed, entitled "Mothering-Motherhood," is a third-year Women Studies course offered through Atkinson college at York University. Atkinson College is a separate faculty for mature and returning students; classes are offered in the evening and students complete their degrees on a part-time basis. The Mothering-Motherhood course, first taught in the 1992 summer session, is to be offered every second academic year. There were 36 students in the first class: all were women and most were white middle-class mothers in their late '30s to early '50s.

Although designed as a Humanities course in the Women's Studies Program, students may also explore Social Science topics in their seminar presentations and research papers. I decided upon a Humanities perspective because I felt a theoretical investigation of the meaning(s) of mothering was most lacking in the Women's Studies curriculum. Empirical studies of motherhood were more readily available in mainstream sociology courses on the family. The central premise of this course is that motherhood is a cultural construction which varies with time and place; there is not one essential or universal experience of motherhood. Along with the recognition that mothering is always/already culturally determined is an emphasis upon the "ideology of the text" in patriarchal and feminist writings on mothering-motherhood; for, just as experiences of mothering are never natural, writings on mothering are never neutral.

In contemporary white western culture, the multiple meanings of what motherhood may signify, both socially and discursively, are erased and impoverished through the construction of an official—ie. patriarchal—definition of motherhood. Patriarchy, therefore, both socially and discursively, defines the meaning of motherhood and determines how women mother. Under patriarchy, a mother is a heterosexual, married, financially dependent woman whose self-definition is derived solely though her maternal role; to be otherwise is to be an abnormality—a *non*-mother.

That is why, of course, the TV character Murphy Brown so unnerved U.S. Republican Vice-President Dan Quayle in the 1992 U.S. presidential campaign. As both a mother and a single career woman Murphy Brown deconstructs the patriarchal discourse of motherhood. This highly publicized event, Quayle's criticism and Brown's later rebuttal in the season premier, marks an important ideological struggle; a contest of meanings between the dominant and enforced "legitimate" definition of motherhood and one marginal, illegitimate meaning of it.

The Mothering-Motherhood course is a site of resistance. In it we challenge the patriarchal monopoly on the meaning of motherhood by exposing the patriarchal definition of motherhood as a specific ideological construction, hence not natural or real, and by claiming and celebrating women's marginalized stories/theories. We deconstruct the patriarchal discourse of motherhood by talking back in mother tongue.

The introductory section of the course, "Gynocentic Mothering and Patriarchal Motherhood," begins with two films, "The Goddess Remembered," an informative and beautifully crafted documentary on early Goddess worship and "The Spring and Fall of Nina Polanski," a short animated film about the "perfect" mother-housewife who is gradually transformed into a fridge and stove. The juxtaposition of these films highlights the crucial distinction Adrienne Rich makes between mothering, "the *potential* relationship of any woman to her powers of reproduction and to children," and motherhood, " … the *institution*, which aims at ensuring that potential—and all women—shall remain under male control" (13). Appropriately, we begin our readings with Rich's classic *Of Woman Born*. The distinction she makes between these two discourses on motherhood—patriarchal motherhood and gynocentric mothering—provides us with a theoretical framework for thinking about women's experiences as mothers.

In the second part of the introductory section we look at one cultural/discursive manifestation of patriarchal motherhood, namely, men's fear of, and control over, female procreation. In her introduction to *The Politics of Reproduction*—the second reading of the course—Mary O'Brien argues that men are "alienated from the seed" (Eliot qtd. in O'Brien 30) and this gives rise to a specific male reproductive consciousness of discontinuity, "between the conception and the creation falls the shadow."[1] Men, however, attempt to compensate for this alienation from genetic continuity—the uncertainty of paternity—through the "social appropriation of the child" and by creating "artificial modes on continuity." This male alienation from the "seed" is further compensated for through a related ideological and later technological construction that I term the patriarchal appropriation of female procreation.

Since the dawn of patriarchy men have attempted to claim for themselves the power of female procreation: in the Bible's first book, Genesis, a male god creates the world by speaking it into being; in Aristotelian science the father is proven to be the true parent of the child because of his warmer blood and, more recently, with the new reproductive technologies, the male seed rather than the female ovum or womb, constitutes parentage. In the course, students consider this theme of patriarchal appropriation of female procreation through a reading of Mary Shelley's classic novel *Frankenstein* and Barbara Rothman's *Recreating Motherhood*. Many students were surprised to learn that *Frankenstein* was on the reading list. *Frankenstein* is usually read as a critique of Man's desire to be Godlike. Indeed, Victor does "play God" but, more specifically and significantly, he creates a human being. He obtains the one power that has been denied to him as a man, the ability to create life. However, Victor's desire to be "the creator of ... a new species" has little to do with giving and nurturing life—he abandons his child the moment he is "born"—and everything to do with the power to create life; once he has proven that he can "do it" he is no longer interested. With the new reproductive technologies the nightmare imagined by Shelley in Frankenstein has become a too familiar reality. The course concludes with a discussion of the new reproductive technologies in terms of the theme of patriarchal appropriation of female procreation developed by O'Brien and dramatized in *Frankenstein*.

The next section, "Mothers in Feminist Theory," is the longest and most difficult. Here the students move from patriarchal discourses on reproduction and motherhood to feminist theories of mothering. In the first part, entitled "Daughter-centricity, Matrophobia and Mother-Blame," we read the works of two early and influential theorists on mothering, Nancy Chodorow's *The Reproduction of Mothering* and Dorothy Dinnerstein's *The Mermaid and the Minotaur*. Chodorow argues that exclusive female mothering engenders particular feminine and masculine psychic configurations; girls develop a sense of self separate from, and superior to, others which reproduces male dominance.

In 1978 Chodorow's feminist revision of Freudian theory was regarded as theoretically ground breaking because it was the first feminist text to tell the daughter's side of the psychoanalytic story. However, in giving voice to the female child, Chodorow writes a psychoanalytic narrative which is told exclusively from the daughter's point of view and in which the mother is described and inscribed as reader and spectator. The mother does not write her own lines or direct her own performance. Recently several theorists have identified what Brenda O. Daly and Maureen T. Reddy appropriately term the "daughter-centricity" (2) of Chodorow's discourse. In the class we discuss how this daughterly subjectivity is responsible for two very disturbing trends in feminist thought: matrophobia and mother blame.[2] With Chodorow, and particularly Dinnerstein, men and patriarchy are exonerated and mothers are held responsible for the oppression of women. That feminist thinkers could blame mothers for the father's crime is surprising and deeply troubling.

Mother-blame and matrophobia upset and angered many students. One wrote in her journal: "It greatly disturbs me when a woman such as Chodorow writes powerful stuff which influences a lot of people. I expect it from Freud but not from someone who calls herself a feminist" (Vicky).[3] Several students came to recognize their own mother-blame by identifying it in Chodorow and Dinnerstein. One wrote: "As I was working on this presentation [on Dinnerstein] I thought about how I had blamed my own mother ... [N]ow I understand that it was terribly wrong of me to blame her for issues which I had with patriarchal values" (Theresa). After recognizing their own mother-blame, many women were able to heal an estranged mother-daughter relationship. One woman, raised by her mother to be strong and self-defined, wrote in her journal: "I always blamed my mother. I believed that if she only raised me like everybody else I would have been a happier person.... I don't blame my mom anymore but rather appreciate her. I appreciate and love the fact that I was raised differently" (Barbara). Another student concluded a journal entry with this insightful and inspirational thought: "Our mothers are ourselves, only so long as we see them relationally, and in terms of ourselves. Within such a psychic structure we hate the part of ourselves which resembles our mothers. It is by re-thinking and re-defining our mothers, not just in terms of, but also set apart from, us that we may love ourselves and free our mothers from our perpetuated blame, hostility and hatred" (Shelly).

The second part of the section on others in Feminist Theory, entitled "The (M)other Side of the Story," begins with Miriam Johnson's *Strong Mothers, Weak Wives*, a book that challenges the daughter-centric mother-blame of Chodorow and Dinnerstein. Johnson's central argument is that "it is the wife role and not the mother's role that organizes women's secondary status." Johnson argues that women's lack of autonomy originates not, as Chodorow argues, from feminine related sense of self which the mother-daughter relationship engenders, but from the daughter's psychological dependency on her father as a male-oriented daddy's girl. Far from prohibiting authentic female autonomy, a daughter's identification with her mother, in fact, produces and promotes authentic female autonomy.

Most students agree with Johnson's argument that a mother-daughter identification empowers women to overcome our psychological authenticity as daddy's girls and our social oppression as women in patriarchy. We discussed how daughters must come to know their mothers as mothers and persons and not as their father's wife. One student wrote in her journal: "I've never thought about listening to her [the mother's] side of the story ... until we started to discuss Johnson's book" (Barbara). While most agreed that a positive daughter-mother identification is the foundation for a strong female-defined identity, several women emphasized how difficult it is to achieve this female solidarity in a patriarchal society. One student noted:

> It's damn hard to "identify with the mother." One can do so intellectually, but emotionally—to really understand on an intuitive and bodily level what your own mother is all about and to come to terms with that knowledge is a life long battle ... There are two people in each of us (actually there are many, but two will do for my current purposes) the daughter and the adult/mother. It is not so hard for the adult within us to understand how easy it is to "fail" one's children, but it is very hard for the child within us.... The adult in us can understand the circumstances that brought about these conditions and realities but the child will always feel wounded and it too deserves a voice. (Carrie)

With the next book in this section, Sara Ruddick's *Maternal Thinking*, we move to the work and thought of maternal practice. Ruddick's central argument is that, "Maternal work ... demands that mothers think; out of this need for thoughtfulness, a distinctive discipline emerges" (24). Ruddick terms this disciplined reflection "Maternal Thinking." We discussed the three demands of maternal practice—preservation, growth, social acceptance—and the characteristics of maternal thinking—scrutiny, humility, resilient cheerfulness, holding attentive love. As well we debated the connections Ruddick makes between maternal thinking and peace politics. Ruddick's distinction between unauthentic and authentic mothering—or what one student appropriately termed right-wing versus feminist mothering—enabled us to conceptualize an empowering experience of mothering apart from the patriarchal institution of motherhood (described by Rich) and the "man-on-top" heterosexual role of wife (described by Johnson). Ruddick and Johnson were, by far, the most popular theorists on the reading list. As one student said of Ruddick: "She has given me the best description of why I am committed to this experience [of mothering]" (Lisa).

The section on "The (M)other Side of the Story" concludes with the new

French feminisms. Helene Cixous celebrates the plurality, multiplicity, and continuity of the mother-daughter pre-Oedipal symbiosis as the source and origin of *l'ecriture feminine*: "In woman there is always, more or less, something of the mother.... She writes in white ink" (93-94). With Julia Kristeva (1984), the maternal is a position for the semiotic pre-Oedipal "jouissance"; a potential or a position which disrupts the symbolic. And for Luce Irigaray the pre-Oedipal mother-daughter jouissance is re-experienced in woman's anatomy and sexuality: "[Female] sexuality, always at least double, goes even further; it is plural ... Woman as sex organs more or less everywhere" (28). Many students commented that this writing from the body was personally and politically empowering. One student commented: "Irigaray and Cixous both emphasize writing to get back to the body, to get in touch with what you suspect but don't know how to say, to mold the foggy hints your body gives you into clear thoughts ... I realize how important it is for women to put that fog on paper, know what it is trying to tell you" (Laura). Another student wrote: "Reading their writing was one of the most powerful experiences I have had, I just kept writing down quotation after quotation" (Lisa). Another student asked us to share with the class our first memories of our mothers, as part of her seminar on *l'ecriture feminine*. We experimented with "writing from the body" and expressed, in a multitude of discourses such as poetry, fictional/autobiographical stories, drawings, a remembering of our mothers (Vicky).

We begin the next section, "Mothers Stories, 'From Margin to Centre,' Race and Class" with Walkerdine and Lucey's *Democracy in the Kitchen* and Tillie Olsen's short story, "I Stand Here Ironing." Walkerdine and Lucey explore how and why the middle-class mode of mothering—what they appropriately term sensitive mothering—came to be naturalized as the normal, true discourse of motherhood over the last 40 years. The duties of the "sensitive mother" are delineated in the following tongue-in-cheek "job description" written by a student for her seminar presentation:

Ten Commandments of Sensitive Mothering

1. Thou shalt not have any needs other than those of thy child's.
2. Thou shalt be sensitive to thy child's needs.
3. Thou shalt know thy child's needs before thy child knows of them.
4. Thou shalt be ready, willing and able to respond to thy child's needs.
5. Thou shalt not do household chores before thy child's needs have been met.
6. Thou shalt drop thy household chores if thy child beckon with any new demands.

7. If thou must do housework, use it to teach thy child an abstract concept.

8. Thou shalt profess undying love and patience for thy child, even in the face of violence.

9. Thou shalt not show displeasure on thy face for it shall damage thy child psychologically.

10. Thou shalt smile at all times and at all costs.[4]

Because working class women do not practise "sensitive mothering," they are deemed unnatural and unfit mothers, in need of regulation. Here we discuss how our class position determines the way we mother. One student produced a video in which she interviewed three different women on their experiences of mothering (Reesa). This video, along with our readings on working class mothering, documented how patriarchal discourses determine and regulate our experiences as mothers.

We conclude our discussion of working class mothers by watching the film, "Would I Ever Like to Work," a very moving story about a young woman who left an abusive marriage and is now on welfare with seven children. She dreams of someday securing subsidized daycare for her children so that she may work as a waitress. Here is a woman who played by patriarchal rules, she got married, followed church teachings and did not practice birth control, stood by her man even though he beat her and her children, and still she is left, alone, poor, and desperate. Her story vividly—and painfully—details the oppressiveness of the patriarchal institution of motherhood.

This film is contrasted to the following film, "Our Dear Sisters," a short documentary about a Native woman performer and the very enriching and empowering relationship she has with her young adopted daughter. The film introduces our topic of Native mothers and the reading, Paula Gunn Allen's *Spider Woman's Granddaughters*, a splendid collection of short stories on Native mothering. Here we explore how and why Native mothering differs from patriarchal *and* feminist discourses on motherhood. Allen's book and the film portray a mother-centered culture in which women are revered and empowered precisely because they are mothers. A culture which cherishes children and assumes a communal responsibility for their well-being. As mothers, Native women are not male-oriented, financially dependent wives who raise children alone in an isolated nuclear family model. One student wrote in her journal: "The stories are filled with a respect of life and of women, especially mothers. They have a distinctively different flavour than Western stories in which women must suffer to be fulfilled" (June). Our discussion concluded with a video on Native mothering produced by a student: she interviewed three Native women about their experiences of mothering and their views on Bill C-31.[5]

In the final part of this section on "Mothers Stories" we look at African-American and African mothering. We read various articles, poems, stories on Black mothering, as well as Toni Morrison's *Beloved* and Buchi Emecheta's *The Joys of Motherhood* . Our readings call into question, time and time again, all the patriarchal and white feminist assumptions about mothering. As one student said of Toni Morrison in her journal: "*Beloved* was a wonderful story. Everything the white reader thinks she understands and knows Toni Morrison deconstructs" (Julie). Two students produced a video on Black mothers and we watched the film "Black Mother, Black Daughter," a beautiful documentary on Black women in Nova Scotia. We explore many themes and topics in our class discussions: Black motherhood under slavery, mothering and colonialism and racism, mother-daughter relationships, communal and surrogate childrearing, mothering as a *cultural* caring for, and healing of, all people, homeplace as a site of resistance, mother as guardian of African-American history and culture, and women's role and status as mothers in African-American society.

Most students wrote on Black mothering for one of their major papers. As well, many students commented in their journal that their readings on Black mothering-motherhood has lead to a greater appreciation of the socio-historical specificity of African-American mothering *and* an increased impatience for feminist thinkers, like Chodorow, who gloss over and/or bracket such lived cultural difference. One student noted: "After reading this material I feel I have a better understanding about why Black women have been reluctant to join white women's feminist movement. Family and motherhood has been a place that many Black women found encouragement and empowerment. Their experience of both these have been very different from white women's experiences as wives and mothers" (Roberta).

In the second section of "Mothers Stories" entitled "Sexuality: With Women, With Men Or On Our Own" we move to the theme of motherhood and sexuality. We open with a theoretical discussion on motherhood and sexuality and view the Hollywood film, "The Good Mother." We discuss how the patriarchal whore/madonna categorization of Woman makes it very difficult for women to reconcile the sexual and maternal in their lives. This led one student to comment in her journal: "Society must accept that a woman, like a man, has the same sexual needs. A woman should be taught to celebrate her body, not hate it the way advertisers make a woman feel" (Sally).

The patriarchal policing of women's sexuality is even more vigilantly enforced when that mother is a lesbian. For our discussion of lesbian mothers we read *Politics of the Heart* (Pollack and Vaughan), a collection of articles and stories on lesbian mothering, and watched "Choosing Children," an informative and inspirational film on lesbian mothers. Many students were enraged and saddened by the patriarchal inquisition of lesbian mothers, particularly those mothers who had suffered the legal violence of the "justice" system and lost custody of their children. One student wrote: "My heart was really touched when reading *Politics*. Some of the stories just make me so angry. You really felt the depths and stranglehold of patriarchy when reading about the allegedly 'unfit' mothers" (Alice). Most students commented that they felt inspired and empowered by lesbian mothers' courageous fight against patriarchy and their radical nonpatriarchal way of mothering. Lesbian women teach others that all mothering may potentially be a "site of resistance"; a place where women may defy patriarchy and be empowered as women through a radical gynocentric mothering.

With the next two books, Fay Weldon's *Down Among the Women*, and Audrey Thomas's *Mrs. Blood*, we examine how heterosexual women—single and married—experience sexuality and mothering. Our discussion of single heterosexual mothers was enriched by the film "Single Woman; Living on the Edge," and a panel of single mothers and an adult son of a single mother put together by a group of students for their seminar presentation. The radical gynocentric mothering, experienced by some lesbian and heterosexual women, contrasts with the oppressive patriarchal institution of motherhood endured by Mrs. Blood/Mrs. Thing in Audrey Thomas's novel.

In the final section of the course entitled "Telling the 'Great Unwritten Story': Mother Daughter Narratives," we explore the mother-daughter relationship. We read Christine Park and Caroline Heaton's *Close Company*, a collection of short stories, and selected poems from Lifshin's *Tangled Vines*. Here we discuss how important it is for women to share and celebrate our stories of mothers and daughters. One student produced a video about her relationship with her eight-year-old daughter, entitled "White Mother, Black daughter," and brought her daughter to class when the video was presented. Another student performed George Egerton's short story "Virgin Soil"—from *Close Company*—with her two teenage daughters as part of her seminar presentation (Julie). The concluding theme of mother-daughter relationships inspired a great deal of writing in students' journals. Stories about ourselves as daughters and mothers written in our mother tongue:

White Mother, Black daughter
she is mine: I am hers
do not deny us our heritage
her story is mine, my story is hers
I share in all her pain

and she in my shame
neither black or white we are both
our world is one
Black daughter, White mother

The night is finally silent, there is now time for me
But who am I?
My mother's daughter or my daughter's mother?
Both to be sure. Yet, is there enough of me?
(June)

Forgive us
our trespasses
For we choose
the path of "other"
Knew not what we did
Once; unboundaried fluid
Liquid surreal
Mother!
We have sinned!
And Oh, how we weep
In the cities of
Our Father!
(Carrie)

The Curse

Once upon a time, a man told me
I was cursed.
I believed and hid the shame.
Perfumes, barriers, "sanitary" things,
obediently I used.
Stop the flow, hide the blood, negate
your body to survive.
Daughter, Stop!
But mother, I bleed …
Your blood is power, your power
life.
But mother, I smell …
It's just the perfume of sacred
rivers.

But mother, I'm cursed ...
No daughter, you're sacred ...
(Vicky)

Dreams of you
are easily
stretched out
with George or all alone
I feel you coming and relax
Reach Between my legs, feel your
soft wet head push through
Mom appears in time to hold you
Sliding out of me
She's there as the Two Me's
Become me and you
I Gather you up greedily
she cuts the chord
Warm blood splatters the side of my face
I wipe it off laughing
In these dreams there is no pain
No tears are cried
Just smiles, our sweat
slimy bodies embrace
clinging to each other
our newly separate selves
(Laura)

We often say of Women's Studies that professors learn more from the students than vice versa. I wrote this article to encourage other teachers to bring the topic of motherhood into the classroom at universities, colleges, and high schools across the country. I believe that by sharing our stories and theories of motherhood and daughterhood we may finally free our bodies and minds from the oppressive patriarchal institution/ideology of motherhood. While I have "known" this for many years on an intellectual and personal level—reading feminist stories/theories on mothering rescued me from patriarchal motherhood—I only began to truly feel it when I re-read my students' journals for this article. In re-reading their stories, poems, thoughts, and questions I experienced a very real and momentous revolution in maternal thinking.

I would like to conclude with some of my students' year-end reflections on the course. They are a testimony to the power that comes from the recovery of our voices from patriarchal discourse—a talking back in our mother tongue.

Thanks for this new perspective on mothering-motherhood. I will never be able to look at anything that I do, or that others do as mothers, as "natural." There is no such thing as a "natural" role for mothers. We are taught what a mother is expected to do, but we have to listen to our hearts, our gut instinct to "know" what is right for our children.

I could not have taken a course that was more relevant. This has allowed me to think about my relationships, as a mom, as a daughter, and as a wife. I feel that I have resolved some of my personal problems (who said university is expensive, think how much 24 therapy sessions would be) and learnt much.

This course has changed me and my life ... This is my first Women's Studies course. I can't imagine I could have started with a better one. At times it was like the course knew my life, it was a very personal experience ... This course has provided me with the image of what is possible—strong women, strong mothers, strong children.

I venture to say that the subjective engagement required of me has changed me in ways I have not yet discovered. I know it has made me take a closer look at who I, as a woman, mother/daughter, am.

This course has filled my life in a way I never knew would be possible ... I can safely say it will be with me for my life time and for that I am thankful, happy and glad.

This article was origianlly published in Paula Bourne et al., eds. Feminism and Education: A Canadian Perspective, *Vol.2, copyright 1994, Centre for Women's Studies in Education, OISE, pp. 221-241. Reprinted with permission.*

[1]The now famous quote of T.S. Eliot was quoted by Mary O'Brien in *The Politics of Reproduction* (Boston: Routledge & Kegan Paul, 1981), p.30
[2]This insightful—and useful—distinction was made by Myrna Clark.
[3]All names have been changed.
[4]Part of seminar presentation on working class mothers and sensitive mothering by Mary Grossi and Lily Ross.
[5]Video made by Charlotte Heminton. Bill C-3 is an amendment to the *Indian*

Act. The Act originally legislated the loss of a woman's Indian status upon marriage to a non-status native man. Native men were not affected in the same way; in fact if they married a non-native woman she could gain status.

CHAPTER THREE

WHAT'S A GIRL LIKE
YOU DOING IN A NICE PLACE LIKE THIS?

MOTHERING IN THE ACADEME

My history as an academic began close to seventeen years ago when I, at the tender age of nineteen, left home to attend university in the big and bad Toronto. My career plans were anything but concrete, though I envisioned myself in a smart and sexy career like law. Given that I had done well in law and economics in high school, such a future seemed possible. However, I made the fatal mistake of enrolling in a course on women and literature; since then, women's writing has been the undying passion of my life. There went the high-powered, and, I may add, high-paying, job. However, I excelled in English and Women's Studies and decided to pursue my studies at the graduate level. Twenty-two, with an A average and a decent boyfriend (a first for me), I felt as if I was finally in control of my life, awaiting a future full of promise and hope. And then I learned that I wasn't just late ... I was pregnant.

Motherhood was something I had planned to do at 30-something, only after both the career and the guy were firmly established. I was not supposed to be pregnant now and certainly not this way: young, poor, and in a dating relationship. Well, we decided to have the baby, and three weeks later I found myself setting up house (if such is applicable to student residence) with this man, obscenely happy, eagerly awaiting the birth of this child. (Fourteen years later we are still together.) I believed my life would go ahead as planned; I reassured my mother that with my child in daycare at six weeks, my studies would resume as scheduled. I did not know then, could not have known, how completely pregnancy and later motherhood would change my life. In the early months of pregnancy I was horribly ill with unrelenting nausea; in the later months I developed a quite serious case of pre-eclampsia, which necessitated the daily monitoring of my blood pressure. I wrote a brilliant paper on the plight of fallen women in Victorian literature as my feet swelled and my back ached; I went into labour having just completed a major paper on sexuality and the empowerment of women; the ironies, in retrospect, are splendid. Labour destroyed any remnant of complacency left over from my pre-

pregnant self. I hemorrhaged during labour. I had never experienced such pain, terror, or aloneness.

Nothing, as any new mother will tell you, can prepare you for the numbing exhaustion and psychic dislocation of new motherhood. Nor can anyone warn you about how deeply you will fall in love with your child. "Motherhood," as Marni Jackson so aptly puts it, "is like Albania—you can't trust the descriptions in the books, you have to go there" (5). Motherhood radicalized and politicized me; it brought me to feminism. Though I had identified as a feminist for a number of years, motherhood made feminism real for me and radically redefined it. At 23, I knew in my gut, though I could not yet fully articulate it, that my feminism was to be about motherhood and that any social or political gains made by women through the repudiation of motherhood were to be seen not as achievements but as compromises and sell-outs. If I had to deny or downplay my maternal self (as if such were possible) to be successful, I was not interested in playing the game. As Audre Lorde reminds us, "the master's tools will never dismantle the master's house." I now realize that, had I been willing to cleave off my maternal self and "pass" as a non-mother, my stay in academia would have been less difficult, though less rewarding. A well-meaning friend advised me, when my son was two, that if I kept my son in daycare longer hours (he attended six hours a day) and if my spouse were to mind him on weekends, I would find mothering less of an interference. That I might want my son in daycare six, as opposed to ten, hours a day and that I might enjoy my weekends with him, had simply not occurred to her. Another friend who had a ten-year-old and a two-year-old confided to me, with much conspiratorial glee, that she had been a student for more than five years and no one in her department had figured out she was a mother. When I became a mother, I realized that feminism was to be about changing the system, not abut securing a niche in it. Getting some of us in, I understood, would not set us free.

The months after my son's birth were spent finishing my honours thesis, due in July. The university agreed, after laborious petitioning, to extend the date to December. With a new baby, poor health (due to complications of birth), and no childcare, I was nonetheless told, in no subtle way, that I should be grateful for their generosity in allowing me the four months to write my hundred-page thesis. My son never slept; as an infant, his naps seldom lasted more than 40 minutes. I remember phoning La Leche League, hysterical about my son's lack of sleep. They reassured me that it was normal ... but then again they didn't have an honours thesis to write. We had planned to enroll our son in daycare when he turned one; but in November we learned that we had a daycare subsidy and that if we turned it down our name would go back to the bottom of the waiting list; motherhood also awakened me to the insensitivities of state bureaucracy. Though our son attended only part-time the first year, he was constantly sick and ended up being hospitalized at six months for bronchitis and at thirteen months underwent an ear operation. The night he was hospitalized, I had a seminar to present in my graduate course. When I explained to my professor that I would be missing class due to my son's stay in hospital and that I would have to reschedule, she suggested that, since my seminar was already prepared, it might be best that I do it as planned. This was one of many moments in which I felt I had to assert my identity as a mother. I spent the night with my son.

In my master's year, I worked nine to three while my son was in daycare. I would cram into six hours what my classmates would do in a full day: no dawdling over the paper and morning coffee, no phone calls, no lunch or TV breaks. My son cried, screamed, and clung to me each and every morning I dropped him off at daycare. I often would see him—my bedroom window overlooked the daycare playground—still standing at the gate where I left him with tears and snot running down his face. These mornings I did not work; I sat and cried, paralyzed by grief and guilt. The day I was to teach my first class as a tutorial assistant, I ran into my son's daycare group out for a walk; of course he wanted to leave with me, and when I left he threw himself into a fury I have seldom seen since. I entered my first classroom as a teacher with his cries still ringing in my ears.

I worked exceptionally hard that year and I was rewarded with A grades and an Ontario Scholarship which I held for four years. My professors were overwhelmingly supportive of my work. But, looking back, I realize that, despite my insistent affirmations of my maternal self, my motherhood had not in any substantial way challenged the way the university worked: I seldom missed class, I was never late, I always had my readings done, and my course papers, though handed in late, were of the highest calibre. I was behaving, for the most part, as the good graduate student I was expected to be. And then I found myself pregnant *again*.

I began my Ph.D. six months pregnant, with a son just turned two. Looking back now, I am amazed at both my defiance and naïvité. I firmly believed that if I just continued to work hard, all would be fine. My daughter was born on December 30; I was back in class on January 4, hospital bracelet still on. There was no maternity leave for graduate students then, though I did have a six-week maternity leave from teaching. My students today are amazed when I tell them this story; they cannot believe that as recently as 1987 a major university lacked maternity provisions for graduate students. The month our daughter was born we lost our daycare subsidy and had to remove our son from daycare. Child Services reasoned that my spouse's contract teaching did not constitute full-time employment, as they counted only in-class teaching hours. We fought, and our eventual victory resulted in a change in municipal policy.

However, for nine months I was a full-time graduate student and a teaching assistant, with two young children and no childcare. To make matters worse, my daughter refused to take a bottle until she was nine months old; this meant that I could not leave her for more than three hours at a time. That term my spouse finished teaching a class at one; my graduate course started also at one on the other side of campus. I would nurse my daughter at twelve-twenty, bundle her and her brother up in their winter apparel, dash to my spouse's classroom (as much as this is possible with as stroller and a toddler in tow), hand them off to him, and then I would quite literally run to class. During this time I managed to attend classes, do my readings, present my seminars, and begin the research for my course papers; lack of childcare prevented me from completing the papers on time. Due to the December birth of my daughter, I had enrolled in one full course and a half course, which ended in December, putting me half a course behind schedule. I had hoped to complete my outstanding course work in the summer. The department, however, argued that since I was a half course behind I should take a course in the summer to get back on schedule. So here I was, taking a full graduate course in four months, again with no childcare and of course, not completing the outstanding papers. In September, though ahead of schedule by a half course, I was put under informal probation because of my incomplete course work. That year I finished my courses and got caught up on some of the earlier incomplete work. Most of the time, I felt as if my life was spiralling out of control; as one assignment was finished, another came due, and the whole time my progress was under constant surveillance. Such stress triggered what we euphemistically term a writer's block; weeks would go by and I could not write a sentence. I was undergoing a crisis of confidence, faith, and no doubt, exhaustion. In the fall of 1988, my status was assessed again, and it was determined that I was to sit my minor field comprehensive exams (an eight-hour exam) in May; by that time all course work would be completed. Failing to honour these commitments would result in my status being changed to part-time. Part-time study is frequently championed as the option of choice for mother students (though, of course, never asked of father students). For me it would mean the end of my academic career; as a part-time student I would lose my scholarship and no longer be entitled to a Teaching Assistantship. As well, I would be ineligible for daycare subsidy, student loans, and even student housing.

Though my children were still quite young (one and four), I was determined to honour my commitments. And then I found myself pregnant *again* (all three pregnancies were the result of birth control failures). I hid my pregnancy all winter, knowing if that if my pregnancy were discovered, my full-time status would be jeopardized. Reflecting back on this, I feel shame, guilt, fear, and, I may add, disbelief. It was 1989 and a straight A student who is an Ontario

Graduate Scholarship recipient, majoring in women's studies, in literature, was compelled to hide her pregnancy. I felt like one of those Victorian fallen women I had been studying. The day of my minor field exam, my pregnancy was discovered; I could hardly hide my protruding belly on a hot day in the middle of May. The chair, as I had feared, applied to have my status changed to part-time that same day after learning that two of my three course papers were still incomplete. I believed he thought that such a gesture was well-meaning and well-intentioned. In reality, it meant the end of my academic career. Fortunately, when my professors learned of this they lobbied on my behalf, struck a committee to investigate the experiences of mother graduate students, and I was awarded a retroactive maternity leave which, appropriately enough, put me two years ahead of schedule.

I *finally* completed my Ph.D. in June 1996. In 1993 I withdrew and wrote my dissertation as I worked full-time as a part-timer, another one of the ironies of university life. I have been quite successful in presenting and publishing my work and I hold what is considered to be an impressive CV. I am hopeful that I will secure a tenure-stream appointment; though, like many women with partners, I am unable to move to obtain such a position. As I look back at my graduate career, I am less bitter than I was a few years ago; though I still mourn for that young woman whose stress, guilt, and anxiety I can still taste today. The requests which that young woman made were quite modest: a recognition she was a mother and that this affected the progress of her studies, and also an extra six months to complete course assignments. Last year I received a call from a graduate student seeking advice on how she should implement her maternity leave. During our conversation, she expressed her incredulity at the difficulties I had experienced as a mother *back then*. I did not have the heart to remind her that *back then* was a mere five years ago, and that, no … I didn't think that we were out of the dark ages quite yet.

CHAPTER FOUR

"AIN'T THAT LOVE?"

ANTIRACISM AND RACIAL CONSTRUCTIONS OF MOTHERHOOD

Dominant ideologies and discourses of mothering and motherhood are racialized and racist; that is, they represent only one experience of mothering, that of white middle-class women, and position this experience as the real, natural, and universal one. Any discussion of mothers and antiracism must, therefore, begin with an understanding of how discourses of motherhood become racially codified and constructed. This essay explores how the development and dissemination of one normative discourse of motherhood—that of so-called sensitive mothering—causes other experiences of mothering—working class, ethnic—to be marginalized and delegitimized.

Motherhood is a cultural construction that varies with time and place; there is no one essential or universal experience of motherhood. However, the diverse meanings and experiences of mothering become marginalized and erased through the construction of an official definition of motherhood. Through a complex process of intersecting forces—economics, politics, cultural institutions—the dominant definition of motherhood is codified as the official and only meaning of motherhood. Alternative meanings of mothering are marginalized and rendered illegitimate. The dominant definition is able to suppress its own construction as an ideology and thus naturalizes its specific construction of motherhood as the universal, real, natural maternal experience.

The dominant discourse of motherhood is, however, historically determined and thus variable. In the Victorian era, for example, the ideology of moral motherhood that saw mothers as naturally pure, pious, and chaste emerged as the dominant discourse. This ideology, however, was race- and class-specific: Only white and middle-class women could wear the halo of the madonna and transform the world through their moral influence and social housekeeping. Slave mothers, in contrast, were defined as breeders, placed not on a pedestal, as white women were, but on the auction block.

After World War II, the discourse of the happy homemaker made the "stay-at-home mom and apple pie" mode of mothering the normal and natural motherhood experience. Again, only white and middle-class women could, in fact, experience what discursively was inscribed as natural and universal. In the 1970s, the era in which many baby boomers became parents, a new hegemonic discourse of motherhood began to take shape, one that authors Valerie Walkerdine and Helen Lucey appropriately term "sensitive mothering" in their landmark book *Democracy in the Kitchen: Regulating Mothers and Socializing Daughters*.

Walkerdine and Lucey examine how the maternal behavior of the middle-class became culturally constructed and codified as the real, normal, and natural way to mother. Natural mothering begins with the ideological presupposition that children have needs that are met by the mother. To mother, therefore, is to be sensitive to the needs of children, that is, to engage in sensitive mothering. The first characteristic of the sensitive mother, Walkerdine and Lucey explain,

> is that her domestic life is centred around her children and not around her housework. The boundaries between this work and children's play have to be blurred.... While the mother is being sensitive to the child's needs, she is not doing any housework. She has to be available and ready to meet demands, and those household tasks which she undertakes have to become pedagogic tasks.... The second feature of the sensitive mother is the way she regulates her children. Essentially there should be no overt regulation; regulation should go underground; no power battles, no insensitive sanctions as these would interfere with the child's illusion that she is the source of her wishes, that she has "free will." (20, 23-24)

The mode of mothering is drawn from the parenting styles of the so-called baby boom generation. Today good mothering is defined as child-centered and is characterized by flexibility, spontaneity, democracy, affection, nurturance, and playfulness. This mode of mothering is contrasted to the earlier stern, rigid, authoritative, "a child should be seen and not heard" variety of parenting.[1]

Working-class mothers, Walkerdine and Lucey emphasize, do not practice so-called sensitive mothering; work does not become play nor do power and conflict go underground. Working-class mothers in the study do play with their children but only after domestic chores have been tended to. In working-class households, the boundaries between mothering and domestic labor are maintained and the very real work of domestic labor is not transformed—or trivialized—into a game for the child's benefit. Nor does the mother abdicate her power and authority to create the illusion of a family democracy. This type of mothering, however, becomes pathologized as deficiency and deviance because the middle-class style of sensitive mothering has been codified, both socially and discursively, as natural. Working-class mothering is, thus, not simply different, it is deemed unnatural, and working-class mothers are deemed unfit mothers in need of regulation. In other words, "there is something wrong with working-class mothering which should be put right by making it more middle-class" (Walkerdine and Lucey, taken from back cover).

Walkerdine and Lucey do not specifically look at African-American mothering in their book. The research that has been done on Black mothering, however, does suggest that Walkerdine and Lucey's observations may be applied to Black women's experiences of mothering, at least among working-class families (see, for example, Steady; Bell-Scott *et al.*; Stack; Collins 1990; hooks 1984, 1990). Patricia Hill Collins, for example, argues, in her many works on Black mothering, that there is a distinct African-American experience of mothering. African-American mothering, what she calls mother-work, is about "maintaining family life in the face of forces that undermine family integrity" while "recognizing that individual survival, empowerment, and identity require group survival, empowerment, and identity" (1994: 47). Central concerns of "racial ethnic" (Collins's term) mothers include keeping the children born to you, the physical survival of those children, teaching the children resistance and how to survive in a racist world, giving to those children their racial/cultural history and identity, and a social activism and communal mothering on behalf of all the community's children. What the research on black mothering suggests is that sensitive mothering is not valued or practiced by African-American mothers, particularly if the family in question is urban and working-class.

In her landmark book *Maternal Thinking*, Sara Ruddick argues that the first duty of mothers is to protect and preserve their children: "to keep safe whatever is vulnerable and valuable in a child" (80). "Preserving the lives of children," Ruddick writes, "is the central constitutive, invariant aim of maternal practice" (19). "To be committed to meeting children's demand for preservation," Ruddick continues, "does not require enthusiasm or even love; it simply means to see vulnerability and to respond to it with care rather than abuse, indifference, or flight" (19). Though maternal practice is composed of two other demands—nurturance and training—this first demand, what Ruddick calls preservative love, is what describes much of economically disadvantaged African-American women's mother-work. For many African-American women, securing food, shelter, and clothing, building safe neighbourhoods, and fighting a racist world is what defines both the meaning and experience of their mother-work and mother-love. However, because sensitive-mothering has been naturalized as the universal, normal experience of motherhood, preservative love is not regarded as real, legitimate, or "good enough" mothering.

In the mothering of my children and in my teaching on motherhood, I seek to challenge the normative discourse of sensitive mothering by inscribing mothering as a culturally determined experience. I bring to this struggle the experience of being raised in a white, middle-class family by a working-class mother. The stories my mother tells me of my early childhood indicate that my mother's mode of mothering was clearly that of working-class 1950s culture. She used to "air" me on the front porch in the pram and, later, in the playpen each morning—summers and winters—as she tended to her housework and the caring of my infant sister. It was the early 1960s, and my mother had an eight-year-old daughter from her first marriage and three children under the age of three from her second marriage.

My mother grew up poor in a working-class family from, what was called in my hometown of Hamilton, Ontario, the "wrong side of the tracks." In the 1950s she found herself divorced with a young baby to raise. At 28 she married my father, a man from an established middle-class family, and moved to middle-class suburbia. My mother has often told me she never really felt she was a part of the suburban culture of young motherhood—the morning coffees in each other's kitchens, afternoons in the park, recipe sharing, and the borrowing of that cup of sugar.

Having had my children in graduate school with no one to share young motherhood with, I envied my mother and could not understand why she kept herself apart from what I imagined to be a feminist utopia of female solidarity. Only recently have I been able to see my mother's experience for what it was: It was the 1950s, and she was an older divorcee with a young daughter, from a poor, working-class family, among young, newly married women from "good" middle-class families. I can only imagine the culture shock she must have experienced and speculate upon how she was received by those "good" middle-class neighbours of hers. The memories of my later childhood reveal that my mother eventually became part of that middle-class culture and practiced, at least occasionally, the so-called sensitive mothering Walkerdine and Lucey discuss.

The struggles of my mother were replayed when I became a mother 30 years later at the relatively young age of 23. While my class affiliation was middle-class, my spouse was working-class; and though we were educated—both of us were pursuing graduate degrees at the time—we were also very poor. At that time, though, my energies were focused on challenging the oppressiveness of motherhood as a patriarchal institution. As a student of women's studies, my perspective was decidedly feminist, and I sought to imagine and achieve an experience of mothering that was empowering or, at the very least, not oppressive to me or my children. What I had not considered in my feminist practice of mothering was how the philosophy of so-called sensitive mothering to which I subscribed was a regulatory discourse as oppressive as the patriarchal one with which I was familiar.

I became conscious of the class and racial dimensions of discourses on mothering only upon reading *Democracy in the Kitchen* (Walkerdine and Lucey) and Toni Morrison's novel *Sula* midway through my early mothering years.[2] What these readings forced me to recognize is that although so-called sensitive mothering is neither real nor universal, it results in the regulation of middle-class mothers and the pathologizing of working-class mothering.

I planned to use the novel *Sula* in my teaching as a way to talk about racist constructions of motherhood and to arrive at an antiracist perspective in the way we perceive and practice mothering. I became more and more convinced that any attempt at teaching antiracism to children and students was doomed to failure as long as our perceptions and practices of mothering were racialized and racist. How can a white middle-class woman who sees her sensitive mothering as more real—and hence superior—possibly teach antiracism to her child? In turn, how can a black mother empower her child to resist racism when that child is encouraged to see her own mother's mode of mothering as insufficient? With these questions in mind I set to work.

I presented a lecture on *Sula* at the conclusion of a first-year humanities course entitled "Concepts of Male and Female in Western Culture" in March 1995, a class made up mostly of mature and returning students. The perspective of the course was thoroughly feminist and issues of race and racism had been discussed in the classroom. My audience was, thus, a highly informed and, for the most part, receptive one.

I spoke with much passion on how the mother's preservative love in the novel had been pathologized by the critics because it did not fit the bill of sensitive mothering. I stressed the need to deconstruct the hegemony of sensitive mothering so that other expressions of mothering are given legitimacy and validity. With this lecture I hoped to generate discussion on the ways in which black and working-class women's mothering is often delegitimized and how white middle-class women are regulated in trying to achieve this sensitive mothering. Instead, what I got was a hazy fog of incomprehension, bewilderment, and indifference.

Interestingly, when I moved from the topic of mothering to other themes in *Sula*—women's friendship, growing up female—I could feel—almost see—a shift in the students' response to my lecture: Suddenly there was a connection, interest, an understanding. I also observed, though could not account for, a noticeable change in the emotional climate of the lecture hall. Inexplicably, during the first part of my lecture on motherhood the atmosphere was serious and noticeably tense, yet in the latter section the mood was lighthearted and relaxed. When we talked about the lecture and text later in tutorial, the students, much to my dismay, replicated the patronizing stance of the critics regarding Eva's mothering—we can't be too hard on her, it wasn't her fault, she would have done it differently had she had the choice and so on. They had missed the whole point of my lecture.

I was troubled, dismayed, and perplexed by my students' misunderstanding/ incomprehension; eventually though I attributed it to a weak lecture. Not until I started working on this essay did I think about the experience again and see it from a different perspective. At the same time, a Caribbean student in a course I was teaching told the class about her family experience. This student's mother, like many Caribbean women, came to Canada in the early 1970s to secure work and left her children back home with her parents in the hope of creating a better life for them. The mother sent her earnings home, visited her children on holidays, and several years later, when she had good, permanent work, had her children join her in Canada. The eldest sister had great difficulty adjusting to this change and blamed her mother for being absent all those years. Good mothers, the daughter told her mother, don't leave their children for a day, let alone for many years. Good mothers, like those of her Canadian friends, did things with their kids, were not always so tired and away so much working. What the daughter was saying is: Why can't you be more like other mothers? Why can't you be normal?

Hearing this student's story I began to make sense of my former students' reaction to my lecture. Though sensitive mothering is a recent ideological construction of motherhood—having been around only two decades—it has very successfully take up residence in the dominant culture. (It reminds one of the aliens in *The Invasion of the Body Snatchers* who enter and take over, en masse, the human population.) Good mothers read to their children, enroll them in ballet and piano lessons, enrich them with theatre, art, and culture; they are patient, nurturing, spontaneous, sensitive and—most importantly— child-centered, transforming even the most mundane task into an entertaining and educational experience for their children.

Now no mother can actually live the ideological script of sensitive mothering, though all mothers are judged by it and many mothers seek to achieve it. And most children, very much cultural creatures, interpret their own mother's mothering from the discourse of sensitive mothering. On several occasions my children have responded to my behavior or comments with the statement: Mothers don't do, or say, that. We have embraced so completely this discourse of mothering that we see it as the best, ideal, normal, and, ultimately, only way to mother. Hence my students' confusion: Why would I problematize something so good, so natural? Why wouldn't I want the characters in this book to partake in such mothering, given how good it is? And why shouldn't we help others to achieve the same experience of sensitive mothering? Why not indeed?

With my own children I struggle to make conscious to them the ways in which mothering is over-determined and regulated by cultural discourses, such as sensitive mothering. Discussions about racism and antiracism have always been part of our children's upbringing. What is more difficult to work through with our growing children is, I think, how practices of mothering are racialized and class-specific. After all, kids don't see mothering as a practice. I strive to challenge that perception in my mothering. What I seek to emphasize to my children, both in word and deed, is that my experience of mothering and their experience of being mothered are culturally determined. I want them to know that children are mothered differently and that one way is not any more real, natural, or legitimate than any other way.

When my kids respond to something I have said or done with the line "Mothers don't do that" or, conversely, "All the other mothers are … so why can't you?" I remind them that there is no one way to mother or be mothered. As I seek to free myself from the regulation of sensitive mothering, I share with my children my critique of this discourse by giving concrete examples of how this discourse is oppressive to me—and by implication to them—and how it results in the "putting down" of other mothers.

In my critique of sensitive mothering I am not suggesting that I am against reading to your child or playing, every now and then, "let's wash the floors" to make enjoyable an otherwise tedious chore. However, what I do find deeply disturbing is the codification of this discourse as the official and only way to mother. Walkerdine and Lucey argue that sensitive mothering is ultimately bad for both mother and child: it trivializes women's domestic labour, causes the mother's workday to be never-ending, and compels her to be manipulative with her children—to make them believe that her wishes are really their own—so as to avoid authoritarianism and conflict. It causes the child to confuse work with play and to see the self as completely in control of circumstances—somewhat problematic lessons, particularly for Black and working-class kids in a racist and capitalist world. While I agree with Walkerdine and Lucey's observations, I am less interested in debating the pros and cons of sensitive mothering than in deconstructing any normative discourse of mothering that pathologizes difference and seeks to regulate it.

What has this to do with mothers acting against racism? My students' incomprehension at my lecture and my student's moving story have brought home to me the intricate relationship between mothering and racism; mothering and antiracism. If that mother could have told her daughter that her survivalist type of mother-love—mothering as separation—*was* an expression of mothering, as good as, if not better than, the dominant mode, perhaps there would have been less blame and more understanding between mother and daughter. With my own lecture I would have been able to talk about an antiracist perspective with respect to mothering far more effectively had the students not been so thoroughly identified with the dominant discourse of mothering.

Adrienne Rich's *Of Woman Born* discusses how motherhood is an institution that is defined and controlled by patriarchy. I would add that ideologies of mothering, and the institutions they create, are also thoroughly racialized and racist. I believe that the teaching and practice of antiracism through mothering can happen if, and only if, the dominant mode of mothering is identified and challenged as racist. It does not help to build an antiracist household on foundations that are racist.

[1]Please refer to the introduction in this volume for a discussion of these two styles of mothering.

[2]The contemporary critical responses to a dialogue in the novel brought home to me how thoroughly identified our culture is with the discourse of sensitive mothering. In this novel, Eva, the mother, is left by her husband in 1895 with "$1.65, five eggs, three beets" and three children to feed. After her baby son nearly dies from constipation Eva leaves her children in the care of a neighbour, saying she will be back the next day, only to return eighteen months later with money and one of her legs gone. It was rumored that Eva placed her leg under a train in order to collect insurance money to support her children. Years later, her now adult daughter, Hannah, asks her mother if "[She] ever love[d] us?" The mother responds: "You settin' here with your healthy-ass self and ax me did I love you? Them big old eyes in your head would a been two holes full of maggots if I hadn't." The daughter then asks: "Did you ever, you know, play with us?" Eva replies: "Play? Wasn't nobody playin' in 1895. Just 'cause you got it good now you think it was always this good? 1895 was a killer, girl. Things was bad. Niggers was dying like flies.... Don't that count? Ain't that love? You want me to tinkle you under the jaw and forget 'bout them sores in your mouth?" (67-69). Many readers of the novel question, with Hannah, whether Eva did in fact mother her children. Her mothering has been called unnatural and untraditional. The words unnatural and untraditional, however, accrue meaning only if both the speaker (writer) and listener (reader) know what is meant by their opposites, the normative terms—in this instance, natural and traditional. When a critic, like Dayle Delancy, laments that Eva has "no time to lavish traditional displays of affection upon her children" or that "she has to work for the

survival of her offspring at the expense of having fun with them" (15, 18) she is working from a very specific discourse of what constitutes good mothering—namely that of sensitive mothering.

CHAPTER FIVE

ACROSS THE DIVIDE

CONTEMPORARY ANGLO-AMERICAN FEMINIST THEORY ON THE MOTHER-DAUGHTER RELATIONSHIP

Sometimes it seemed as if we were engaged in an Olympic competition to decide whose mother was absolutely the worst. We ground them up in our long conversations and spit them out.
—Anne Rophie, *Fruitful: A Real Mother in the Modern World*

I cannot forget my mother. Though not as sturdy as others, she is my bridge. When I needed to get across, she steadied herself long enough for me to run across safely.
—Renita Weems, "Hush, Mama's Gotta Go Bye-Bye"

"The cathexis between mother and daughter, essential, distorted, misused," wrote Adrienne Rich in 1976, "is the great unwritten story." I am a daughter and I am a mother of daughters. My feminism as it is lived and as it is practised in my scholarship and teaching is decidedly mother-centred; its aim is to recover, narrate, and theorize the unwritten stories of mothers and daughters. What I discovered close to ten years ago, when I began my work on motherhood and the mother–daughter relationship, was that our stories as mothers and daughters had in fact *already* been written—narrated by the larger patriarchal culture that scripted the roles mothers and daughters were expected to play. The received view of mothers and daughters, or what author Toni Morrison calls in another context, the master narrative, is that this relationship, particularly in the daughter's adolescent years, is one of antagonism and animosity. The daughter must distance and differentiate herself from the mother if she is to assume an autonomous identity as an adult. The mother, in turn, is perceived and understood only in terms of her maternal role, viewed either as devouring shrew or devoted madonna, bitch or victim; her own subjectivity as woman is eclipsed by her maternal identity. The mother represents for the daughter, according to the received narrative, the epitome of patriarchal oppression that she seeks to transcend as she comes to womanhood; and yet the daughter's failings, as interpreted by herself and the culture at large, are said to be the fault of the mother. This is the patriarchal narrative of the mother–daughter relationship.

The lives of mothers and daughters as they are lived are shaped by these larger cultural narratives even as mothers and daughters live lives different from, and in resistance to, these assigned roles. The aim of my research and teaching is to deconstruct this patriarchal narrative by first exposing this narration as precisely that: a narrative, an ideology, that, by definition, is a construction not a reflection of the actual lived reality of mothers and daughters, hence neither natural nor inevitable. Second, my work is concerned with how daughters and mothers may unravel the patriarchal script to write their own stories of motherhood and daughterhood. As part of this larger project, I designed a first year course on mothers and daughters that I taught at York University for years.[1] The objective of this course, entitled "Mothers and Daughters: From Estrangement to Empowerment," is to situate the mother–daughter relationship as a *cultural* construction. Students are taught to think critically and consciously about the cultural meanings assigned to the mother–daughter relationship; they are taught to explore how their own experiences of being mothered, and their perceptions of motherhood in general and of their own mothers in particular, are shaped by the larger patriarchal narrative of motherhood and daughterhood. The course aims to identify, challenge, and dismantle the patriarchal narrative of mother–daughter estrangement; in particular, it asks students to uncover the historical/ psychological origins of this narrative. Students track the manifestations of patriarchal narrative in various cultural practices as diverse as media, education, government policy, and psychological theory; analyze its workings in their own personal relationships; imagine ways it may be deconstructed; and finally construct an alternative mother–daughter narrative scripted for empowerment as opposed to estrangement.

An in-class writing assignment at the beginning of the course asks students to reflect upon their relationship with their mother. They are asked to describe this relationship at three points in their lives and are given a series of instructions and questions to help them do this: Describe your mother both inside and outside her role as mother. What do you want/need from your mother? What does she want/need from you? Are you like your mother? Do you want to be like your mother? Describe how your mother has helped or hindered you in achieving your life goals. This assignment serves as the first entry in the students' course journals: weekly written reflections on course readings, discussions, and so forth.

One student, reflecting upon this assignment at the close of the course, commented:

When I look back to the beginning of the course only eight months ago I realize how different I was—how naive I was. To gain some perspective as to how my attitudes have changed concerning my own mother, I reread my first journal entry. I still agree with most of what I wrote, however after looking at the questions you asked us to answer, I realized that I had overlooked the most crucial of all the questions posed. I neglected the questions, "Do you know your mother as a person other than your mother? Who is your mother?" I think at the time I didn't really understand the significance of these questions nor could I have answered them for I didn't know my mother as a person. I didn't even know that I didn't know.[2]

This student's reflections, and in particular her comment "I didn't even know that I didn't know," serve as an appropriate epigraph for our positioning as daughters in the patriarchal narrative of mother–daughter estrangement. So thoroughly do we identify with this script that its cultural staging has been rendered invisible to us and we see it as merely "the way things are"—hence natural and inevitable. African-American essayist and poet Audre Lorde once said we must "name the nameless so that it can be thought" (37). The aim of this course, for daughters and mothers alike, is to render visible the "invisible hand of patriarchy" so as to see how thoroughly our lives are produced and shaped by patriarchal ideologies that are not of our own making.

Matrophobia, Mother-Blame and Daughter-Centricity

I begin the course with Nancy Chodorow's (1989) classic essay "Family Structure and Feminine Personality," and a lecture on her "reproduction of mothering" thesis as it is developed in her book of the same name (Chodorow 1978). Nancy Chodorow, as Penelope Dixon noted in her feminist annotated bibliography on mothers and mothering, "was one of the first to write on the subject [of mothering] and subsequently has authored more books and articles on this subject than any other feminist writer" (4). Indeed, Chodorow's writings, particularly her now classic *The Reproduction of Mothering*, have influenced the way in which a whole generation of scholars view motherhood. What is less acknowledged, however, is how this influential writer, who is identified as a feminist, reinscribes the patriarchal narrative of mother–daughter estrangement even as she seeks to dismantle it. Chodorow contends that female mothering constructs gendered identities that are both differentiated and hierarchical. The pre-Oedipal mother–daughter attachment, she argues, is more prolonged and intense than the mother–son relationship. Because the daughter and the mother are the same gender, the mother perceives and treats her daughter as identical to and continuous with herself. The sameness and continuity of the pre-Oedipal mother–daughter symbiosis engenders a feminine psychic structure that is less individuated and differentiated. The daughter's sense of self is relational; she experiences herself as connected to others. The relational sense of self that women inherit from their mothers and bring to their own mothering, Chodorow goes on to argue, exacerbates female self-effacement and frustrates women's achievement of an authentic autonomous identity. Relationality, Chodorow concludes, is problematic for women because it hinders autonomy, psychological and otherwise, and since daughter–mother identification is the cause of this relationality in women, it is, in her words, "bad for mother and [daughter] alike" (217).

Chodorow has been criticized heavily in the 20 years since the publication of *The Reproduction of Mothering*. What concerns critics most is Chodorow's bracketing of the "real" world in her psychoanalytic abstractions of family patterns and gender formations. Critics have pointed out that Chodorow's mother-involved, father-absent family is quite specifically a white, urban, middle-class family structure of the first world. The gendered personalities that this specific family structure might create should not be used, as Chodorow does, to account for universal male dominance and gender difference. Moreover, Chodorow's theory of mother–daughter mutual psychological over-identification, used to explain women's subordination, far too readily glosses over women's lived powerlessness in a patriarchal world. While I argue wholeheartedly with the above criticisms, I am nonetheless disturbed by the fact that among the hundreds of articles written about Chodorow's theory only a handful assume as their focus of critique what I find to be the most troubling premise of Chodorow's reproduction thesis; namely, the pathologizing of mother–daughter identification/intimacy, particularly in positioning it as the cause of women's inadequacy, psychological and otherwise. One early critic of Chodorow, Marcia Westkott faulted Chodorow for failing to understand that women's relationality and dependency result not from psychology but from culture: "The need of mothers to remain close to their daughters arises because mothers are given few other choices, not just because of an infantile personality structure" (17). Here, as with Chodorow, mother–daughter identification is construed as a liability.

In *Don't Blame Mother*, Paula Caplan writes, "women love connection. But in a society that is phobic about intimacy and extols the virtues of independence, we mistakenly regard connection and closeness as dependency, fusion, and merging" (113). The aim of the introductory section is to expose the pervasiveness of the pathology of mother–daughter intimacy and identification in contemporary culture. The sanction against mother–daughter intimacy observed in Chodorow is one of the many cultural practices that render mother–daughter estrangement natural and inevitable. It also originates from and reinscribes another central tenet of mother–daughter estrangement— mother-blame and the devaluation of motherhood.

Across cultures and throughout history most women mother in the institution of motherhood; that is, women's mothering is defined and controlled by the larger patriarchal society in which they live. Mothers do not make the rules, Rich emphasizes—they simply enforce them. Mothers are policed by what theorist Sara Ruddick calls the "gaze of others."[3] The institution of motherhood is predicated upon inauthentic mothering and the abdication of maternal authority.[4]

A daughter, Ruddick emphasizes, perceives this inauthenticity and understands the powerlessness that underpins her mother's compliance and complicity. In *Of Woman Born*, Rich speaks of the rage and resentment daughters feel toward this powerlessness of their mothers. However, at the same time, the daughter feels rage toward her mother, she is expected to identify with her because the daughter is also a woman who, it is assumed, will some day become a mother/wife as her mother did. The daughter resists this identification because she does not want a life like her mother, nor does she wish to be aligned with someone who is oppressed and whose work is so devalued. "Thousands of daughters," writes Rich, "see their mothers as having taught a compromise and self-hatred they are struggling to win free of, the one through whom the restrictions and degradations of a female existence were ... transmitted" (235). Rich calls this distancing between mothers and daughters matrophobia: "the fear not of one's mother or of motherhood but of *becoming one's mother*" (236, emphasis in original). Matrophobia, she writes, can be seen as a womanly splitting of the self in the desire to become purged once and for all of our mothers' bondage, to become individuated and free. The mother stands for the victim in ourselves, the unfree woman, the martyr. Our personalities seem dangerously to blur and overlap with our mothers, and in a desperate attempt to know where mother ends and daughter begins, we perform radical surgery (Rich 236). When daughters perform this radical surgery they sever themselves from their attachment with their mother.

The institution of motherhood and the cultural devaluation/subordination of mothers, and the practice of inauthentic mothering on which it is predicated, gives rise to mother-blame. Paula Caplan argues that mother-blame is rampant in contemporary culture, among both professionals and the population at large. "The biggest reason daughters are upset and angry with their mothers," writes Caplan, "is that they have been *taught* to do so" (2, emphasis in original). Similar to the feeling of matrophopia identified by Rich, mother-blame distances daughters from mothers because mothers come to be seen not as sources of empowerment but as the cause of all and any problems that may ail the daughter. Marianne Hirsch, in her highly acclaimed book *The Mother/ Daughter Plot: Narrative, Psychoanalysis, Feminism*, argues that the feminist theory written in the 1970s is characterized by a daughterly perspective or subjectivity that Maureen Reddy and Brenda Daly call "daughter-centricity" (2).[5] "It is the woman as daughter," Hirsch writes, "who occupies the center of the global reconstruction of subjectivity and subject-object relation. The woman as mother remains in the position of other, and the emergence of feminine daughterly subjectivity rests and depends on that continued and repeated process of othering the mother" (136). She goes on to say, "The adult woman who is mother continues to exist only in relation to her child, never as a subject in her own right. And in her maternal function, she remains an object, always distanced, always idealized or denigrated, always mystified, always represented through the small child's point of view" (167). Hirsch argues that such ambivalence expresses itself in the rhetoric and the politics of the 1970s movement:

> Throughout the 1970s, the metaphor of sisterhood, of friendship or of surrogate motherhood has been the dominant model for female and feminist relationships. To say that "sisterhood is powerful," however, is to isolate feminist discourse within one generation and to banish feminists who are mothers to the "mother-closet." In the 1970s, the prototypical feminist voice was, to a large degree, the voice of the daughter attempting to separate from an overly connected or rejecting mother, in order to bond with her sisters in a relationship of mutual nurturance and support among women. With its possibilities of mutuality and its desire to avoid power, the paradigm of sisterhood has the advantage of freeing women from the biological function of giving birth, even while offering a specifically feminine relational model. "Sisters" can be "maternal" to one another without allowing their bodies to be invaded by men and the physical acts of pregnancy, birth, and lactation. In this feminist family romance, sisters are better mothers, providing more nurturance and greater encouragement of autonomy. In functioning as mutual surrogate mothers, sisters can replace mothers. (164)

Thus, while mothering as nurturance was celebrated amongst 1970s feminists, real mothers and the biological processes of mothering were displaced and disparaged.

Hirsch identifies four reasons for the 1970s "avoidance and discomfort" with the maternal. First, for daughters motherhood represented a compliance with patriarchy of which they wanted no part. Second, feminists feared the lack of control associated with motherhood. Third, feminists suffered from what critic Elizabeth Spelman has identified as "somatophophia"—fear and discomfort with the body (qtd. in Hirsch). And nothing, as Hirsch has observed, "entangles women more firmly in their bodies than pregnancy, birth, lactation, miscarriage, or the inability to conceive" (166). Fourth, and characteristic of much feminist theorizing in the 1970s, was an ambivalence about power, authority, and anger—all of which are part of mothering and associated with the maternal. "Feminist theoretical writing in the U.S.," writes Hirsch, "is permeated with fears of maternal power and with anger at maternal powerlessness" (167). Caplan argues that men fear maternal power. It would seem that women, too, fear it. The sisterhood metaphor of the 1970s thus may be read as a gesture of displacement or containment. The maternal power that is feared is rendered safe by transforming it into mothering between sisters—no power imbalance—and by objectifying and "otherizing" the person who seems to wield this power, the mother.

To a young child, the powers of the mother appear limitless. Our own individual flesh-and-blood mother is also connected to the primordial Great Mother, who held very real life and death powers over mortal men. In our individual and collective unconscious we remember that time when we lived under the mother's power in the pre-Oedipal and pre-patriarchal world. In *The Mermaid and the Minotaur*, Dorothy Dinnerstein argues that the fear of maternal power and the hatred of women generally originate from infant experiences which, in turn, come to structure adult consciousness. The mother, Dinnerstein reasons, cannot satisfy all of the child's needs and desires. The inevitable dissatisfaction, discomfort, frustration, and anger felt by the child directs itself at the person whose responsibility it was to meet those needs. In contrast to Dinnerstein's view, I would suggest that the experiences of infancy, given that they include both pain and pleasure, engender not misogyny but a deep ambivalence that becomes organized around polarized constructions of the mother. The Good Mother and the Bad Mother are created; all that we find desirable about mothers is signified by the former, and all that we fear and hate is marked by the latter. This delineation is, I would suggest, mapped along an already established historical topography of separation and specialization. I refer here to what we speculate occurred at the dawn of patriarchy when the many diverse qualities of the original Great Goddess were separated and used to create several distinct goddesses. That which mortal men feared in the original Goddess—particularly her powers over life and death—was displaced upon a terrible mother goddess, like the Hindu goddess Kali, who represented death and destruction while that which was desired was retained and assigned to a beneficent power. In Catholicism, for example, Mary, the mother of Jesus, is such a woman. The polarization and specialization of the maternal self continue to structure our ambivalence.

The fear of maternal power is at the heart of such disparagement and idealization. However, as Ruddick reminds us: "All power lies at least partly in the eye of the beholder. To a child, a mother is huge—a judge, trainer, audience, and provider whose will must be placated.... A mother, in contrast to the perception her children have of her, will mostly experience herself as relatively powerless" (34).[6] However, as we speak to and about the very real powerlessness of mothers, we must not forget the power a mother does possess. Ruddick writes:

> There are many external constraints on [a mother's] capacity to name, feel, and act. But in the daily conflict of wills, at least with her children, a mother has the upper hand. Even the most powerless woman knows that she is physically stronger than her young children. This along with undeniable psychological power gives her the re-sources to control her children's behaviour and influence their perceptions. If a mother didn't have this control, her life would be unbearable. (35)

Mothering is a profound experience of both powerlessness and power; it is this paradox of motherhood that helps explain women's ambivalence about motherhood. This ambivalence about maternal power—along with fear of the maternal, mother-blame, cultural devaluation of motherhood, and matrophobia— distance daughters from their mothers and scripts the relation-ship of mother and daughters as one of disconnection and estrangement.

Mother–Daughter Connection and Empowerment: Theories and Narratives

Once students have identified these cultural practices that distance daughters from the mothers, they explore ways in which these practices can be resisted. The sanction against mother–daughter identification, with which I began this chapter, is challenged by Elizabeth Debold, Marie Wilson, and Idelisse Malavé, in their important work, *Mother Daughter Revolution*. They argue that psychological theories of development are organized around the assumption that adolescence is a "time of separation when daughters are struggling to be independent, particularly from their mothers; and daughters in adolescence don't want to listen to their mothers or be like them in any way" (36). Separation from parents is mandated in developmental theory to enable the emerging adult to achieve an autonomous sense of self. *Mother Daughter*

Revolution calls into question this "sacred cow" of developmental theory—the equivalency of separation and autonomy—and argues that it constitutes a betrayal of both mothers and daughters:

> Separation and autonomy are not equivalent: a person need not separate from mothers emotionally to be autonomous. Under the dominion of experts, mothers are urged to create a separation and disconnection from daughters that their daughters do not want. Early childhood and adolescence are the two stages of life where separation has been decreed as imperative to the independence and autonomy of children. To mother "right," women disconnect from their daughters and begin to see them as society will. Rather than strengthen girls this breach of trust leaves girls weakened and adrift. (22)

Mothers want to "do right" by their daughters so, as dictated by developmental theory, they distance themselves from their daughters when the daughters reach adolescence. At the same time, they propel the daughters out of the maternal space of childhood and into the heterosexual realm of adulthood. What is most disturbing about this pattern of separation and betrayal is its timing. "In childhood, girls have confidence in what they know, think, and feel" (Debold, Wilson and Malavé 11). With the onset of adolescence, girls between the ages of nine and twelve come up against what Debold, Wilson, and Malavé call "the wall." "The wall is our patriarchal culture that values women less than men.... To get through the wall, girls have to give up parts of themselves to be safe and accepted within society" (12).[7] Before adolescence, girls are, in their words, "fully themselves," but at the crossroads between childhood and adolescence,

> girls come to label their vitality, desires, and thoughts as "selfish," "bad," or "wrong." They lose the ability to hold on to the truth of their experience.... They begin to see themselves as others see them, and they orient their thinking and themselves towards others .... [They] have to give up their relationship with the world of girls and women, the world that they have lived and loved in, and also give up relationship with parts of themselves that are too dangerous to keep in the adult world of male desire. Girls give up these relationships for the sake of the relationships that have been prescribed for them in male-led societies. The wall of patriarchy expects girls to separate from what they know, from each other, and from the women who care for them. (Debold, Wilson and Malavé 15)

Central to *Mother Daughter Revolution* is the belief that mothers can help their daughters resist being influenced by the wall. With her mother beside her, the daughter is empowered and can learn to compromise less of herself. The key to the mother's ability to do this is the reclamation of her own girl self. The authors write:

> If mothers decide to join with daughters who are coming of age as women, mothers must first reclaim what they themselves have lost. Reclaiming is the first step in women's joining girls' resistance to their own dis-integration. Reclaiming is simply the process of discovering, describing, and reappropriating the memories and feelings of our preadolescent selves .... The goal is not to become a preadolescent girl. That wouldn't be desirable even if it were possible .... But women can reclaim and, thus, reintegrate the vital parts of themselves that they discarded or drove underground. (Debold, Wilson and Malavé 101)

This reclamation empowers the mother and enables her to help her daughter in her resistance. As *Mother Daughter Revolution* suggests, if mothers reclaim their driven-underground pre-patriarchal selves, their reclaimed selves can join their daughters, and empower them to withstand the loss or compromise of their own female selfhood. Mothers and daughters together "can claim the power of connection, community, and choice. And this power just might bring down the wall" (Debold, Wilson and Malavé 38).

Another contemporary theorist read in my course champions mother–daughter connectedness as a mode of resistance. Miriam Johnson, the author of *Strong Mothers, Weak Wives*, emphasizes how daughters may connect with their mothers to withstand what may be called the heterosexualizing behaviour of the father. In Chodorow's psychoanalytical account, the differential treatment of sons and daughters by their mothers is said to be the cause of both gender difference and male dominance. Johnson challenges this argument. She writes: "It is the wife role and not the mother role that organizes women's secondary status" (6). Women's secondary status, she maintains, originates not from the maternal core of women's subjectivity (Chodorow's relational self) but from their heterosexual identity as wives of men. In contrast to Chodorow, Johnson maintains that male dominance originates not from the mother–child attachment, but from the father–daughter relationship.

The relationship of father and daughter, Johnson asserts, "trains daughters to be wives who are expected to be secondary to their husbands" (8). She argues that fathers often romanticize the father–daughter relationship and interact with their daughters as a lover would. Fathers feminize their daughters: daddies teach their girls to be passive, pleasing, and pretty for men. In Johnson's words, the father–daughter relationship "reproduce[s] in daughters a disposition to please men in a relationship in which the male dominates." In other words, "daddy's girls are in training to be wives" (184). Because daddy's girls are trained and rewarded for pleasing and playing up to men, they grow up to be male-defined and male-orientated women. In most so-called normal (male-dominant) families what is experienced is psychological incest. "The incest ... is psychological, not overtly sexual. The father takes his daughter over. She looks up to him because he is her father. He is the king and she is the princess. It is all OK because the male is dominant in 'normal' adult heterosexual relations" (Johnson 173).

Johnson argues that these princesses are in need of rescue, and that the rescuer is the mother: "If daddy's girls are to gain their independence they need to construct an identity as the daughters of strong mothers as well" (184). In *The Reproduction of Mothering*, Chodorow attributes women's lack of autonomy to the feminine-related sense of self which the mother–daughter relationship engendered. In contrast, Johnson argues that women's lack of autonomy originates from the daughter's psychological dependency on her father as a male-orientated daddy's girl. According to Johnson, a daughter's identification with her mother, far from prohibiting authentic female autonomy, produces and promotes that authenticity and autonomy. Chodorow suggested in her earlier sociological work that daughters are empowered by identification with their mothers in matrifocal cultures. Johnson believes that an empowering mother–daughter identification is also possible under patriarchy if the daughter relates to her mother as a mother and friend, not as the father's wife. Johnson contends that the mother–daughter relationship is the key to overcoming women's psychological inauthenticity as daddy's girl and, by implication, women's social oppression in patriarchy. Thus the daughter achieves authentic autonomy not through greater involvement with the father, but through a heightened identification with the mother.

For Johnson, the daughter must identify with the maternal part of her mother's identity rather than the heterosexual one. This identification empowers the daughter in two ways: first it allows her to step outside her oppressive daddy's girl role; and second, it allows her to identify with an adult woman's strength rather than her weakness. In Johnson's view, women are strong as mothers but made weak as wives. In identifying with her mother as mother, the daughter may construct a strong female identity outside of the passive heterosexual one patterned for her by her father and by society at large. In *Mother Daughter Revolution*, the emphasis is on the mother joining the daughter, while the focus of *Strong Mother, Weak Wives* is the daughter connecting to the mother. Though different, both positions are mapped along what feminist writer Naomi Ruth Lowinsky calls "the motherline." In *Stories from the Motherline: Reclaiming the Mother–Daughter Bond, Finding Our Feminine Souls*, Naomi Ruth Lowinsky explores "a worldview that is as old as humankind, a wisdom we have forgotten that we know: the ancient lore of women—the Motherline." She goes on to say:

> Whenever women gather in circles or in pairs, in olden times around the village well, or at the quilting bee, in modern times in support groups, over lunch, or at the children's party, they tell one another stories from the Motherline. These are stories of female experience: physical, psychological, and historical. They are stories about the dramatic changes of woman's body: developing breasts and pubic hair, bleeding, being sexual, giving birth, suckling, menopause, and of growing old. They are stories of the life cycles that link generations of women: Mothers who are also daughters, daughters who have become mothers; grandmothers who also remain granddaughters. (1-2)

Most women today, Lowinsky contends, are cut off from their motherline; they suffer from what she calls "the feminist ambivalence about the feminine" (30). "Women," she writes, "seemed to want to live their father's lives. Mother was rejected, looked down upon.... In the headlong race to liberate those aspects of ourselves that had been so long denied, we left behind all that women had been.... Many of us," she continues, "who joyfully accepted the challenge of new opportunities discovered in retrospect that we had cut ourselves off from much of what was meaningful to us as women: our mothers, our collective past, our passion for affiliation and for richness in our personal lives. We felt split between our past and our future" (29). Lowinsky asks that women integrate their feminine and feminist selves: women "must connect the historical self that was freed by feminism to live in the 'real' world, with the feminine self that binds us to our mothers and grandmothers" (32).[8]

Daughters of the so-called baby boom are the first generation of women, at least among the middle classes, whose lives are radically different from those of their mothers. These daughters, Lowinsky argues, have "paid a terrible price for cutting [them]selves off from [their] feminine roots" (31). By disconnecting themselves from their motherline, these daughters have lost the authenticity and authority of their womanhood. Women may reclaim that authority and authenticity by reconnecting to the motherline:

> When a woman today comes to understand her life story as a story from the Motherline, she gains female authority in a number of ways.

First, her Motherline grounds her in her feminine nature as she struggles with the many options now open to women. Second, she reclaims carnal knowledge of her own body, its blood mysteries and their power. Third, as she makes the journey back to her female roots, she will encounter ancestors who struggled with similar difficulties in different historical times. This provides her with a life-cycle perspective that softens her immediate situation .... Fourth, she uncovers her connection to the archetypal mother and to the wisdom of the ancient worldview, which holds that body and soul are open and all life is interconnected. And, finally, she reclaims her female perspective, from which to consider how men are similar and how they are different. (13)

Virginia Woolf wrote in *A Room of One's Own*: "[W]e think back through our mothers if we are women" (72). Writing about Lowinsky's motherline in her book *Motherless Daughters: The Legacy of Loss*, Hope Edelman emphasizes that "motherline stories ground a ... daughter in a gender, a family, and a feminine history. They transform the experience of her female ancestors into maps she can refer to for warning or encouragement" (201).

These stories are made available to daughters through the female oral tradition, or what we call gossip and old wives' tales. These feminine discourses, however, have been trivialized, marginalized and discredited; they are, to borrow French theorist Michel Foucault's term, "subjugated knowledge[s]" that circulate outside the master narrative. Moreover, the language of the motherline is rendered in a specifically feminine discourse or dialect that has been discursively and culturally marginalized by patriarchal culture.

In *Motherless Daughters*, Edelman studies daughters who lost their mothers between infancy and their early '30s, and considers the impact this loss had on the daughters' lives.[9] The daughters' narratives speak of feelings of incompleteness and fragmentation. "Our mothers," Edelman explains, "are our most direct connection to our history and our gender. Regardless of how well we think they did their job, the void their absence creates in our lives is never completely filled again" (61). When the mother dies daughters lose their connection to the motherline. "Without a mother or mother-figure to guide her," writes Edelman, "a daughter has to piece together a female self-image on her own" (xxv).[10] A girl who loses her mother has little readily available, concrete evidence of the adult feminine to draw from. She has neither a direct guide for sex-typed behaviour nor an immediate connection to her own gender. Left to piece together her own feminine identity, she looks to other females for signs that she's developing along an appropriate gendered path (178).

Motherless daughters long to know and to be connected to, what Lowinsky calls, the deep feminine, or in Edelman's words: "that subtle unconscious source of feminine authority and power we mistakenly believe is expressed in scarf knots and thank-you notes but instead originates from a more abstract gendered core" (179). "Without knowledge of her own experiences, and the relationship to her mother's," Edelman continues, "a daughter is snipped from the female cord that connects the generations of women in her family, the feminine line of descent ... the motherline" (200).

Adrienne Rich writes in *Of Woman Born*, "The loss of the daughter to the mother, the mother to the daughter, is the essential female tragedy" (237). In Hope Edelman's work, this loss refers to the daughter losing her mother through death, abandonment, or neglect. In these instances, separation occurs as a result of the mother's leaving the daughter. More frequent, in patriarchal culture, is the loss of the daughter to the mother: daughters become disconnected from their motherline through specific cultural practices, notably the devaluation of motherhood and the reinforcement of maternal powerlessness, fear of the maternal, motherblame and matrophopia, discussed earlier.

Journalist Marni Jackson calls maternal space "the mother zone; [the] hole in culture where mothers [go]" (13). Motherhood, she writes, "is an unexplored frontier of thought and emotion that we've tried to tame with rules, myth, and knowledge. But the geography remains unmapped " (9). She emphasizes that "[m]otherhood may have become an issue but it's not yet a narrative" (3). Maternal stories are forgotten and lost before they are spoken because "[m]others in the thick of it have not the time or brain cells to write it down, to give it life. [When they] have the time, amnesia moves in ... all the raw extremes of emotion are smoothed over and left behind.... Culture," she continues, "encourages this amnesia, by excluding mothers from its most conspicuous rewards—money, power, social status" (4,9). Because our mothers' stories remain unspoken, she argues, "the true drama of mother and child is replaced by the idealization of motherhood" (4,9). Julia Kristeva identifies the maternal with the unspeakable. The maternal is found outside and beyond language, "spoken" only in the extralinguistic, nonverbal discourse of the semiotic. Perhaps, the maternal is, as Hirsch speculates in *The Mother/Daughter Plot*, "unnarratable" (179). Or, as Ruddick writes,

> maternal voices have been drowned by professional theory, ideologies of motherhood, sexist arrogance, and childhood fantasy. Voices that have been distorted and censored can only be developing voices. Alternatively silenced and edging toward speech, mothers' voices are not voices of mothers as they are, but as they are becoming. (401).

Much of current feminist writing and activism is concerned with the recovery of the maternal voice. While recognizing how difficult it is to speak that which has been silenced, disguised, and marginalized, writers today seek to make the maternal story narratable. In earlier times the ancient lore of the motherline was told around the village well or at the quilting bee; today, the oral tradition of old wives' tales is shared through written narratives. In *Writing a Woman's Life*, Carolyn Heilbrun observes, "Lives do not serve as models, only stories do that. And it is a hard thing to make up stories to live by. We can only retell and live by stories we have heard.... Stories have formed us all: they are what we must use to make new fictions and new narratives" (32).

Recent writings on the mother–daughter relationship call upon the mother to speak and the daughter to listen. Debold, Wilson, and Malavé argue in *Mother Daughter Revolution* that the compromise of the female self in adolescence may be resisted or, at the very least, negotiated, when the mother connects with the daughter through stories. The mother, in recalling and sharing with her daughter her own narrative of adolescence, gives the daughter strategies of resistance and, hence, an alternative script for coming into womanhood. Caplan, in *Don't Blame Mother*, emphasizes that only by speaking and hearing the mother's story can women move beyond mother-blame.[11] In turn, Lowinsky and Edelman argue that a daughter's very identity as a woman is acquired through connection to, and knowledge of, her mother and the motherline of which she is a part. Rich writes, "mothers and daughters have always exchanged with each other—beyond the verbally transmitted lore of female survival—a knowledge that is subliminal, subversive, pre-verbal: the knowledge flowing between two alike bodies, one of which has spent nine months inside the other" (220). The lore Rich refers to here is, of course, the lore of the motherline that constructs female experience outside the patriarchal narrative.

Conclusion

The theories and narratives read by the students in this course expose the cultural practices that underpin the patriarchal narrative of mother–daughter estrangement—sanction against mother–daughter intimacy, mother-blame, daughter-centricity, matrophobia, and fear of maternal power—and offer various strategies by which mothers and daughters may deconstruct the patriarchal narrative so as to write their own stories of motherhood and daughterhood, ones scripted from relations of empowerment as opposed to estrangement. As another student remarked in her journal at the conclusion of the course:

I want to tell you how much your course has meant to me and how much my life has changed because of it. I feel almost as if I am a different person now. You helped me break the cycle instilled in me by a patriarchal society that I was doomed to repeat. Most significantly, you provided me with the means to eliminate mother–blame from my life, and for that I am eternally grateful.

Through this course, I hope to create a dialogue between mothers and daughters that in turn will help them build a bridge over which they can cross the patriarchal divide that separates them. By doing so, mothers and daughters can construct a truly lasting politics of empowerment.

[1]The course described in this chapter was designed and taught from 1993 to 1997 at York University as part of the college course programme. In the first two years, the course examined the mother–daughter relationship from a cross-cultural perspective: students read selected novels and poetry by Anglo-American, Anglo-Canadian, Caribbean, African, Native, Chinese, Jewish, African-American, and African-Canadian women writers. In 1995, the focus of the course became an in-depth and detailed study of the representation of the mother–daughter relationship in the dominant Anglo-American feminist tradition. In the second term of the course, students were introduced to theory and literature on mothers and daughters by African- American and Caribbean women writers, in order to problematize the received feminist tradition. This chapter explores only the first part of the course. My research on the mother–daughter in African-American women's theory and literature may be found in Chapter Four of this book, "'Ain't that Love?': Anti-racism and Racial Constructions of Motherhood"; "'In Search of My Mother's Garden, I Found My Own': Motherlove, Healing and Identity in Toni Morrison's *Jazz*" (1996); "Talking Back in Mother Tongue: A Feminist Course on Mothering and Motherhood" (Chapter Two in this book). See also my book, *Toni Morrison and Motherhood: Politics of the Heart* (2004b). Also see Jenkins; Hamilton. Regrettably, in 1996, York administration made the decision to cancel the College Course Programme as part of its cost-cutting and restructuring initiative and practice. This was a great loss to the students and faculty at York.
[2]Journal entry from a student in my "Mothers and Daughters" class, York University, April 1995. All other student writings used in this chapter are taken from journal entries in this class.
[3]"Teachers, grandparents, mates, friends, employers, even an anonymous passerby," writes Ruddick, "can judge a mother by her child's behaviour and find her wanting" (111– 112).

[4]Please refer to the introduction for a discussion on inauthentic mothering.
[5]"In psychoanalytic studies," write Daly and Reddy, "we frequently learn less about what it is like to mother than what it is like to be mothered, even when the author has both experiences" (2).
[6]Many, many works have examined women's feelings of powerlessness in the institution of motherhood. See, for example, Luxton.
[7]Several feminist scholars have written on the loss of the female self in adolescence. See, for example, Brown and Gilligan; Hite; Mann; Pipher; de Waal.
[8]It is important to emphasize that Lowinsky does not advocate "turning back the clock" and pushing women once again out of historical time.
[9]Edelman's book, *Motherless Daughters*, includes several types of absences— "premature death, physical separation, mental illness, emotional abandonment, and neglect" (xxv).
[10]One woman, whose mother died when she was eight, spoke about the longing for guidance of a mature, experienced woman who would teach her "how to be."
[11]Caplan writes: "[Women] must humanize [their] image of [their] mother ... [in order] to see the real woman behind the mother-myths" (147). Significantly, Caplan argues that such may be achieved through listening to the mother's story and writing a biography of her life.

II. MOTHERING

CHAPTER SIX

"HOME IS WHERE THE REVOLUTION IS"[1]

WOMANIST THOUGHT ON AFRICAN-AMERICAN MOTHERING

"During the early stages of contemporary women's liberation movement," bell hooks writes, "feminist analyses of motherhood reflected the race and class biases of participants" (1984: 133). "Some white, middle class, college educated women argued," hooks continues, that motherhood was:

> the locus of women's oppression. Had black women voiced their views on motherhood, it would not have been named a serious obstacle to our freedom as women. Racism, availability of jobs, lack of skills or education ... would have been at the top of the list—but not motherhood. (1984: 133)

Feminist theory on motherhood, as hooks identifies, is racially codified. Drawing upon contemporary womanist thought on black motherhood, this chapter will argue that there exists a distinct African-American tradition of motherhood. Two interrelated themes or perspectives distinguish the African-American tradition of motherhood. First, mothers and motherhood are valued by, and central to African-American culture. Secondly, it is recognized that mothers and mothering are what make possible the physical and psychological well-being and empowerment of African American people and the larger African American culture. Black women raise children in a society that is at best indifferent to the needs of black children and the concerns of black mothers. The focus of black motherhood, in both practice and thought, is how to preserve, protect and more generally empower black children so that they may resist racist practices that seek to harm them and grow into adulthood whole and complete. For the purpose of this discussion, I employ African-Canadian theorists Wanda Thomas Bernard and Candace Bernard's definition of empowerment: "empowerment is naming, analyzing, and challenging oppression on an individual, collective, and/or structural level. Empowerment, which occurs through the development of critical consciousness, is gaining control, exercising choices, and engaging in collective social action" (46). To fulfill the task of empowering children, mothers must hold power in African-American culture, and mothering likewise must be valued and supported. In turn, African-American culture, understanding the importance of mothering for individual and cultural well-being and empowerment, gives power to mothers and prominence to the work of mothering. In other words, black mothers require power to do the important work of mothering and are accorded power because of the importance of mothering.

The African-American tradition of motherhood centres upon the recognition that mothering, in its concern with the physical and psychological well-being of children and its focus upon the empowerment of children, has cultural and political import, value and prominence and that motherhood, as a consequence, is a site of power for black women. This chapter will examine this tradition of African-American mothering under five interrelated topics: "Othermothering and Community Mothering," "Motherhood as Social Activism and a Site of Power," "Matrifocality," "Nurturance as Resistance: Providing a Homeplace" and "The Motherline: Mothers as Cultural Bearers." Next it will examine this tradition in the context of mothers' relationships with their children. Specifically, the chapter will consider how daughters seek identification or connection with their mothers due to the cultural centrality and significance of the mother role and how this connection gives rise to the daughters' empowerment in African-American culture.[2]

Othermothering and Community Mothering

Stanlie James in "Mothering: A Possible Black Feminist Link to Social Transformation" defines othermothering as "acceptance of responsibility for a child not one's own, in an arrangement that may or may not be formal" (45). Othermothers usually care for children. In contrast, community mothers, as Njoki Nathani Wane explains, "take care of the community. These women are typically past their childbearing years" (112). "The role of community mothers," as Arlene Edwards notes, "often evolved from that of being othermothers" (88). James argues that othermothering and community mothering developed from, in Arlene Edwards's words, "West African practices of communal lifestyles and interdependence of communities" (88). Consequently, as Patricia Hill Collins has observed, "Mothering [in West Africa] was not a privatized nurturing 'occupation' reserved for biological mothers, and the economic support of children was not the exclusive responsibility of men" (1993: 45). Rather, mothering expressed itself as both nurturance and work, and care of children was viewed as the duty of the larger community. Collins argues that these complementary dimensions of mothering and the practice of communal mothering/othermothering give women great influence and status in West African societies. She elaborates:

> First, since they are not dependent on males for economic support and provide much of their own and their children's economic support, women are structurally central to families. Second, the image of the mother is culturally elaborated and valued across diverse West African societies.... Finally, while the biological mother-child bond is valued, childcare was a collective responsibility, a situation fostering cooperative, age-stratified, woman centered 'mothering' networks. (1993: 45)

These West African cultural practices, Collins (1993) argues, were retained by enslaved African-Americans and gave rise to a distinct tradition of African-American motherhood in which the custom of othermothering and community mothering was emphasized and elaborated. Edwards, in her article "Community Othermothering: The Relationship Between Mothering and the Community Work of Black Women," explains:

> The experience of slavery saw the translation of othermothering to new settings, since the care of children was an expected task of enslaved Black women in addition to the field or house duties.... [T]he familial instability of slavery engendered the adaptation of communality in the form of fostering children whose parents, particularly mothers, had been sold. This tradition of communality gave rise to the practice of othermothering. The survival of the concept is inherent to the survival of Black people as a whole ... since it allowed for the provision of care to extended family and non blood relations. (80)

The practice of othermothering remains central to the African-American tradition of motherhood and is regarded as essential for the survival of black people. bell hooks, in her article "Revolutionary Parenting," comments:

> Child care is a responsibility that can be shared with other childrearers, with people who do not live with children. This form of parenting is revolutionary in this society because it takes place in opposition to the idea that parents, especially mothers, should be the only childrearers. Many people raised in black communities experienced this type of community-based child care. Black women who had to leave the home and work to help provide for families could not afford

to send children to day care centers and such centers did not always exist. They relied on people in their communities to help. Even in families where the mother stayed home, she could also rely on people in the community to help.... People who did not have children often took responsibility for sharing in childrearing. (1984: 144)

"The centrality of women in African-American extended families," as Nina Lyon Jenkins concludes in "Black Women and the Meaning of Motherhood," "is well known" (206).

The practice of othermothering, as it developed from West African traditions, becomes, in African-American culture, a strategy of survival in that it ensured that all children, regardless of whether the biological mother was present or available, would receive the mothering that delivers psychological and physical well-being and makes empowerment possible. Collins concludes:

Biological mothers or bloodmothers are expected to care for their children. But African and African-American communities have also recognized that vesting one person with full responsibility for mothering a child may not be wise or possible. As a result, "othermothers," women who assist bloodmothers by sharing mothering responsibilities, traditionally have been central to the institution of Black motherhood. (1993: 47)

Community mothering and othermothering also emerged in response to black mothers' needs and served to empower black women and enrich their lives. "Historically and presently community mothering practices," Erica Lawson writes, "was and is a central experience in the lives of many Black women and participation in mothering is a form of emotional and spiritual expression in societies that marginalize black women" (26). The self defined and created role and identity of community mother also, as Lawson explains, "enabled African Black women to use African derived conceptions of self and community to resist negative evaluations of Black women" (26).

The practice of othermothering/community mothering as a cultural sustaining mechanism and as a mode of empowerment for black mothers has been documented in numerous studies. Carol Stack's early but important book, *All Our Kin: Strategies for Survival in a Black Community*, emphasizes how crucial and central extended kin and community are for poor urban blacks. "Black families in The Flats and the non-kin they regard as kin," Stack writes in her conclusion, "have evolved patterns of co-residence, kinship-based exchange networks linking multiple domestic units, elastic household boundaries, lifelong bonds to three-generation households, social controls against the formation of marriages that could endanger the network of kin, the domestic authority of women, and limitations on the role of the husband or male friend within a woman's kin network" (124).[3] Priscilla Gibson's recent article, "Developmental Mothering in an African American Community: From Grandmothers to New Mothers Again," provides a study of grandmothers and great grandmothers who assumed the caregiving responsibilities of their (great) grandchildren as a result of the parent being unable or unwilling to provide that care. Gibson argues that "[in]creasingly grandmothers, especially African American grandmothers, are becoming kinship providers for grandchildren with absent parents. This absent middle generation occurs because of social problems such as drug abuse, incarceration, domestic violence, and divorce, just to name a few" (33). In "Reflections on the Mutuality of Mothering: Women, Children and Othermothering," Wane explores in her research study of women in Kenya how pre-colonial African beliefs and customs gave rise to a communal practice of childrearing and an understanding that "parenting, especially mothering, was an integral component of African traditions and cultures" (111). "Most of pre-colonial Africa" explains Wane, "was founded upon and sustained by collectivism.... Labour was organized along parallel rather than hierarchical lines, thus giving equal value to male and female labour. Social organization was based on the principle of patrilineal or matrilineal descent, or a combination of both. Mothering practices were organized as a collective activity" (108). Today, the practice of othermothering, as Wane notes, "serves[s] to relieve some of the stresses that can develop between children and parents [and] provides multiple role models for children; [as well] it keeps the traditional African value systems of communal sharing and ownership alive" (113). Othermothering and community mothering, Wane concludes, "can be understood as a form of cultural work or as one way communities organize to nurture both themselves and future generations" (113).

Motherhood as Social Activism and as a Site of Power

The practices of othermothering and in particular community mothering serve, as James argues, "as an important Black feminist link to the development of new models of social transformation" (45). Black women's role of community mothers, as Collins explains, redefines motherhood as social activism. Collins explains,

> Black women's experiences as other mothers have provided a foundation for Black women's social activism. Black women's feelings of responsibility for nurturing the children in their extended family

networks have stimulated a more generalized ethic of care where Black women feel accountable to all the Black community's children. (1993: 49)

In *Black Feminist Thought: Knowledge, Consciousness and the Politics of Empowerment*, Collins develops this idea further:

> Such power is transformative in that Black women's relationships with children and other vulnerable community members is not intended to dominate or control. Rather, its purpose is to bring people along, to—in the words of late-nineteenth-century Black feminists— "uplift the race" so that vulnerable members of the community will be able to attain the self-reliance and independence essential for resistance. (1991: 132)

Various and diverse forms of social activism stem from and are sustained by the African American custom of community mothering. Community mothering, as Edwards explores in her article "Community Mothering: The Relationship Between Mothering and the Community Work of Women" has been expressed in activities and movements as varied as the Black Clubwomen, and Civil Rights movements and Black women's work in the church. Drawing upon the research of Gilkes, Edwards elaborates: "In reporting on Black community workers, Gilkes found that these women often 'viewed the Black Community as a group of relatives and other friends whose interest should be advanced, and promoted at all times, under all conditions, and by almost any means'" (88). Bernard and Bernard theorize Black women's work as educators as a form of social activism. "Education," they argue, "is considered a cornerstone of Black community development, and as such Black women, as community othermothers, have placed a high value on education and have used it as a site for activism" (68). Academic mothers, they continue, "also value education, and use their location to facilitate the education of others. [As well] academic othermothers who operate within an Africentric framework, are change agents who promote student empowerment and transformation" (68). They go on to elaborate:

> Collins' definition of othermothers extends to the work we do in the academy. Othermothering in the community is the foundation of what Collins calls the "mothering the mind" relationships that often developed between African American women teachers and their Black female and male students. We refer to this as mothering in the academy, and see it as work that extends beyond traditional defini-

tions of mentorship. It is a sharing of self, an interactive and collective process, a spiritual connectedness that epitomizes the Africentric values of sharing, caring and accountability. (68)

Collins argues that this construction of mothering as social activism empowers black women because motherhood operates, in her words, as "a symbol of power." "A substantial portion of Black women's status in African-American communities," writes Collins, "stems not only from their roles as mothers in their own families but from their contributions as community othermothers to Black community development as well" (1993: 51). "More than a personal act," write Bernard and Bernard,

Black motherhood is very political. Black mothers and grandmothers are considered the 'guardians of the generations.' Black mothers have historically been charged with the responsibility of providing education, social, and political awareness, in addition to unconditional love, nurturance, socialization, and values to their children, and the children in their communities. (47)

Black motherhood, as Jenkins concluded, "is a site where [Black women] can develop a belief in their own empowerment. Black women can see motherhood as providing a base for self-actualization, for acquiring status in the Black community and as a catalyst for social activism" (206).

Matrifocality

The African-American model/practice of mothering, according to Collins (1993), differs from Eurocentric ideology in three important ways:

First, the assumption that mothering occurs within the confines of a private, nuclear family household where the mother has almost total responsibility for child-rearing is less applicable to Black families. While the ideal of the cult of true womanhood has been held up to Black women for emulation, racial oppression has denied Black families sufficient resources to support private, nuclear family households. Second, strict sex-role segregation, with separate male and female spheres of influence within the family, has been less commonly found in African-American families than in White middle-class ones. Finally, the assumption that motherhood and economic dependency on men are linked and that to be a "good" mother one must stay at home, making motherhood a full-time "occupation," is similarly uncharacteristic of African-American families. (43-44)

Miriam Johnson in *Strong Mothers, Weak Wives* argues that the wife role and not the mother's role occasions women's secondary status in a patriarchal culture. In contrast, matrifocal cultures, such as African-American culture, according to Johnson, emphasize women's mothering and are characterized by greater gender equality.[4] In matrifocal societies, Johnson writes, "women play roles of cultural and social significance and define themselves less as wives than as mothers" (226). "Matrifocality," Johnson continues,

> however, does not refer to domestic maternal dominance so much as it does to the relative cultural prestige of the image of mother, a role that is culturally elaborated and valued. Mothers are also structurally central in that mother as a status "has some degree of control over the kin unit's economic resources and is critically involved in kin-related decision making processes." ... It is not the absence of males (males may be quite present) but the centrality of women as mothers and sisters that makes a society matrifocal, and this matrifocal emphasis is accompanied by a minimum of differentiation between women and men. (226)

The wife identity, according to Collins, is less prevalent in African-American culture because women assume an economic role and experience gender equality in the family unit. She writes:

> African-American women have long integrated their activities as economic providers into their mothering relationships. In contrast to the cult of true womanhood, in which work is defined as being in opposition to and incompatible with motherhood, work for Black women has been an important and valued dimension of Afrocentric definitions of Black motherhood. (1993: 48)

"Whether they wanted to or not," Collins continues, "the majority of African-American women had to work and could not afford the luxury of motherhood as a noneconomically productive, female 'occupation'" (1993: 49). Thus, Black women, at least among the urban poor, do not assume the wife role that Johnson identified as that which structures women's oppression. Moreover, in African-American culture, motherhood, not marriage, emerges as the rite of passage into womanhood. As Joyce Ladner emphasizes in *Tomorrow's Tomorrow*: "If there was one common standard for becoming a woman that was accepted by the majority of the people in the community, it was the time when girls gave birth to their first child. This line of demarcation was extremely clear and separated the girls from the women" (215-6).[5] In African-American culture, motherhood is the pinnacle of womanhood. The matrifocal structure of black families with its emphasis on motherhood over wifedom and black women's role as economic provider means that the wife role is less operative in the African-American community and that motherhood is site of power and empowerment for Black women.

Nurturance as Resistance: Providing a Homeplace

The fourth way that African-American mothering differs from the dominant model is the way in which nurturance of family is defined and experienced as a resistance. In African-American culture, as theorist bell hooks has observed, the black family, or what she terms homeplace, operates as a site of resistance. She explains:

> Historically, African-American people believed that the construction of a homeplace, however fragile and tenuous (the slave hut, the wooden shack), had a radical political dimension. Despite the brutal reality of racial apartheid, of domination, one's homeplace was one site where one could freely confront the issue of humanization, where one could resist. Black women resisted by making homes where all black people could strive to be subjects, not objects, where one could be affirmed in our minds and hearts despite poverty, hardship, and deprivation, where we could restore to ourselves the dignity denied to us on the outside in the public world. (1990: 42)

hooks emphasizes that when she talks about homeplace she is not speaking merely of Black women providing services for their families; rather, she refers to the creation of a safe place where, in her words, "black people could affirm one another and by so doing heal many of the wounds inflicted by racist domination ... [a place where] [they] had the opportunity to grow and develop, to nurture [their] spirits" (1990: 42).[6] In a racist culture that deems Black children inferior, unworthy and unlovable, maternal love of Black children is an act of resistance; in loving her children the mother instills in them a loved sense of self and high self-esteem, enabling them to defy and subvert racist discourses that naturalize racial inferiority and commodify blacks as other and object. African Americans, hooks emphasizes, "have long recognized the subversive value of homeplace and homeplace has always been central to the liberation struggle" (1990: 42). Like hooks, Collins maintains that children learn at home how to identify and challenge racist practices and it is at home that children learn of their heritage and community. At home they are empowered to resist racism, particularly as it becomes internalized. Collins elaborates:

> Racial ethnic women's motherwork reflects the tensions inherent in trying to foster a meaningful racial identity in children within a society that denigrates people of color.... [Racial ethnic] children must first be taught to survive in systems that oppress them. Moreover, this survival must not come at the expense of self-esteem. Thus, a dialectal relationship exists between systems of racial oppression designed to strip a subordinated group of a sense of personal identity and a sense of collective peoplehood, and the cultures of resistance extant in various ethnic groups that resist the oppression. For women of color, motherwork for identity occurs at this critical juncture. (1994: 57)

The empowerment of minority children through resistance and knowledge occurs at home and in the larger cultural space through the communal mothering and social activism spoken of earlier. This view of mothering differs radically from the dominant discourse of motherhood that configures home as politically neutral space and views nurturance as no more than the natural calling of mothers.

The Motherline: Mothers as Cultural Bearers

The motherline, the fifth and final theme, considers the role black mothers play as cultural bearers and tradition keepers. Anglo-American feminist writer Naomi Lowinsky, author of *The Motherline: Every Woman's Journey to Find her Female Roots*, defines the motherline:

> When a woman today comes to understand her life story as a story from the Motherline, she gains female authority in a number of ways. First, her Motherline grounds her in her feminine nature as she struggles with the many options now open to women. Second, she reclaims carnal knowledge of her own body, its blood mysteries and their power. Third, as she makes the journey back to her female roots, she will encounter ancestors who struggled with similar difficulties in different historical times. This provides her with a life-cycle perspective that softens her immediate situation.... Fourth, she uncovers her connection to the archetypal mother and to the wisdom of the ancient worldview, which holds that body and soul are one and all life

is interconnected. And, finally, she reclaims her female perspective, from which to consider how men are similar and how they are different. (13)

Writing about Lowinsky's motherline in her book *Motherless Daughters: The Legacy of Loss*, Hope Edelman emphasizes that "Motherline stories ground a ... daughter in a gender, a family, and a feminine history. They transform the experience of her female ancestors into maps she can refer to for warning or encouragement" (201). Motherline stories, made available to daughters through the female oral tradition, unite mothers and daughters and connect them to their motherline. Lowinsky argues that many women today are disconnected from their motherline and have lost, as a consequence, the authenticity and authority of their womanhood. For Lowinsky, female empowerment becomes possible only in and through reconnecting to the motherline.

In African-American society the motherline represents the ancestral memory, traditional values of African-American culture. Black mothers pass on the teachings of the motherline to each successive generation through the maternal function of cultural bearing. Various African-American writers argue that the very survival of African America depends upon the preservation of black culture and history. If Black children are to survive they must know the stories, legends and myths of their ancestors. In African-American culture, women are the keepers of the tradition: they are the culture bearers who mentor and model the African-American values essential to the empowerment of Black children and culture. "Black women," Karla Holloway continues,

> carry the voice of the mother—they are the progenitors, the assurance of the line ... as carriers of the voice [black women] carry wisdom—mother wit. They teach the children to survive and remember. (Holloway and Demetrakopoulos 123)

Black mothers, as Bernard and Bernard conclude,

> pass on the torch to their daughters, who are expected to become the next generation of mothers, grandmothers, or othermothers, to guard future generations. (47)

The above five themes demonstrate that mothers and motherhood are valued by and regarded as central to African-American culture; as well mothers and mothering are recognized as that which make possible the physical and psychological well-being and empowerment of African-American people and the larger African-American culture. The following section will detail how the centrality and significance of black motherhood gives rise to the empowerment of daughters. Black women, in connection with powerful mothers, become empowered as daughters. "I come from / a long line of / Uppity Irate Black Women" begins Kate Rushin's poem, "Family Tree." "And [when] you ask me how come / I think I'm so cute," Kate Rushin replies, "I cultivate / Being uppity, / It's something / My Gramon taught me" (qtd. in Bell-Scott *et al.* 176-7).

African-American Mothers and Daughters

Gloria Joseph and Jill Lewis in their early but important work,[7] *Common Differences: Conflicts in Black and White Feminist Perspectives*, contrast Anglo-American and African-American women's experiences of motherhood and daughterhood. Joseph argues that respect for the mother was a central and organizing theme of the mother-daughter relationships examined. She also found that female socialization centered upon the teaching of survival skills and an insistence upon independence:

> What was startlingly evident, as revealed in the mother/daughter questionnaire, was the teaching of survival skills to females for their survival in and for the survival of the Black community. Intra-group survival skills were given more importance and credence than survival skills for dealing with the White society at large. There is a tremendous amount of teaching transmitted by Black mothers to their daughters that enables them to survive, exist, succeed, and be important to and for the Black communities.... Black daughters are actually "taught" to hold the Black community together. (Joseph and Lewis 106)[8]

The independence that mothers insist upon for their daughters is to be achieved through education and effort. This may be contrasted to the dominant narrative of Anglo-American feminine achievement that scripts marriage as the avenue through which women will "get ahead." The African-American mothers' insistence upon independence for their daughters includes a critique of marriage, particularly the dependency inherent in the wife role. These mothers recognize with Miriam Johnson that it is the wife role and not the mother role that organizes women's secondary status. "Through Mom's guidance and direction," comments Candace Bernard in "Passing the Torch," "I learned the value of hard work, self-determination, goal-setting, and shared responsibility.... I experienced empowerment through Mom's ability to survive in a climate that was not conducive to survival." The daughter adds, "It is empowering to know that I have come from such a long line of strong Black women.... I feel honored that ... I am able to carry on the struggle you began a generation ago" (48-9).

A Black daughter also, as Barbara Turnage discusses in her article, "The Global Self-Esteem of an African-American Adolescent Female and Her Relationship with Her Mother," develops high self-esteem through a secure and close attachment with her mother and knowledge of her African-American heritage. Her study of 105 African-American young women ranging in age from sixteen to eighteen, found that the most significant variable was "trust of the mother": "African-American mothers play an important role in their daughters self-esteem development. That is, the young women in this study who had high self esteem also trusted their mothers to be there for them" (184). The second significant variable for self-esteem was "acknowledgment of an African ancestry": "For an adolescent African-American female knowl-edge of her African heritage helps her define her body image and structure her expectations" (Turnage 184). The message of this study, Turnage emphasizes, can not be "overstated":

> The relationship between these African-American young women and their mothers instilled in them the knowledge that they are competent and lovable. Based on their trust in their mothers, these young women believed, when confronted with difficult situations, that they could rely on their mothers' assistance. Thus, as they grow into black womanhood, they grow with the knowledge that they can accomplish their goals and that they are worthy of love and respect. (184)

These daughters, connected with their mothers and motherline (awareness of heritage), develop a strong and proud identity as black women and secure empowerment.

Contemporary African-American women's writing also celebrates mothers as mentors and role models and illustrates the power daughters obtain in connection with their mothers and motherline. Readers of Black women's literature have long observed a deeply rooted matrilineal tradition in which daughters think back through their mothers. In Marianne Hirsch's words, "[there is] in much of contemporary black women's writing, a public celebra-tion of maternal presence" (177). In a 1980 article, appropriately entitled "I Sign My Mother's Name," Mary Helen Washington speaks of a "generational continuity" among African-American women in which "a mother serves as the female precursor who passes on the authority of authorship to her daughter and provides a model for the black woman's literary presence in this society"

(147). "For black women writers," as Dolana Mogadime observes in "A Daughter's Praise Poem for her Mother," "the idea of thinking back through our mothers is rooted in the notion of revisiting and learning about maternal knowledge and female-centred networks as expressions of African continuities in contemporary society" (87). Respect and gratitude for "women who made a way out of no way" is repeated time and time again in the recent collection of writings on black mothers and daughters, appropriately entitled *Double Stitch: Black Women Write About Mothers and Daughters* (Bell-Scott *et al.*).

In an introductory section to this collection, Beverly Guy-Sheftall writes: "In selection after selection, daughters acknowledge how their mothers provided road maps and patterns, a 'template,' which enabled them to create and define themselves.... Though daughters must forge an identity which is separate from the mothers, they frequently acknowledge that a part of themselves is truly their mothers' child" (61). Margaret Walker in her poem appropriately entitled "Lineage" pays tribute to her grandmothers who "were strong / ...full of sturdiness and singing" (175). Sonia Sanchez writes: "My life flows from you Mama. My style comes from a long line of Louises who picked me up in the night to keep me from wetting the bed.... A long line of Lizzies who made me understand love.... A long line of Black people holding each other up against silence" (25-6). Judy Scales-Trent writes: "my mother opened the door/ ... and set me free" (213). The first stanza of Irma McClaurin's poem, "The Power of Names," reads:

I slip my mother's name on like a glove
and wonder if I will become like her
absolutely.
Years number the times I have worn her pain
as a child, as a teenager, as a woman – my second skin –
as she sat, silver head bowed
silent
hedging the storm. (63)

In her moving autobiographical narrative, *Pushed Back to Strength: A Black Woman's Journey Home* (some of which is excerpted in *Double Stitch*), Gloria Wade-Gayles argues that in the segregated south of the forties "Surviving meant being black, and being black meant believing in our humanity, and retaining it, in a world that denied we had it in the first place" (6). The survival of black culture and black selfhood was sustained by the motherline. "The men in my family were buttresses and protectors," writes Wade-Gayles, "but it was the women who gave meaning to the expression 'pushed back to strength'" (13). Whether named mentor, role model, guide, advisor, wise woman or advocate, the mother represents for the daughter a sturdy bridge on which to cross over. Even the author Renita Weems, who was abandoned by her alcoholic mother, writes: "Though not as sturdy as others, she is my bridge. When I needed to get across she steadied herself long enough for me to run across safely" (129).

Alice Walker's classic essay, "In Search of Our Mothers' Garden," is a moving tribute to her African-American foremothers who, in her words, "handed on the creative spark, the seed of the flower they themselves never hoped to see: or like a sealed letter they could not plainly read" (240). "[S]o many of the stories that I write," Walker emphasizes, "that we all write, are my mother's stories" (240). Walker delineates here a theory of creative identity that juxtaposes the male paradigm of literary achievement that demands separation and individuation. As Dannabang Kuwabong observes about Africaribbean women's writing, but germane I argue to all black female diaspora literature, "the mother-daughter relationship ... is central to the development of identity and voice" (132). Cassie Premo Steele's observation about Audre Lorde is likewise applicable to many black women writers: "Grounding her narrative in matrilineal history and myth allows Lorde to find and take root: to form her identity" (8). Black female subjectivity generally, and creativity specifically, are formed, nurtured and sustained through women's identification with, and connection to, their motherline. As Sylvia Hamilton, noted documentary writer and director, commented in the film *Black Mother, Black Daughter*, "[Our foremothers] created a path for us...we are bound to something larger than our selves.... I am moved by the example of their lives."

African-American daughters seek and hold connection with mothers and the motherline; they achieve empowerment through this identification because motherhood is valued by and is central to African-American culture and because the motherline bestows to the daughter affirming and empowering lessons of black womanhood. In *Not Our Kind of Girl: Unraveling the Myths of Black Teenage Motherhood*, Elaine Bell Kaplan, proposes a "poverty of relationship" thesis to account for the high incidence of black unwed teenage pregnancy. "[T]eenage mothers," she writes, "describe being disconnected from primary family relations, abandoned by their schools and by the men in their lives...at the time of adolescence, when it is most important that they experience positive relationships" (11). The absence of relationships in the adolescent girl's life, Kaplan argues, results from the loss of black neighbourhood and community occasioned by the economic restructuring of the 1970s. In the 1950s and 1960s a strong sense of family and community prevailed in black neighbourhoods; there was also a low incidence of unwed teenage pregnancy. Whether the two are causally related as Kaplan maintains, her argument explicates, albeit inadvertently, the connection-empowerment the-sis advanced here. Disconnection, a word Kaplan herself uses, is at the core of the adolescent girl's aloneness and at the center of the community's despair. As African-American women celebrate the power acquired through connec-tion to a strong mother and a strong motherline, Kaplan's words remind us that the very survival of African-American culture may depend on it.

Conclusion

Reflecting upon the themes of this chapter, I am reminded of the chorus from Canadian singer-songwriter Jann Arden's song "Good Mother":

I've got a good mother
and her voice is what keeps me here
Feet on ground
Heart in hand
Facing forward
Be yourself.

African-American motherhood, in the five themes detailed above, bestows upon black children a loved, strong and proud selfhood. The mother, in fulfilling these tasks of black motherhood, becomes, to borrow the metaphor from the song, "the voice that keeps [the children] here." She is the "heart in the hand" that enables the children to "face forward with feet on the ground and be themselves." In other words, mothering in black culture is what ensures physical and psychological survival and well-being and is what makes resist-ance possible.

[1] I am thankful to Heather Hewett for drawing my attention to this quote by Cecelie Berry. Please see Hewett's forthcoming article, "Third-Wave Era Feminism and the Emerging Mothers' Movement," *Journal of the Association for Research on Mothering* 8 (1,2) (Summer 2006) and Cecelie Berry's article, "Home is Where the Revolution Is" (September 1999), online: salon.com.
[2] Please see Chapter Eight for a discussion of African-American mothers and sons.
[3] "Childbearing and children are valued by members of this community and black women in The Flats," Stack continues, "unlike many other societies ... feel few if any restrictions about childbearing. Unmarried black women, young and old, are eligible to bear children, and frequently women bear their first children when they are quite young" (47). Many of these teen-age mothers,

however, do not raise their first born. This responsibility is left to the mother, aunt, or elder sister with whom the biological mother resides. The child thus may have both a "Mama," the woman "who raised him up," and the biological mother who birthed him. The mama, in Stack's terminology, is the "sponsor" of the child's personal kinship network; the network is thus matrilineal and matrifocal.

[4]Johnson's argument is that contemporary African-American culture is matrifocal; at no time does she suggest that black family or culture is matriarchal. Nonetheless, any discussion of matrifocality must locate itself in the infamous Moynihan report and the controversy it generated (see Rainwater and Yancey). The report described the Black family as dysfunctional and argued that the mother was to blame for the purported pathologies of the race: "In essence, the negro community has ... a matriarchal structure which ... seriously retards the progress of the group as a whole" (qtd. in Rainwater and Yancey 75). Or, as critic Michele Wallace put it, "The Moynihan report said that the black man was not so much a victim of white institutional racism as he was of an abnormal family structure, its main feature being an employed black woman" (12). Swiftly and abruptly the report was condemned for its failure to take into account institutionalized racism to explain under/unemployment, family "breakdown" and so forth, not to mention the report's blame-the-victim rhetoric and mother-blaming stance. For an excellent discussion of the Moynihan report in terms of the ideological constructions of black womanhood see Morton, particularly chapter nine, "Rediscovering the Black Family: New and Old Images of Motherhood." Morton argues that, "[T]he 1970's saw a veritable revolution in interpretation of the modern Afro-American family ... [with] an emphasis on familial health. In contrast to the old equation of black deviance from white middle-class norms as pathologized and dysfunctional, the new black family studies increasingly emphasized Afro-American diversity—including familial and sexual departures from white norms—as a positive thing" (126).

The revisionist family scholarship set out to debunk the Black matriarchy thesis by documenting the poverty and powerlessness experienced by Black women. At the same time, the revisionist Black family studies argued that it was precisely the strength and resiliency of black motherhood that enabled blacks to remain whole and intact in a racist world. Paradoxically, the new scholarship exposed Black matriarchy as a myth while emphasizing the strength of Black mothers. This paradox underscores the difference between matrifocality and matriarchy and points to the ideological impasse of the *Moynihan Report* that linked strength with domination.

Scholars today often downplay the strengths of the Black mother so as to appear that they are staying clear of the controversial black matriarchy thesis.

This is evident in historical accounts of slavery, particularly the research of Herbert Gutman, *The Black Family in Slavery and Freedom, 1750-1925*, where he emphasizes that the slave family remained, for the most part, intact by which he means father-headed and nuclear. "It may be," Morton writes, "that matrifocality and strong slave women were too akin to the myth of the black matriarchy to be acceptable to contemporary historians" (133). Such a perspective keeps us locked in the Moynihan framework, pathologizing the very thing that keeps black families viable and resilient, namely black motherhood. Such a viewpoint also curtails honest and appreciative study of black women. For readings in revisionist black family studies refer to: Ballingsley 1968, 1992; Staples and Boulin; McAdoo 1981, 1993.

[5]Ladner continues: "This sharp change in status occurs for a variety of reasons. Perhaps the most important value it has is that of demonstrating the procreative powers that the girls possess. Children are highly valued and a strong emphasis is placed on one's being able to give birth. The ultimate test of womanhood, then, is one's ability to bring forth life. This value underlying child bearing is much akin to the traditional way in which the same behaviour has been perceived in African culture. So strong is the tradition that women must bear children in most West African societies that barren females are often pitied and in some cases their husbands are free to have children by other women. The ability to have children also symbolizes (for these girls) maturity that they feel cannot be gained in any other way" (216).

For white middle-class culture, marriage, rather than motherhood, is what ushers girls into womanhood. The elaborate, ritualized—and I may add costly—customs of the wedding ceremony, bridal showers, bridal shows, wedding service and receptions and so forth, bear testimony to the place of the wedding in that culture.

[6]bell hooks continues: "[The] libratory struggle has been seriously undermined by contemporary efforts to change that subversive homeplace into a site of patriarchal domination of black women by black men, where we abuse one another for not conforming to sexist norms. This shift in perspective, where homeplace is not viewed as a political site, has had a negative impact on the construction of black female identity and political consciousness. Masses of black women, many of whom were not formally educated, had in the past been able to play a vital role in black liberation struggle. In the contemporary situation, as the paradigms for domesticity in black life mirrored white bourgeois norms (where home is conceptualized as politically neutral space), black people began to overlook and devalue the importance of black female labour in teaching critical consciousness in domestic space. Many black women, irrespective of class status, have responded to this crisis of meaning by imitating leisure-class sexist notions of women's role, focusing their lives on

meaningless compulsive consumerism" (1984: 47).

[7]For a discussion of the African-American mother-son relationship, please see Chapter Eight in this volume.

[8]Joseph's research—a 1979-1980 survey—revealed that the majority of black daughters (94.5 per cent) said that they respected their mothers (Joseph and Lewis). Joseph's research identified different issues and trends in the Anglo-American mother-daughter relationship. She found a greater belief in romance amongst white mothers, as expressed in the commonly offered advice "Marry for love." Joseph discovered further that: "the ways in which the White daughters said they feared their mothers disclosed an area that was rarely, if ever, mentioned by the Black daughters. The response was, 'I fear I might be like her. I want to be independent of her'" (Joseph and Lewis 125). Here the Anglo-American daughters bespeak matrophobia first defined by Rich in *Of Woman Born*. "White women were included" in the survey, but because of "the small number of respondents," Joseph writes, "it was not possible to conduct a comparative study between White subjects and Black ones" (Joseph and Lewis 125). Joseph discovered in her analysis that class was an important variable to the degree that working-class white mothers gave responses similar to the black mother's responses.

CHAPTER SEVEN

"A POLITICS OF THE HEART"

TONI MORRISON'S THEORY OF MOTHERWORK

Motherhood is a central theme in Toni Morrison's fiction and is a topic she returns to time and time again in her many interviews and articles. In her reflections on motherhood, both inside and outside her fiction, Morrison articulates a fully developed theory of African-American mothering that is central to her larger political and philosophical stance on black womanhood. Building upon black women's experiences of, and perspectives on, motherhood, Morrison develops a view of black motherhood that is, in terms of both maternal identity and role, radically different than the motherhood practised and prescribed in the dominant culture. Morrison defines and positions maternal identity as a site of power for black women. From this position of power, black mothers engage in a maternal practice that has as its explicit goal the empowerment of children. This chapter will introduce Morrison's theory of motherhood, what I have termed "A Politics of the Heart." Drawing upon Patricia Hill Collins' standpoint theory, and building upon the five traditions of black motherhood discussed in the previous chapter, I will explore how and in which ways Morrison defines motherwork as a political enterprise that assumes as its central aim the empowerment of children. This discussion will be developed from Sara Ruddick's theory of maternal practice. The central question of Morrison's writing, I will argue, is how mothers, raising black children in a racist and sexist world, can best protect their children, instruct them in how to protect themselves from the racism, and, for daughters, the sexism that seeks to harm them. This, is Morrison's theory of motherhood as a "Politics of the Heart."

Patricia Hill Collins' Standpoint Theory

In *Black Feminist Thought: Knowledge, Consciousness and the Politics of Empowerment*, Patricia Hill Collins writes "every culture has a worldview that it uses to order and evaluate its own experiences" (1990: 10). Black women, Collins goes on to explain,

> fashioned an independent standpoint about the meaning of Black womanhood. These self definitions enabled Black women to use African-derived conceptions of self and community to resist negative evaluations of Black womanhood advanced by dominant groups. In all, Black women's grounding in traditional African-American culture fostered the development of a distinctive African American women's culture. (1990: 11)

The black female standpoint develops in opposition to and in resistance against the dominant view or what Collins calls the controlling images of black womanhood. Collins argues that "the dominant ideology of the slave era fostered the creation of four interrelated, socially constructed controlling images of Black womanhood, each reflecting the dominant group's interest in maintaining Black women's subordination" (1990: 71). The four controlling images that Collins examines include the mammy, the matriarch, the welfare mother, and the Jezebel. By way of controlling images, as Collins explains, "certain assumed qualities are attached to Black women and [... then] used to justify [that] oppression" (7). "From the mammies, Jezebels, and breeder women of slavery," Collins writes, "to the smiling Aunt Jemimas on pancake mix boxes, ubiquitous Black prostitutes, and ever-present welfare mothers of contemporary popular culture, the nexus of negative stereotypical images applied to African-American women has been fundamental to Black women's oppression" (7). Black women, according to Collins, may resist these derogatory stereotypes through the creation of a distinct black female standpoint that is based on black women's own experiences and meanings of womanhood.

The black female standpoint, Collins argues, develops through an interplay between two discourses of knowledge: "the commonplace taken-for granted knowledge" and the "everyday ideas" of black women as they are clarified and rearticulated by black women intellectuals or theorists. This gives rise to a specialized Black feminist thought. In turn, as Collins explains, "the consciousness of Black women may be transformed by [this] thought" (20). She elaborates:

> Through the process of rearticulation, Black women intellectuals offer African-American women a different view of themselves and their world from that forwarded by the dominant group [...]. By taking the core themes of a Black women's standpoint and infusing them with new meaning, Black women intellectuals can stimulate a new consciousness that utilizes Black's women's everyday, taken-for

granted knowledge. Rather than raising consciousness, Black feminist thought affirms and rearticulates a consciousness that already
exists. More, important, this rearticulated consciousness empowers
African-American women and stimulates resistance (1990: 31-32).

In other words the black female standpoint, emerging from black women's
everyday experiences and clarified by black feminist theory, not only provides
a distinct "angle of vision on self, community and society" but also, in so doing,
enables black women to counter and interrupt the dominant discourse of black
womanhood.

The formation and articulation of a self-defined standpoint, Collins emphasizes, "is [thus] key to Black women's survival" (1990: 26). As Audre Lorde
argues "it is axiomatic that if we do not define ourselves for ourselves, we will
be defined by others –for their use and to our detriment" (qtd. in Collins, 1990:
21). However, as Collins emphasizes the importance of self-definition, she
recognizes that black women, as an oppressed group, inevitably must struggle
to convey this self-definition positioned as they are at the periphery of the
dominant white, male culture. Collins writes: "An oppressed group's experiences may put its members in a position to see things differently, but their lack
of control over ideological apparatuses of society makes expressing a self-
defined standpoint more difficult" (26). The black female standpoint is thus,
in Collins' words, "an independent, viable, yet subjugated knowledge" (13).

Collins' standpoint thesis provides a useful conceptual framework for
viewing Morrison as a maternal theorist. To borrow from Collins' paradigm:
Morrison is an intellectual who takes the core themes of black motherhood and
develops from them a new consciousness of black motherhood that empowers
African-American women and engenders resistance. Furthermore, Morrison's
standpoint on black motherhood enables black women to challenge the
controlling images of black motherhood, which Collins has defined as the
mammy, the matriarch, and the welfare mother. Morrison's standpoint on
black motherhood enables black women to resist these negative evaluations of
black motherhood by rearticulating the power that is inherent in black
women's everyday experiences of motherhood. This rearticulation centres
upon a reaffirmation of the traditional roles and beliefs of black motherhood
discussed in the previous chapter that gives rise to Morrison's theory as
motherwork as profoundly political undertaking.

Morrison's Theory of Maternal Practice: Motherwork as Concerned with the Empowerment of Children

Morrison's maternal standpoint on black motherhood as a site of power gives rise to a particular model of maternal practice that I will be calling motherwork. This section of the chapter will explore how and in which ways motherwork in Morrison centres upon the empowerment of children. In particular, I will examine how Morrison defines the responsibilities of motherwork in terms of four distinct yet interrelated tasks; namely, preservation, nurturance, cultural bearing, and healing. Together these four tasks enable mothers to 1) protect their children, physically and psychologically; 2) teach children how to protect themselves; and 3) heal adults who were unprotected as children and hence harmed. This discussion will be built from Sara Ruddick's theory of maternal practice and maternal thinking.

Sara Ruddick's Theory of Maternal Practice and Maternal Thinking

In *Maternal Thinking: Toward a Politics of Peace*, Sara Ruddick argues that the work of mothering "demands that mothers think; out of this need for thought-fulness, a distinctive discipline emerges" (24). Ruddick elaborates:

> I speak about a mother's thought—the intellectual capacities she develops, the judgements she makes, the metaphysical attitudes she assumes, the values she affirms. Like a scientist writing up her experiment, a critic poring over a text, or a historian assessing documents, a mother caring for her children engages in a discipline. She asks certain questions—those relevant to her aims—rather than others; she accepts certain criteria for the truth, adequacy, and relevance of proposed answers; and she cares about the findings she makes and can act on. The discipline of maternal thought, like other disciplines, establishes criteria for determining failure and success, sets priorities, and identifies virtues that the discipline requires. Like any other work, mothering is prey to characteristic temptations that it must identify. To describe the capacities, judgements, metaphysi-cal attitudes, and values of maternal thought presumes not maternal achievement, but a *conception* of achievement. (24)

Ruddick argues that mother-work is characterized by three demands: pres-ervation, growth and social acceptance. "To be a mother," continues Ruddick, "is to be committed to meeting these demands by works of preservative love, nurturance, and training" (17).

The first duty of mothers is to protect and preserve their children: "to keep safe whatever is vulnerable and valuable in a child" (80). "Preserving the lives of children," Ruddick writes, "is the central constitutive, invariant aim of maternal practice: the commitment to achieving that aim is the constitutive maternal act" (19). "To be committed to meeting children's demand for preservation," Ruddick continues, "does not require enthusiasm or even love; it simply means to see vulnerability and to respond to it with care rather than abuse, indifference, or flight" (19). "The demand to preserve a child's life is quickly supplemented," Ruddick continues, "by the second demand, to nurture its emotional and intellectual growth" (19). Ruddick explains:

> To foster growth ... is to sponsor or nurture a child's unfolding, expanding material spirit. Children demand this nurturance because their development is complex, gradual, and subject to distinctive kinds of distortion or inhibition .... Children's emotional, cognitive, sexual, and social development is sufficiently complex to demand nurturance; this demand is an aspect of maternal work ... and it structures maternal thinking. (83)

The third demand of maternal practice is training and social acceptability of children. This third demand, Ruddick writes:

> is made not by children's needs but by the social groups of which a mother is a member. Social groups require that mothers shape their children's growth in "acceptable" ways. What counts as acceptable varies enormously within and among groups and cultures. The demand for acceptability, however, does not vary, nor does there seem to be much dissent from the belief that children cannot "naturally" develop in socially correct ways but must be "trained." I use the neutral, though somewhat harsh, term "training" to underline a mother's active aims to make her children "acceptable." Her training strategies may be persuasive, manipulative, educative, abusive, seductive, or respectful and are typically a mix of most of these. (21)

"In any mother's day," Ruddick concludes, "the demands of preservation, growth and acceptability are intertwined. Yet a reflective mother can separately identify each demand, partly because they are often in conflict" (23).

The many and various children's needs that arise from each demand of mother-work and the various and many responses of the mother coalesce to form the discipline of maternal thought. Specifically, mother-work gives rise to particular cognitive styles, particular ways of seeing and dealing with the world. For example, because the job of raising children is complex, and often contradictory, where there is seldom a right or wrong—and because the mother's own feelings about her children are so ambivalent—mothers become accepting of ambiguity. Moreover, because so much of mother-work is beyond the control of the mother, mothers develop what Ruddick calls humility: "In a world beyond one's control, to be humble is to have a profound sense of the limits of one's actions and of the unpredictability of the consequences of one's work" (72). Mother-work also gives rise to what Ruddick calls "cheerfulness": "To be cheerful means to respect chance, limit, and imperfection and still act as if it is possible to keep children safe" (74). Humility, cheerfulness, and acceptance of ambiguity are only a few of the many attitudes that mothers learn and develop as they respond to the demands of mother-work. "Mothers, like gardeners or historians," writes Ruddick, "identify virtues appropriate to their work. But to identify a virtue is not to possess it" (25). Ruddick explains further:

> Mothers meeting together at their jobs, in playgrounds, or over coffee can be heard thinking. This does not necessarily mean that they can be heard being good. Mothers are not any more or less wonderful than other people—they are not especially sensible or foolish, noble or ignoble, courageous or cowardly … . When mothers speak of virtues they speak as often of failure as of success. Almost always they reflect on the *struggles* that revolve around the temptations to which they are prey in their work. What they share is not virtuous characteristics but rather an identification and a discourse about the strengths required by their ongoing commitments to protect, nurture, and train. (25)

When mothers set out to fulfil the demands of mother-work—to protect, nurture, train—they are engaged in maternal practice; and this engagement, in turn, gives rise to a specific discipline of thought—a cluster of attitudes, beliefs, values—which Ruddick calls maternal thinking.

Morrison's Theory of Motherwork

Toni Morrison, in a manner similar to the model developed by Sara Ruddick, positions motherwork as a practice committed to meeting specific tasks. Like Ruddick, Morrison foregrounds the aims of preservation and nurturance in her theory of mothework. As well, Morrison is attentive to the task of "training" children so that they are acceptable to their social group. However, with Morrison the aim of training is amplified to include the African-American maternal custom of cultural bearing discussed in the previous chapter: raising children in accordance with the values, beliefs, and customs of traditional African-American culture. In each of these tasks—preservation, nurturance, cultural bearing—Morrison is concerned with protecting children from the hurts of a racist and, for daughters, sexist culture, and with teaching children how to protect themselves so they may be empowered to survive and resist the racist and patriarchal culture in which they live and develop a strong and authentic identity as a black person. Finally, Morrison advances a fourth aim, healing, that is developed from the African-American maternal practice of nurturance as resistance discussed earlier. With this aim, Morrison's focus is upon those adults who never received protection, nurturance, and cultural bearing as children and thus grew to be adults psychologically wounded by the hurts of racism and/or sexism. In Morrison's reformulation of these tasks, maternal practice is defined and represented specifically as a political under-taking with the explicit objective of empowering children and/or healing adults so that may survive and resist racism and sexism through the creation of a strong self-defined identity. In other words, Morrison building upon the African-American maternal practices of nurturance as resistance and cultural bearing discussed in Chapter Six, argues that motherwork, through the tasks of preservation, nurturance, cultural bearing and healing, is what makes survival and resistance possible for African-American people.

Morrison's theory of motherwork as concerned with the empowerment of children means that mothering, in Morrison's view, is profoundly a political act with social and public connections and consequences. In this, Morrison's theory counters and challenges the dominant view that mothering is an individualized and private act, focussed upon the nurturance of children, and having no or little political import, social significance, or cultural value. The aim of this section is to explore how Morrison positions motherwork—in the functions of preservation, nurturance, cultural bearing and healing—as com-mitted to the empowerment of children and how Morrison in doing so deconstructs the "master narrative" of motherhood. Morrison, building upon the traditions of black motherhood discussed in the previous chapter, positions motherwork in African-American culture as a political undertaking in its commitment to the empowerment of children and thus can not be understood or appreciated from the ideological lens of the normative discourse of moth-erhood. In the pages that remain I will detail how Morrison positions motherwork, through the tasks of preservation, nurturance, cultural bearing, and healing, as committed to the empowerment of children.

Preservation

Central to Morrison's counter narrative of motherhood and her critique of the dominant discourse is a challenge to the received view that links 'good' mothering solely with nurturance. Morrison, in her model of motherwork as empowerment, foregrounds the importance of preservation, a dimension of motherhood minimized and trivialized in the dominant discourses of mother-hood, most notably with intensive mothering discussed in Section I. Sara

Ruddick argued, as noted above, that the first duty of mothers is to protect and preserve their children: "to keep safe whatever is vulnerable and valuable in a child" (1989, 80). "Preserving the lives of children," Ruddick writes, "is the central constitutive, invariant aim of maternal practice" (1989, 19). Though maternal practice is composed of two other demands—nurturance and training—this first demand, what Ruddick calls preservative love, is what describes much of African-American women's motherwork. In a world in which, to use Patricia Hill Collin's words, "racial ethnic children's lives have long been held in low regard" (1994: 49), mothering for many black women, particularly among the poor, is about ensuring the physical survival of their children and those of the larger black community. Securing food and shelter, struggling to build and sustain safe neighbourhoods is what defines both the meaning and experience of black women's motherwork. Preservation, as, Collins explains further is, "a fundamental dimension of racial ethnic women's motherwork" (1994: 48-49). However, normative discourses of motherhood particularly in their current configuration as sensitive mothering define motherwork solely as nurturance. "Physical survival," writes Collins, "is assumed for children who are white and middle class. The choice to thus examine their psychic and emotional well-being … appears rational. The children of women of color, many of whom are 'physically starving' have no such choices however" (1994: 49). While exclusive to middle-class white women's experiences of mothering, the normative discourse of mothering as nurturance has been naturalized as the universal normal experience of motherhood. Consequently, preservative love, such that practised by Eva in *Sula* and Mrs. MacTeer in *The Bluest Eye* is often not regarded as real, legitimate or "good enough" mothering. However, for Morrison, keeping children alive through preservative love is an essential and integral dimension of motherwork.

Nurturance

The aim of black mothering, once preservation has been ensured, is to nurture children so that they may survive and resist the maiming of racism and, for daughters, sexism and grow into adulthood whole and complete. Nurturance requires that black mothers immunize their children from racist ideologies by loving them so that they may love themselves in a culture that defines them as not deserving or worthy of love. In loving her children the mother instils in them a loved sense of self and self-esteem, enabling them to defy and subvert racist discourses that naturalize racial inferiority and commodify blacks as object and other. This maternal nurturance is described in *Paradise*: "Parents who wiped the spit and tears from their children's faces and said 'Never mind, honey. Never you mind. You are not and never will be a nigger, a coon, a jog, a jungle bunny nor any other thing white folks teach their children to say. What you are is God's'" (Morrison 1998: 212). Morrison's thinking on nurturance as an act of resistance builds upon the African- American view of homeplace as a site of resistance. Homeplace, as discussed ealier, refers to a haven or refuge, where "black people could affirm one another and by so doing, heal many of the wounds inflicted by racist domination ... [a place where they] had the opportunity to grow and develop, to nurture their spirits" (hooks 1998: 42).

Time and time again in her writing Morrison emphasizes the need for the parent to have a strong sense of self so that he or she may nurture the same in the growing child. The nurture of self-love in children, Morrison believes, depends on self-love in parents. Morrison argues that self-love depends on the self first being loved by another self. Before the child can love herself, she must experience herself being loved and learn that she is indeed valuable and deserving of affection. Informing Morrison's writing is her belief that mothering is essential for the emotional well being of children because it is the mother who first loves the child and gives to that child a loved sense of self. Rich writes in *Of Woman Born*: "The nurture of the daughters in a patriarchy calls for strong sense of self-nurture in the mother" (247). The self-love that Morrison deems as essential for the motherlove is derived from the ancestral memory and ancient properties discussed in detail below in the section on the task of cultural bearing. Parents, and in particular mothers, Morrison argues, must identify with the ancestral memory and ancient properties of the African-American motherline in order to love themselves as black people and to teach the same to their children so that they can develop a strong and proud black identity. This is particularly true for girl children. Daughters need strength and confidence from their mothers because, in patriarchy, female selves are susceptible to erasure and displacement. In an interview Morrison commented: "Women sabotage themselves.... They locate the true beloved out of themselves." These women, Morrison goes on to say "have girl children ... [they] bring them up to be broken in half..to loath themselves." Mothers must, Morrison emphasizes, "take their daughters in their arms and hold them and say, you are just fine the way you are" (qtd. in Ross C1). Rich writes in *Of Woman Born* that "[what] women [need] growing into a world so hostile to us ... [is] a very profound kind of loving in order to love ourselves" (246). Morrison's children thus move from mother-love to self-love to selfhood. This is why the comment about Gideon in *Tar Baby* upsets Son "[It] bothered him that everybody called Gideon Yardman, as though he had not been mothered" (1981: 161). Son's statement makes clear the connection between mothering and selfhood.

Frequently in Morrison, a woman other than the child's biological mother is the one who provides this nurturance. Building upon the African-American tradition of othermothers and woman-centred networks discussed above, Morrison defines mothering to include, as Patricia Hill Collins has observed, a "generalized ethic of caring and personal accountability among African-American women who often feel accountable to all the Black community's children" (1990: 129). Speaking of the character Hagar in *The Song of Solomon*, Morrison writes: "She needed what most colored girls needed: a chorus of mamas, grandmamas, aunts, cousins, sisters, neighbors, Sunday school teachers, best girl friends, and what all to give her the strength life demanded of her and the humor with which to live it" (311). In Morrison, surrogate mothers or a community of women mother the child in the event of the mother's death or abandonment, psychological or otherwise. These mothers are also, as with Pilate in *Song*, the singing teachers or story tellers who tell the orphaned or neglected child the stories and provide them with nurturance not made available by the biological mother. The act of nurturance whether it be conveyed by the biological mother or an othermother bestows upon the child a loved sense of self that both shields him/her from the hurts of a racist and sexist culture and fortifies that child to survive and resist racism and sexism.

Cultural Bearing

The third aim, cultural bearing, is the central and most significant task in Morrison's theory of motherwork. Cultural bearing refers to the task of raising children in accordance with the values and beliefs of traditional African-American culture. The aim of nurturance is to develop in the child a loved sense of self so that he/she will see themselves as worthy and deserving of love in a culture that largely deems them otherwise. In this way nurturance could be seen as an act of immunization in that it shields children from the disease of racism and sexism and then fortifies them so that children are able to protect themselves from this same disease to survive and resist racism/sexism. The task of cultural bearing functions in a similar manner: by way of cultural bearing, mothers pass on to each successive generation of children African-American culture and instill in their children knowledge about and pride in their African-American heritage. More specifically, mothers pass on what I will be calling the motherline: the ancestral memory and the ancient proprieties of traditional black culture. By way of cultural bearing or what may be termed mothering from the motherline, mothers transmit ancestral memory and the ancient proprieties to their children. In so doing, cultural bearing or motherline mothering confers affirming images of black people and their history that, in turn, impedes the internalization of the controlling images of blackness put forward by the dominant culture and allows the child to develop a strong and authentic selfhood as a black person. Therefore, as with nurturance, cultural bearing both protects black children from racism and sexism and enables children to protect themselves.

The Motherline: The Ancient Properties and Ancestral Memory

There is "a worldview," writes Naomi Lowinsky, "that is as old as humankind, a wisdom we have forgotten that we know: the ancient lore of women—The Motherline" (1). The motherline, as noted in Chapters Five and Six, enables daughters to derive strength from their identities as women. In Morrison, the motherline signifies the ancient properties of traditional black womanhood and ancestral memory more generally of black culture. Mothers pass on the ancient properties of black womanhood and ancestral memory through the maternal task of cultural bearing. Women however, are often, as Naomi Lowinsky, has observed, "cut off from their motherline, and [have] paid a terrible price for cutting [themselves off from] [their] feminine roots" (26). What is lost, she emphasizes, is female authenticity and authority. Morrison, likewise, argues that fullness and completeness of being are assured only in connection with the motherline and by living life in accordance with the ancient properties ancestral memory. According to Morrison, daughters need mothers to become women and mothers need women to stay daughters. "A woman," Morrison argues, "has to be a daughter before she can be any kind of woman. If she doesn't know how to relate to her ancestors, to her tribe, so to speak, she is not good for much" (qtd. in Taylor-Guthrie 184). "When I talked to a very young black girl recently," Morrison continues, "it seemed to me that she had never heard of anything. They've grown up like they never had grandmothers. Or if they had them, they never paid them any attention. Kill your ancestors, you kill all" (qtd. in Taylor-Guthrie 73).

One could argue that the main theme of Morrison's fiction is summed up in her oft-cited quotation: "When you kill the ancestor you kill yourself. I want to point out the dangers, to show that nice things don't always happen to the totally self-reliant if there is no conscious historical connection" (1984: 344). "From the outset of her literary career," critic Angelita Reyes emphasizes, "Toni Morrison ... has been deeply concerned with the preservation of black folklore, and with sustaining positive black cultural values" (19). Speaking specifically of Morrison's fourth novel *Tar Baby*, but applicable to all of her writings, Reyes maintains that what Morrison asks is that "Black people of the New World diaspora must not lose sight of their African consciousness" (19). In a conversation with Elsie B. Washington (1987), Toni Morrison comments:

[Grandparents and ancestors are] DNA, it's where you get your information, your cultural information. Also it's your protection, it's your education. They were responsible *for* us, and we have to be responsible *to* them ... . You can't just *take*. Our ancestors are part of that circle, an ever widening circle, one hopes. And if you ignore that, you put yourself in a spiritually dangerous position of being self-sufficient, having no group that you're dependent on. (qtd. in Taylor-Guthrie 238)

Toni Morrison describes the memory of black people as a "spoken library":

The spoken library was ... children's stories my family told, spirituals, the ghost stories, the blues, and folk tales and myths, and the everyday ... instruction and advice of my own people.... . I wanted to write out of the matrix of memory, of recollection, and to approximate the sensual and visceral response I had to the world I lived in ... to recreate the civilization of Black people ... the manners, judgements, values, morals.... (qtd. in Holloway and Demetrakopoulos 104-5)

Morrison, thus, as critic Theodore Mason has observed:

is an example of the novelist as *conservator*. She is a writer particularly interested in depicting, and thereby preserving and perpetuating, the cultural practices of black communities. Her work displays a commitment to the capacity of fiction to provide ways of maintaining and communicating important cultural values which otherwise might be lost. The novelist, then, is not a figure isolated form history and culture but rather is someone who conserves cultural forms and practices by depicting them in the public act of fiction. (172, emphasis in original)

The motherline in Morrison signifies ancestral memory; therefore men, as well as women, must live their lives in accordance with the values of the motherline, or more specifically the ancestral memory of black culture. In this, Morrison differs radically from conventional thinking on the mother-son relationship. Psychoanalytic discourse, childrearing manuals, literature from the men's movement, and popular wisdom argue that sons must separate from their mothers in order to assume a "normal" masculine identity. A close and caring relationship between a mother and her adolescent son is pathologized as somehow aberrant—she's making a mama's boy out of him—while a relationship structured upon separation is naturalized as the real, normal and hence natural way to experience mother-son attachment. In contrast to this, Morrison argues that men are made complete and whole through connection to the mother and identification with the motherline and the ancestral memory it conveys and embodies. In Morrison, to use the words of Baby Suggs from *Beloved*: "A man ain't nothing but a man …. But a son well now, that's *somebody*" (1987: 23). Therefore, sons as well as daughters must live their lives in accordance with the values of the motherline to develop a healthy sense of self. And it is the mother who, in the task of cultural bearing, models and mentors the teachings of the African-American motherline. To this task I now turn.

Cultural Bearing: Mothering from Motherline

In *Maternal Thinking*, Sara Ruddick writes: "Many mothers find that the central challenge of mothering lies in training a child to be the kind of person whom others accept and whom the mothers can actively appreciate" (104). With Morrison, training or more specifically cultural bearing means socializing children in the values of the African-American motherline so that a child will not only be accepted by African-American values but more significantly develop self-esteem as a black person that will enable him/her to survive and challenge the racism of the dominant culture.

Karla Holloway observes that there are "archetypal children's needs, and these show in Black children's special need for memory" (Holloway and Demetrakopoulos 104) if black children are going to survive they must know the stories, legends, and myths of their ancestors. Black women, writes Barbara Hill Rigney, "are the primary tale-tellers and the transmitters of history, as well as the singing teachers" (10). Trudier Harris describes these women as "keepers of the tradition" and "culture bearers … they are women who have kept their funkiness intact" (41). "These women are free," Harris continues, "but the freedom they experience is one wrought in nurturing their children and grandchildren, not in defiance and destruction of them" (40). Speaking to Nellie McKay (1983) about her ancestors, Morrison commented: "What is uppermost in my mind … is that my life seems to be dominated by information about black women. They were the culture bearers, and they told us [children] what to do … " (qtd. in Taylor Guthrie 140). "Black women," critic Karla Holloway writes, "carry the voice of the mother— they are the progenitors, the assurance of the line … . Women as carriers of the voice," Holloway continues, "carry wisdom—mother wit" (Holloway and Demetrakopoulos 123). In an interview with Bessie Jones and Audrey Vinson (1985), Morrison talks about her own mother's soliloquies: "[She had the] habit of getting stuck like a record on some problem, going on for days and days and then singing in between … just like a saga" (qtd. in Taylor Guthrie

172). Stories also bestow, in Holloway's words, "endurance, staying power, and spiritual dominion" (114). In this cultural bearing function, mothers by way of storytelling, song or soliloquies impart important life lessons about black strength and courage as well as instill knowledge about, and pride in African-American heritage that enable children to refuse the controlling images of blackness put forward by the dominant culture.

Healing

In meeting the three tasks of motherwork, whether it be in the form of nurturance, preservation or cultural bearing, mothers seek to protect children and teach them how to protect themselves from the hurts of the racist and, for daughters, sexist culture in which they live by enabling the child to develop a loved and proud sense of self as a black person. In this, these three functions of motherwork may be viewed as preventive or pro-active acts in so far as mothers through preservation, nurturance and cultural bearing empower children to survive and resist. Alive and armed with the self-esteem of a beloved child who is proud of his/her black identity, this son or daughter is physically and psychologically readied and prepared to keep his selfhood intact and withstand the many and varied racist and sexist assaults that threaten to harm him or her physically and psychologically. Morrison's final task of motherwork, what I have termed healing, may be read as a re-active or restorative practice in so far as it seeks to repair those people, in particular women, whose selfhood has been displaced or damaged by the hurts of a racist and a patriarchal culture.

In her interviews Morrison has spoken about the tendency in women to place, what she calls, the beloved outside of themselves. In her interview with Gloria Naylor (1985), Morrison tells of how she became, in her words, "obsessed ... with fragments of stories" she had heard of women who displaced their selves. The first was the story of Margaret Garner, the fugitive slave mother who chose to kill her children rather than see them returned to slavery. The second was the photo of a young dead girl from Van der Zee's *The Harlem Book of the Dead* (in Taylor-Guthrie 207). This young girl was shot and, as she lay dying, she was asked, "What happened to you?" To which she responded, "I'll tell you tomorrow" giving the man responsible time to get away. "[I]n both instances" Morrison explains,

> something seemed clear to me. A woman loved something other than herself so much. She had placed all the value of her life in something outside herself. That woman who killed her children loved her children so much; they were the best part of her and she would not see

them sullied. She would not see them hurt.... And ... this woman had loved a man or had such affection for a man that she would postpone her own medial care or go ahead and die to give him time to get away so that, more valuable than her life, was not just his life but something else connected with his life. (qtd. in Taylor-Guthrie 206-208)

Morrison goes on to say:

Now both of those incidents seem to me ... very noble, you know, in that old-fashioned sense, generous, wide-spirited, love. This is peculiar to women. And I thought, it's interesting because the best thing that is in us is also the thing that makes us sabotage ourselves, sabotage in the sense that our life is not as worthy, or our perception of the best part of ourselves.... [W]hat is it that really compels a good woman to displace the self, her self ... [W]hat I started ... thinking about ... was to project the self not into the way we say "yourself," but to put a space between those words, as though the self were really a *twin* or a thirst or a friend or something that sits right next to you and watches you. (qtd. in Taylor-Guthrie 208)

In this conversation with Gloria Naylor, Toni Morrison described her writing as a "process of reclamation"—a journey of remembering which brings into being the life of the dead girl:

bit by bit I had been rescuing her [the dead girl] from the grave of time and inattention. Her fingernails may be in the first book; face and legs, perhaps, the second time. Little by little bringing her back into living life. So that now she comes running when called—walks freely around the house, sits down in a chair; looks at me, listens.... She cannot lie. Doesn't know greed or vengeance. Will not fawn or pontificate.... She is here now, alive. I have seen, named and claimed her—and oh what company she keeps. (qtd. in Taylor-Guthrie 217)

Eight years later during a radio interview with Eleanor Wachtel on *Jazz* (1993), Morrison was asked about the relationship between the dead girl inside who is brought back to life through writing and the dead girl that is killed by Violet and yet lives with her. Morrison responded:

[Violet's] dead in the sense of being asleep. No one can bring that person back to life except the person who has enfolded it. The soul or spirit ... what ... we mean when we say me. [It] is so ignored, so silent, so unappreciated by forces that are in the world.... That is where self esteem is born or destroyed ... need to release ... honor that part of our selves.... That seems to be critical and very important for human beings to be able to do that.... [The] search for that person, concept or idea informs a great deal of my work. (Wachtel)

Morrison's writings call upon her readership to recognize, affirm and celebrate the "me"; and to love, as Baby Suggs preaches in Beloved, the person we are. The self must be known and loved, in Morrison's terms, "honored and released." When we do not name or nurture our own authentic self, we lose, forget about or put to sleep the person we are. Morrison comments further: "[What concerns me] is when you displace the self, so completely that you do not have value if you are not worried about someone else. When are you going to worry about your self?" She goes on to ask:

Who is Beloved? ... Where is that part of you that you know loves you and will never let you down.... Why are we ignoring that part of ourselves—we keep strangling it every minute and we know that one will always be there, will always love and no judgement. That is the one we put to sleep all the time and transfer energy of that into the thing outside. (Wachtel)

Morrison asks us to recognize, as Sethe eventually does in Beloved, that our "me" is indeed our "best thing" (1987: 73).

In her 1993 radio interview, Morrison spoke about the need to "honor and release the soul or spirit ... what we mean when we say me, the part of you that you know, loves you and will never let you down" (Wachtel). In a 1990 interview with Bill Moyers, Morrison commented: "We have to embrace ourselves [and have] Self regard" (qtd. in Taylor-Guthrie 57). In her 1983 interview with Nellie McKay, Morrison described the woman in yellow from Tar Baby as:

a real, a complete individual who owns herself—another kind of Pilate. There is always someone who has no peer, who does not have to become anybody. Someone who already "is." ... She is the original self—the self that we betray when we lie, the one that is always there. And whatever that self looks like—if one ever sees that thing, or that image—one measures one's other self against it" (qtd. in Taylor-Guthrie 147-148).

In her 1985 conversation with Gloria Naylor, Morrison discusses again the woman in yellow and says:

> [She] is somehow transcendent and whatever she really was, what she
> was perceived as by Jadine, is the real chic. The one that authenti-
> cates everything. The one that is very clear in some way about what
> her womanhood is.... [T]he memory of that one is somehow a basis
> for either total repression or a willingness to let one's true self surface.
> (qtd. in Taylor-Guthrie 194)

The interviews collected in *Conversations with Toni Morrison* (Taylor-
Guthrie), cover a ten-year period, and yet in each the idea of an authentic or
true self is emphasized. This authenticity of self is specifically the selfhood
made possible through the preservation, nurturance, and cultural bearing of
motherwork. Morrison's emphasis on an authentic or true self informs all of her
writings and has particular relevance for her women characters.

In Morrison's work, children who do not receive the preservation, nurturance,
and cultural bearing of motherwork never develop the authentic selfhood
Morrison champions and thus grow to be psychologically wounded as adults.
Never having been loved—protected, nurtured, and sustained through cultural bearing—by their mothers, unmothered children never learn how to love
themselves. Without this self-love, the "me" of which Morrison speaks is lost,
forgotten, or "put to sleep." The aim of healing, the fourth task motherwork,
is to mend the unmothered and wounded children. Normally, this healing
takes place when these children have become adults and centres upon the
recovery of displaced selfhood for those individuals who were denied nurturance
and cultural bearing in childhood. Specifically these adults finally acquire self-
love and achieve selfhood by being remothered as adults. This remothering is
achieved by way of a spiritual or physic reconnection with a lost mother and
by way of a reclamation of a lost or displaced mother/daughter selfhood. This
reconnection and reclamation is achieved through what Morrison has termed
rememory. Healing occurs when the son or daughter is able to remember the
mother, mourn her loss, reconnect with her and recreate for themselves an
identity as a mothered child. This connection, however, is not with an actual
flesh-blood mother but with the spirit or memory of the lost mother. This
psychic journey of return, reconnection, and reclamation, while directed to a
spirit of a lost mother, is often initiated and overseen by an actual mother
figure, a close female friend of the troubled woman who serves as an othermother
for her. "Black women," as Carol Boyce Davies has observed, "at certain
junctures in their lives, require healing and renewal and ... Black women
themselves have to become the healers/mothers for each other when there is
such a need" (41). The othermother heals the woman by prompting her to take

this journey of rememory and reconnection and assisting, comforting and sustaining her as she does so. The me-ness that Morrison argues is central to well-being therefore is either imparted to us as children through cultural bearing and nurturance or restored to us as adults through healing. And it is this me-ness that empowers the child to survive and resist. In both instances it is women, though not necessarily or exclusively a biological mother or even a real flesh-and-blood mother, who provide this healing that makes possible the achievement of this sustaining selfhood.

Conclusion

Motherwork in Morrison is explicitly and profoundly a political undertaking concerned as it with the empowerment of children. By way of motherwork, children develop a loved and proud African-American identity that makes survival and resistance possible. However, this theoretical trajectory of Morrison's is not delineated in the fiction itself.[1] Only with the task of healing is the redemptive power of mothering conveyed and in this instance such is achieved by a child's psychic return to his lost mother rather than by an actual woman mothering her children (though an othermother does oversee this adult child's journey of remembering, return and reconnection). From this perspective, it would seem that there is a disparity or divergence between the idealized view of motherhood put forward in Morrison's theory and the "ineffectual" mothering portrayed in her fiction, that the promise of the power of mothers and motherhood celebrated in her theory is not delivered in her fiction.

However, I argue, and as I explore at length in my book on Toni Morrison (O'Reilly 2004b), that the reverse is, in fact, the case. Morrison affirms and confirms the importance of mothers and motherwork by describing in poign-ant and often agonizing detail the personal and cultural suffering and loss that occurs when children are not mothered and do not receive the preser-vation, nurturance, and cultural bearing needed for personal resistance and cultural renewal. Morrison, in her many interviews, explains why and how motherwork empowers children. In contrast, Morrison's novels, as fiction, do not describe or prescribe how such motherwork is to be performed; rather they portray mothers' despair at not being able to fulfil the essential tasks of motherwork and the inevitable suffering of children and the larger African-American culture in the absence of maternal preservation, nurturance, and cultural bearing. Frequently, we understand or appreciate the importance of something or someone only when that something or someone is lost or absent. Morrison's dedication in Sula bespeaks this theme: "It is sheer good fortune to miss somebody long before they leave you. This book is for Ford and Slade, whom I miss although they have not left me." This is the strategy of Morrison's fiction.

[1]Please see my book, *Toni Morrison and Motherhood: Politics of the Heart*, for a discussion on this topic.

CHAPTER EIGHT

IN BLACK AND WHITE

AFRICAN-AMERICAN AND ANGLO-AMERICAN FEMINIST
PERSPECTIVES ON MOTHERS AND SONS

In "Man Child: A Black Lesbian Feminist's Response," African-American poet and essayist Audre Lorde asks us to "consider the two western classic myth/ models of mother/son relationships: Jocasta/Oedipus, the son who fucks his mother, and Clytemnestra/Orestes, the son who kills his mother" (1987:76). These ancient myths are continually retold and reenacted in Western culture and function, in Louis Althusser's terms, as ideological apparatuses that interpolate mothers and sons into specific relationship positions that are most fully dramatized in the narratives of Clytemnestra and Jocasta. The sanction against mother–son closeness and connection is signified and achieved by the incest taboo, while the enforcement of mother–son separation is represented and enforced by the murder of Clytemnestra. Both patriarchal narratives are enacted through the denial and displacement of the maternal presence.

I open this chapter referencing the above narratives because it is my contention that maternal erasure and disconnection are central not only to patriarchal thinking on mothers and sons but also to Anglo-American *feminist* thought on mothers and sons as well. Through a close reading of three early, classic, Anglo-American, feminist texts on mothers and sons, I examine how the early Anglo-American perspective on mothers and sons scripted mother–son attachment in terms of these hegemonic narratives of maternal erasure and disavowal. Next, I consider how recent Anglo-American feminist writings on mothers and sons call into question this patriarchal and early feminist view of maternal displacement to emphasize mother–son connection. Finally, I will review recent African-American feminist theory on mothers and sons to explore both its emphasis on maternal presence (as opposed to maternal erasure) and its specific, racially determined, mode of rearing sons.

Patriarchal Narratives

The story of Oedipus and his mother Jocasta was first told by the playwright

Sophocles, but is known to us today through Freud's psychological theory of the Oedipal complex. The son's first love object, according to Freud, is the mother, but the son renounces this love upon the realization that this desire is forbidden and will result in his castration by the father. In the story of Clytemnestra and her son Orestes, the mother, as most accounts tell it, kills her husband Agamemnon upon his return from Troy to avenge his sacrificial killing of their daughter, Iphigenia, and because he has brought home with him a concubine. In retaliation against his father's death, Orestes kills his mother, which he defends as just vengeance for the death of his father. The Furies, the female chorus who are judge and jury, excuse the mother's crime because "the man she killed was not of her own blood." The son retorts: "Am I of my mother's blood?" To which they respond: "She nourished you in the womb ... do you disown your mother's blood?" Apollo, called in to settle the dispute, states that: "the mother is not the parent of the child which is called hers. She is the nurse who tends the growth of the young seed planted by its true parent, the male." Finally, Athena, a female goddess born from the head of Zeus, is asked to decide the verdict and rules: "No mother gave me birth. Therefore, the father's claim and male supremacy in all things wins my whole heart's loyalty." With her vote the son is pardoned, and the Furies, the last representatives of the mother right of ancient goddess times, are banished. These myths narrate the consolidation of patriarchal power through the son's identification with the patrilineal line, and script mother–son separation as the precondition of manhood.

These ancient myths, functioning as ideological apparatuses, are continually reenacted and retold in our contemporary culture. A cursory review of twentieth-century popular culture reveals many and diverse manifestations of the ancient patriarchal narratives of forbidden Jocasta/emasculated Oedipus, and of triumphant Orestes/defeated Clytemnestra. Philip Wylie in his immensely popular *Generation of Vipers* coined the term "momism": "Our land," writes Wylie, "subjectively mapped, would have more silver cords and apron strings crisscrossing it than railroads and telephone wires. She is everywhere and everything.... Disguised as good old mom, dear old mom, sweet old mom ... she is the bride at every funeral and the corpse at every wedding" (185). In the 1960s, the Moynihan "report" advanced the now infamous black matriarchy thesis that described the black family as dysfunctional and argued that mothers were to blame for the pathologies of the race. "In essence," wrote Daniel Moynihan, "the Negro community has ... a matriarchal structure which ... seriously retards the progress of the group as a whole" (75). Or, as African-American writer/critic Michele Wallace puts it "The Moynihan report said that the black man was not so much a victim of white institutional racism as he was of an abnormal family structure, its main feature being an employed black woman" (12). The 1980s gave us Robert Bly, the father of the men's mytho-poetic movement and author of the best-selling *Iron John*, the notorious thesis which suggests the American man has grown up with too much mothering and not enough fathering; they suffer from what Bly diagnosed as "father hunger." "[The modern man] is not happy," laments Bly, "he is life-preserving but not life-giving, he is full of anguish and grief" (1990: 2–4). Men have discovered their "feminine side," but have left unexplored their true essential masculine identity. For Bly, healing occurs only when the son "cut[s] his soul away from his mother-bound soul" and moves, again in Bly's words, "from the mother's realm to the father's realm" (1990: ix).

Feminism has long critiqued Wylie's momism, Moynihan's black matriarchy, and Bly's father hunger for their blatant misogyny and virulent mother blame. From a sociohistorical perspective, they are clearly backlash texts. A *Generation of Vipers*, popular after World War II when women were being reprogrammed from workers back into mothers, articulates the culture's uneasiness with what Miriam Johnson has called the white, middle-class matrifocality of the 1950s. The minimal involvement of fathers in those postwar years meant that the home was a maternal dominion where sons grew to manhood under the mother's influence, with little or no involvement from the father. The matrifocality of the home in the 1950s is what is said to have caused, according to many social commentators, the "feminine" men of the 1960s—how Alan Alda came to replace John Wayne as the ideal identity of manhood. The Moynihan report was written in the 1960s, the decade that witnessed the civil rights movement and the beginnings of the feminist movement. *Iron John* takes as its cultural context the 1980s, that witnessed increased economic independence for women, skyrocketing divorce rates, and, significantly, the beginning of the father's rights movement.[1]

Early Anglo-American Feminist Theory on the Mother–Son Relationship

The purpose of this chapter is not to detail the patriarchal script of maternal displacement and denial. Rather, I am interested in exploring how this displacement and denial are represented, recast, and resisted in *feminist* theory on mothers and sons. The first and longest section of this chapter offers a close and detailed reading of three classic Anglo-American texts on the mother–son relation: Judith Arcana's *Every Mother's Son: The Role of Mothers in the Making of Men* (1983); Linda Forcey's *Mothers of Sons: Toward an Understanding of Responsibility* (1987); and Babette Smith's *Mothers and Sons: The Truth About Mother-Son Relationships* (1995),[2] in order to examine how this literature mimicked, albeit unintentionally, the patriarchal dictate of maternal displacement and denial. The three books, though spanning fifteen years, can be grouped together as a representative writing of the earlier Anglo-American feminist perspective on mothers and sons.

Judith Arcana's *Every Mother's Son* (1983)

In the prologue to *Every Mother's Son*, Arcana asserts that: "mothers need to understand that we are creating and nurturing the agents of our own oppression; once we make them, their education as men in this misogynist society will pull them from our arms, set them above us, and make them the source of our degradation" (1983: 3). She goes on to argue that: "we would prevent this if we could, and to do so we must enter into conscious struggle with our sons, actively seeking to change what is currently defined as male and female behavior" (1983: 34). This book, developed from sixty interviews with mothers and with sons, and from Arcana's own personal reflections on raising her son, Daniel, during his first ten years, explores how current practices of masculine socialization give rise to expectations of entitlement as boys grow into men, and how they result in the disavowal of all things feminine in the adult male psyche.

Over the course of her interviews with mothers and sons, Arcana discovered that most mothers reject traditional definitions of masculinity. However, the sons of these same women had assumed, for the most part, a conventional gender identity, or were aware that such was expected of them. What accounts for this disparity between intent and consequence? A small number of sons in Arcana's study reported that their mothers consciously and enthusiastically socialized them to be masculine, while another small group said that while their mothers did not engage in overt gender socialization, it was done unconsciously and indirectly. However, the majority of sons in Arcana's study stated that they could not recall any incident in which their mother had explicitly or implicitly directed them to be "men." The disparity, Arcana argues, may be attributed to three factors of masculine socialization.

The first is that mothers, for the most part, are lesser agents in the socialization of sons. Many of the sons identified "culture" or "the father" as where they learned patriarchal masculinity. "Basic sex-role conditioning," as Arcana observes, "is not in mothers' hands, but in the hands of men who've made this culture" (120). Second, mothers raise children but they do not determine the material or ideological conditions of their mothering. Women, as Adrienne Rich (1986) reminds us, mother in motherhood, the latter being a patriarchal institution which is male-defined and -controlled. Mothers raise boys but they don't make men, because, as Arcana explains, mothers are "contractors rather than architects, following specifications not of our design" (115). Women, Arcana continues, "are relatively powerless in this culture, and though we raise the children we bear, almost none of us are free to bear and raise them *if or when we choose*, much less *as we choose*" (115).

Finally, while mothers may not initiate or enforce the gender socialization of their sons, they do accommodate it. A central and constitutive demand of mothering, as Sara Ruddick explains in her book, *Maternal Thinking*, is "training children in the behaviour acceptable to their social and cultural group" (110). Thus, while mothers may reject patriarchy and its constructions of masculinity, they realize, consciously or otherwise, that their sons must take their place in that world. "The fear of alienating a male child from 'his' culture," writes Adrienne Rich, "seems to go deep, even among women who reject that culture for themselves every day of their lives" (205). Rich goes on to ask: "What do we fear? That our sons will accuse us of making them into misfits and outsiders? That they will suffer as we have suffered from patriarchal reprisals? Do we fear they will somehow lose their male status and privilege, even as we are seeking to abolish that inequality?" (205). "As mothers in this time," Arcana writes, "we are faced with a dilemma: we see that the old ways are not good; we wish to raise our children differently—but we fear they'll suffer ostracism, alienation, and loneliness in a society that has by no means given up its old definitions and restrictions" (1).

Another explanation Arcana offers to account for this discrepancy between aim and consequence centers on maternal practice itself. Mothering is about caring for and catering to the needs of children, and about nurturing self-esteem so that children see themselves as special and deserving; what Ruddick defines as the second demand of maternal practice (83). However, with sons this nurturance may be, according to Arcana, interpreted as privilege and entitlement: "Though children of both sexes put their mothers in the positions of servants ... mothers of sons are, whether we feel it in the moment or not, inadvertently reinforcing the sexist premise that women exist to serve men .... Men learn from infancy to expect and solicit selfishness and cherishing care at the hands of women" (101, 102). While "[d]aughters learn from our mothers to *be mothers*, to give in that disastrously self-destructive way that has been honored by men as true motherhood; sons learn *to expect such treatment from women*" (102). Women in patriarchal culture are expected to devote their time and attention to children and men; sons thus, as Arcana identifies, derive double benefits from these patriarchal imperatives as both men and children. Given that women's secondary status is enforced in both the gender arena (service to men) and in the maternal realm (service to children), mothers must, if they hope to raise non-sexist men who reject traditional masculinity, challenge both patriarchal imperatives. Women, Arcana writes, "need to live out of ourselves. We wrong ourselves and our children if we subordinate our lives to theirs" (235).

Mothers must, Arcana continues, "reject [the] traditional mother role [and] ... accept ... our sons into our daily lives" (247). In so doing, the mother will enable her boy child to see her outside and beyond her maternal identity that positions her as secondary to, and in service to, children and men. Coming to know their mothers outside motherhood, sons learn to view and appreciate their mothers as, in Arcana's words, "whole people."

According to Arcana, mothers must, therefore, reject traditional motherhood if they hope to raise non-traditional sons; that is, men who have renounced patriarchal masculinity and the entitlement and privilege that such accords. No longer can mothers be, or be seen as, "the primary source of praise, encouragement, and selfless service" (1983: 280). However, as mothers reject this role of selfless service to sons, traditional male socialization, as Arcana explains, teaches boys "that they are to be the beneficiaries of a male culture: they will grow up to power, status, and the admiration and support of women.... When [a mother] moves to change that pattern with her son, he understands that she wants him to give up power .... [A] boy has to begin by *losing*" (280). In other words to become more human, he must become less male. This, then, is the second paradox of feminist male child rearing: sons gain by losing, and mothers are better mothers by "being less of a mother." This, in Arcana's view, is both the challenge and contradiction of feminist mothering of sons.

Arcana maintains that the patriarchal institution of motherhood oppresses women, impedes mother–son equality, and fosters both sexism and patriarchal masculinity. Women thus must reject traditional motherhood and become, in Rich's words, "outlaws from the institution of motherhood" in order to effect the gender transformations they wish for themselves and their sons, for women and men. Arcana perceptively identifies the many ways traditional motherhood oppresses women and perpetuates traditional masculinity. However, less clear in this critique is a distinction between motherhood and mothering. Patriarchal motherhood, however, does not negate the possibility and potentiality of gynocentric mothering. Mothers have always mothered against, beyond, and outside patriarchal motherhood. In dismissing motherhood, Arcana, I would suggest, loses sight of the radical potentiality of mothering; if you will, she throws the baby out with the bathwater.

Arcana also finds problematic the way mothering places mothers in service to children and in particular to sons. However, I would argue that maternal practice, as Ruddick argues, is by necessity concerned with meeting the physical, psychological, and social needs of children. "These three demands— for preservation, growth, and social acceptance," writes Ruddick, "constitute maternal work; to be a mother is to be committed to meeting these demands by works of preservative love, nurturance and training" (17). Service, the word

Arcana uses to describe such work, is what one (a woman or man) must do when one engages in maternal practice; however "service" does not necessarily require the subordination and enslavement of the mother. Moreover, care of children does not preclude care of self, nor does service equal servitude or require self-erasure. However, because service becomes confused in Arcana with servitude, as does the distinction between mothering and motherhood, motherhood is represented as an essentially oppressive state and hence rejected. This in turn results in the displacement and disparagement of the maternal.

Linda Forcey's *Mothers of Sons: Toward an Understanding of Responsibility* (1987)

The teaching of antisexism and the undermining of masculine socialization are, according to Arcana, the explicit goals of feminist mothering of sons. This is to be achieved by challenging both traditional practices of male socialization *and* traditional ways of mothering. Linda Forcey's *Mothers of Sons: Toward an Understanding of Responsibility*, the second book-length feminist work on mothers and sons, considers, as the title suggests, the issue of responsibility. The position advanced in her 1987 book differs significantly from Forcey's current thinking on mothers and sons. Thus the following exposé and critique of Forcey's responsibility thesis is pertinent only to this early work—as it laid the foundation for contemporary thinking about motherhood—and not to Forcey's subsequent research.

Mothers of Sons, based on the oral histories of one hundred women from various socioeconomic backgrounds, examines, in Forcey's words, "how mothers perceive their relationships with their sons. That is, what do they have to tell us about the relationship, and their responsibility to and for it?" (3). Her book opens with a review of early feminist thought on motherhood—the writings of de Beauvoir, Friedan, Bernard—and argues that these early feminist texts question "the sagacity of the assignment of solitary responsibility for 'mothering' to mothers [and] find it harmful to children of both sexes but especially sons" (32). Forcey recognizes that children must be nurtured; this is, in her words, "beyond dispute." However, Forcey goes on to argue that "what is not beyond dispute ... is who should be responsible for seeing that the requisite nurturing gets done, and precisely what constitutes effective nurturing in order to promote this preservation and growth" (42). Traditional "malestream" mother-blaming thought, as feminists have rightly argued, is preoccupied with the so-called failures of mothers to fulfill their maternal responsibilities. However, Forcey maintains that this perspective informs *feminist* thinking on mothering as well; it too operates as a regulatory discourse, reinscribing mothers in the traditional ideological matrix of responsibility and blame:

> The differences between the traditional and the recently revised feminist approach to the mother–son relationship center on the reasons why mothers mother the way they do, and what it means to be a "good" mother. For these feminists, the "good" mother is she who, in spite of her oppression, assumes the responsibility for raising sons who are physically, emotionally, and socially well-adjusted and who do not separate from her, do not identify with their fathers, and do not assume the traditional masculine values.... As with the conventional wisdom on mothers of sons, this recent feminist scholarship implicitly assumes that mothers are all powerful. It calls on women to assume their rightful responsibility for their children's welfare in order to affect a nonpatriarchal society. (46, 47)

Feminists, in Forcey's view, have merely redefined the meaning of "good mothering" and have left unquestioned the "wisdom of the responsibility assignment itself" (46). As well they have failed to challenge the patriarchal premise that assumes "[that women] are more relational than men [and thus] should be assigned the primary responsibility for the care of children" (59).

Recent feminist writings, notably Nancy Chodorow's feminine relationality argument and the different voice theory advanced by Carol Gilligan, work to reconstitute women, Forcey maintains, as natural mothers, while in the feminist instance it is psychology and not wombs that predispose women to nurturance. The challenge of feminism should not be to determine how women may fulfill their responsibility as feminist mothers, Forcey argues, but rather to question the responsibility assignment itself. "No person," Forcey writes, "can successfully be responsible for the meaning of another's being. Not even mothers of sons" (59). Such a view, Forcey continues, "is personally and politically damaging for both mothers and sons, women and men" (59).

Most of the women in Forcey's study "perceived themselves to have the primary responsibility for the well-being of their sons, a responsibility they find to be enormous and never-ending" (47). Nevertheless, women experience their identity and work as mothers as "responsibility" because such a role accords women a purpose and power not otherwise available to them in a patriarchal culture. Forcey explains: "Many women, particularly those in mid-life, do express their satisfaction in life in terms of how they view the results of their years as mothers as measured by the happiness of their sons. For many women being the 'essential' one in the family is a hard role to give up" (59). However, mothers must, Forcey argues, for the good of their sons *and* themselves, reject this maternal self-definition, and come to define themselves outside and beyond their maternal identity, as well as learn to share the work of child rearing with others.

In her final chapter, appropriately entitled "Jocasta Unbound," Forcey argues, in a manner similar to Arcana, that women must develop identities outside their maternal role; the three locations she identifies are school, work, and women's friendship. When women balance "caring and selfhood" they are less likely to define their identity and worth in the context of the responsibility assignment that, Forcey argues, is damaging to both mothers and sons. It is important to note that Forcey calls for the "unboundness" from motherhood in order to free *mothers* from the matrix of blame and responsibility, while Arcana champions unboundness, or in her words, rejection of traditional motherhood, so that *sons* do not see women exclusively in service to children and secondary to men. However, both agree that mothering must be shared; as Forcey concludes her book: "When the sons of tomorrow are the responsibility of the many instead of the one they will grow freer, stronger, and more caring, as will their mothers" (151). Thus both Arcana and Forcey advocate "less mothering" in order to effect the desired transformations in gender relations/roles for both men (Arcana) and women (Forcey).

Forcey maintains, as examined above, that the traditional and revised feminist view of the responsibility of mothers for sons "is personally and politically damaging to mothers and sons, women and men" (59). She exhorts mothers to renounce the exclusive and essentialist responsibility role through the formation of self-identities other than that of mother, and by sharing the task of childrearing. The task of responsibility is, no doubt, "enormous" and "never-ending," as Forcey argues. However, I would suggest that the problem rests not so much with responsibility as with the way motherhood becomes defined in the dominant Anglo-American culture. A therapist interviewed by Forcey, and who worked with poor and "struggling" mothers, observed that "[such mothers] are just too busy. Their whole lives cannot be wrapped up in their sons.... If you are very, very busy, she argues, you don't put quite the same emotional burden on the child." (67). "The major difference between middle-class and working-class mothers of sons," she speculates, "was that in the case of the latter the mother was not the central person in the son's life and sons were not the central people in the mothers' lives" (67).

It would seem that the problem is not responsibility per se but rather that motherhood, as it is defined in Anglo-American culture, assigns this responsibility exclusively to mothers. Furthermore, the work of mothering is assumed to preclude or take precedence over any other work, and is defined solely as nurturance; paid employment is not seen as an aspect of mothering but rather as something that prevents women from mothering. Forcey apparently recognizes this, as suggested by her insistence upon the need for both shared childrearing and non-maternal work and identities. Nonetheless her book, as its subtitle suggests, focuses on the responsibility assignment rather than on the way motherhood is organized in Anglo-American culture. Moreover, in Anglo-American culture mothers are assigned the responsibility but given no power—and accorded no real status— for the maternal work they do. Mothers do not make the rules, they simply enforce them. Again, it would seem that motherhood becomes oppressive to women not because of the responsibility assignment, as Forcey would argue, but rather because this responsibility comes with little or no power and prestige and because maternal responsibility— defined exclusively as care rather than work in Anglo-American culture— confines mothering and mothers to the home. Finally, as discussed earlier, mothering does, and must, mean being responsible for the children in your care; those who engage in maternal practice assume this task upon the arrival of the child, by birth or adoption. However, because Forcey, in her early work, identifies the responsibility assignment as the problem, her argument, as does Arcana's, advances "less mothering" as the solution and partakes in the displacement and disparagement of the maternal.

Babette Smith's *Mothers and Sons: The Truth About Mother-Son Relationships* (1995)

The final book on the mother–son relationship under consideration is Babette Smith's *Mothers and Sons: The Truth About Mother-Son Relationships*. Smith's research, developed from a comparative study of post-war and post-1960s mothers and sons, explores how mothers' and sons' perceptions of one another and of their relationship have changed over the last 50 years. This study focuses on two interrelated questions: How do mothers perceive masculinity? And how do sons, in turn, perceive their mothers and their mothering? Of interest to us here in the discussion of the way motherhood is represented in feminist thought on the mother–son relation is Smith's second concern: sons' perceptions of maternal practice.

The post-war sons' reflections on their mothers and mothering were both startling and sad. These sons, Smith writes, "were struggling to love where they had little respect, to believe they *were* loved when they remembered no affection, to justify their love by saying their mother was *not typical*" (33). While the ideology of "the Good Mother," particularly as it was represented in the 1950s, demanded that mothers be selfless, moral, pleasing, passive, and subservient to their husbands, and led mothers to believe that they would be honored and appreciated for this, the views expressed by the now middle-aged sons interviewed by Smith reveal the contrary: the mothers were neither admired nor respected for their maternal devotion. As one son commented: "The worst thing I think was the way she made herself a martyr to what everyone else wanted" (34). The few sons who spoke or wrote favourably about their relationship with their mothers remembered their mothers as "female people rather than [just] 'mothers'" (50). The memories of these sons "reveal that these women had also developed wide-ranging interests beyond the home, 'artistic and intellectual curiosity,' 'stories from work,' 'has published a book'" (50). They felt their mothers were "adaptable," or they had "broadness of outlook and knowledge," qualities that their sons celebrated (50).

In contrast, the post-1960s sons genuinely liked their mothers and enjoyed being in their company. Smith writes:

> The male experience of the mother–son relationship changed sub-
> stantially. The consensus which emerged from these younger sons'
> opinions was a reversal of the past. The percentage which once ran
> 70:30 negatively about a man's mother, had turned right around to
> run approximately 70:30 positively. Most sons of this age group spoke
> enthusiastically about their mothers, the percentage as well as the
> tone of the assessment, holding good among those who explored the
> subject in some depth and those who answered a briefer question-
> naire. These sons loved their mothers, as their fathers had loved
> theirs, but the younger generation also liked them. (175)

The reasons, the interviews would suggest, are: (a) the mothers of these sons were less invested in the ideology of the Good Mother; (b) as a result of increased education, work, and travel opportunities for women, these mothers had more in common with their sons; and (c) the familial, economic, and cultural changes occasioned by feminism gave women more confidence and clout. As well, and of particular significance to the discussion at hand, according to Smith, for the post-1960s son "it was noticeably easier for [him] to agree that he admired or respected his mother when he did not have to pass judgement on her parenting at the same time ... [in contrast], [1950s] sons had no choice but to evaluate their mothers in her maternal role" (182). Smith elaborates:

> [When they could,] sons of all ages nominated their mothers' achieve-
> ments outside the home. Younger men who had this option more
> often were more readily admiring. They could avoid the ambivalence
> caused by passing judgement on the women's parental success in their
> own lives and external yardsticks, such as occupation, income, or
> title, were concrete evidence that society endorsed their personal

opinion. This was the benefit which a woman's outside work could bring to the mother–son relationship—not as a role model, as it was for daughters (although these young sons did not automatically exclude their mothers as a role model), but by providing the boys with something about their mother which was understood and valued in their male world. (182)

Mothers who exhibited attributes valued in male culture, and/or achieved what was deemed success from the masculine standpoint, were more readily respected and admired by their sons. As one schoolteacher observed of the sons in the class:

> Boys identify with mothers who are independent, freethinking, nice people, not only for security and emotional reasons, but also because they happen to like their mothers as people. These are mothers who actually present themselves to their sons as people *without overt[ly] "being Mother."* (185, emphasis added).

And while Smith argues that the variable is not so much paid employment as self-confidence, she nonetheless concludes that women's work outside the home benefited the mother–son relationship because it, as noted above, "[provided] the boys with something about their mother which was understood and valued in their male world" (182). Male respect and admiration for mothers, Smith goes on to argue, is essential "because, without those elements, there is no basis for equality between them" (185).

Though not always explicitly acknowledged or addressed, the "beyond motherhood" thesis, if you will, of Arcana, Forcey, and Smith begins with the recognition that motherhood in patriarchal culture is neither valued nor respected, and that mothers do not acquire any real or substantive power, status, or agency— economic, cultural, or otherwise—for the work they do as mothers. Thus, as a mother, the woman is not able to secure the respect of her son. Though this is a concern for all three, it is of particular importance for Smith because her theoretical platform for improving gender relations hinges upon sons respecting and admiring their mothers.

The problem, according to Smith, is "[how do] sons ... hold their own mothers dear in a society which has little regard for mothers" (180). Smith argues, as we saw earlier, that this problem may be remedied through mothers fashioning an identity and role "beyond motherhood" in the public, male realm of work so as to, in Smith's words "provid[e] [their sons] with some-thing about their mother which [is] understood and valued in their male world" (182). Smith's argument here resonates with earlier liberal feminist thinking on motherhood. Smith recognizes that motherhood is devalued in our culture, but instead of addressing this larger problem, she exhorts women, as did much of earlier liberal feminist theory, to abandon the private realm of motherhood and obtain personhood, power, and prestige by entering the public arena of (paid) work. Smith's argument thus reinscribes, as did much of 1970s liberal feminism, the hierarchal gender opposition that privileges masculine values over those that are associated with the feminine, and in so doing both mimics and perpetuates the patriarchal disparagement and displacement of the maternal.

As Smith's argument seeks to distance mothers from motherhood and downplay their maternal role and identity, it also calls for the abdication of maternal authority and power. Smith argues that post-1960s mother–son relationships are more successful because they are based on equality, and that this equality is what makes possible the respect Smith deems essential for a successful mother- son relationship. While equality in relationships is generally understood to be a good and desired thing, in the mother-child relationship such equality is problematic because it denies the mother the power and authority that is rightly hers as the mother of the child. "There are," as Sara Ruddick observes, "many external constraints on [a mother's] capacity to name, feel, and act. But in the daily conflict of wills, at least with her children, a mother has the upper hand.... *If a mother didn't have this control, her life would be unbearable*" (1989: 55, italics added). The mode of mothering advocated by Smith is what Valerie Walkerdine and Helen Lucey define in their book, *Democracy in the Kitchen*, as "sensitive mothering": "[A defining characteristic] of the sensitive mother is the way she regulates her children. Essentially there should be no overt regulation; regulation should go underground; no power battles, no insensitive sanctions as these would interfere with the child's illusion that she is the source of her wishes, that she had 'free will'" (25, 24).[3] While sensitive mothering may make possible the mother–son equality so valued by Smith, it centers on and depends upon the abdication of maternal power and authority.

Smith argues, as did Forcey and Arcana ten years earlier, that the less a mother relates to her son as "mother," the greater the chances will be of raising non-sexist, non-masculine (as it is traditionally defined) boys and improving relations between mothers and sons and men and women generally. This will allow sons to see their mothers as other than secondary persons subservient to men and children, according to Arcana; will undercut the responsibility assignment, according to Forcey; and will enable boys to respect and admire their mothers, according to Smith. Each downplays, denies, and in some instances, disparages, the responsibility, authority, and power of mothers as mothers of sons, while according the same to women as women. In so doing

Smith, Arcana, and Forcey script the mother-relation, albeit subtly and no doubt inadvertently, in terms of the patriarchal imperatives of maternal erasure and displacement, as enacted in the narratives of Clytemnestra and Jocasta.

New Anglo-American Feminist Perspectives on the Mother–Son Relationship

Feminist theory on mothers and sons has been informed by and has developed in the context of feminist thinking on mothering and motherhood over the last 30 years. More specifically, Anglo-American feminist theory on mothers and sons mirrors and re-enacts the theoretical trajectory of Anglo-American feminist thought on the mother–daughter relationship. In the 1970s, the received view—or master narrative—of mothers and daughters was that this relationship, particularly in the daughter's adolescent years, was one of antagonism and animosity. The daughter must differentiate herself from the mother if she is to assume an autonomous identity as an adult. The mother, in turn, is perceived and understood only in terms of her maternal identity. The mother represents for the daughter, according to the received narrative, the epitome of the patriarchal oppression that she seeks to transcend as she comes to womanhood; the daughter's failings, as interpreted by herself and by the culture at large, are said to be the fault of the mother. This is the patriarchal narrative of the mother–daughter relationship. The lives of mothers and daughters are shaped by these cultural narratives even as mothers and daughters live lives different from, and in resistance to, these assigned roles. Feminist Anglo-American writers, most notably Nancy Chodorow, author of the influential *The Reproduction of Mothering*, and Nancy Friday, author of the best-selling *My Mother/My Self*, argue that mother–daughter identification is ultimately detrimental to the daughter's attainment of autonomy. For Chodorow, writing from a psychoanalytic perspective, this is because mother–daughter identification results in the daughter having weak "ego-boundaries"; with Friday, separation is required to enable the daughter to assume an adult sexual identity as a woman.

The 1970s feminist view that problematizes if not pathologizes mother–daughter identification has now fallen out of favour among Anglo-American feminist theorists. Indeed most Anglo-American feminists, since at least the mid-1980s, regard mother–daughter connection and closeness as essential for female empowerment. From the early 1980s, feminists, both lay and academic, have increasingly linked female power to mother–daughter connection. Today, Anglo-American feminist writers challenge the normative view of mother–daughter attachment that scripts estrangement as both natural and inevitable; they argue that identification empowers mothers and daughters alike, giving rise to the transformation of patriarchal culture. Drawing upon the ancient Elyeusis rites of Demeter and Persephone, recent feminist writings on the mother–daughter relation celebrate mother–daughter connection, and explore how such is achieved and sustained through maternal narratives, the motherline, feminist socialization of daughters, and gynocentric mothering. To this end, feminist theorists identify and challenge the various cultural practices and assumptions that divide mothers and daughters, and seek an alternative mother–daughter narrative scripted for empowerment as opposed to estrangement.[4]

A similar trajectory may be observed in Anglo-American feminist writing on the mother–son relation, with an approximate ten-year time lag. The texts examined above tend to downplay women's maternal role and identity. In contrast, the contemporary Anglo-American feminist view emphasizes mother–son connection, and positions it as central to the reconfiguration of traditional masculinity. Similar to the new Anglo-American feminist literature on mothers and daughters that recasts connection as empowerment by referencing the mythic mother–daughter dyad Demeter and Persephone, the contemporary Anglo-American feminist emphasis on the mother–son connection is also frequently conveyed through a mythic mother–son relation, that of Thetis and Achilles.

Thetis, according to the myth, dipped her son Achilles into the river Styx to render him immortal. However, fearing that he might be lost to the river, she held onto him by his ankle. Achilles, as the story goes, remains mortal and vulnerable to harm. Thetis would be forever blamed for her son's fatal flaw, his Achilles heel. However, contemporary feminist theorists reinterpret the traditional reading of this narrative to argue, as Cate Dooley and Nikki Fedele do in their article, "Raising Relational Boys," that "the holding place of vulnerability was not, as the myth would have us believe, a fatal liability to Achilles. It was the thing that kept him *human and real*. In fact, we consider it *Thetis' finest gift* to her son" (357, emphasis in original). Dooley and Fedele's research with mothers and sons, as discussed later in this volume, reveals that "boys with a secure maternal connection develop stronger interpersonal skills and enjoy healthier relationships as adults" (360). Mother–son connection, they conclude, is what makes possible the new masculinity we desire for our sons and men in general.

The Thetis and Achilles model of mother–son attachment advanced by Dooley and Fedele is examined fully in Olga Silverstein and Beth Rashbaum's 1994 book, *The Courage to Raise Good Men*. The book opens with a poem about Thetis and Achilles that Silverstein wrote many years ago for her now middle-aged son upon his birth. Presenting herself as Thetis, Silverstein worries that her love, like that of Thetis, might damage her son's manhood:

> Even Thetis, dipping her mortal boy
> In Styx, dreaming of armouring him
> Against both worlds, gripping her joy
> In fatal fingers, allowed the dim
> Danger of her handhold on his heel ...
> If immortal mothers are to such folly prone,
> How am I to guard against the thumbprints
> On my own?
> (Silverstein and Rashbaum 1)

As a young mother whose views on childrearing were very much shaped by the larger patriarchal culture of 1940s America, Silverstein believed, as do many mothers, that she, like Thetis, "might fail to let [her son] go, and the love [she] felt for him might in some way damage the armour of his manhood, rendering him as vulnerable as Achilles—who of course died of a wound to that very heel by which his mother had once clung to him" (Silverstein and Rashbaum 1). "Hands and thumbs off is the warning to mothers of son," Silverstein notes, "so that to mother a son is to engage in a continuous process of pulling back" (1–2).

Silverstein challenges this received view of mother–son relation and argues that the mandate of disconnection and the taboo against mother–son intimacy is the root cause of sons' difficulties as adults. The assumption is that boys, as scripted by the Freudian Oedipal scenario, gradually withdraw and distance themselves from their mothers as they grow into manhood. A close and caring relationship between a mother and a son is pathologized as aberrant, while a relationship structured upon separation is naturalized as the real and normal way to experience mother–son attachment. Silverstein explains:

> [Our culture believes] that a male child must be removed from his mother's influence in order to escape the contamination of a close relationship with her. The love of a mother—both the son's love for her, and hers for him—is believed to "feminize" a boy, to make him soft, weak, dependent, homebound.... [O]nly through renunciation of the loving mother, and identification with the aggressor father, does the ... boy become a man. (Silverstein and Rashbaum 11)

In other words, the majority of us in western culture see mother–son separation as both inevitable and desirable.

Silverstein challenges the central, organizing premise of patriarchally mandated mother–son separation, namely that this process is both natural, hence inevitable, and "good" for our sons. She emphasizes that what we interpret as a normal process is, in fact, a culturally scripted and orchestrated act. Moreover, she argues that it is mothers and not boys who both initiate and direct the separation. "By expecting our sons to cut off from us," she writes, "we make sure that they do" (Silverstein and Rashbaum 159). The mother, aware that mother–son connection and closeness is disparaged and pathologized in our culture, is ever vigilant that she not be "overclose" with her son. While her son nurses in her arms, she may worry about the intimacy and stiffen, pull back, or look away; so too when her eight-year-old scrambles onto her lap she will laugh proudly and nudge him off, saying that he is now a big boy and cannot fit in her lap; and when she is kissed by her teenage son, she will turn her cheek, tense her body, and mumble to hurry and not be late. The gestures of distancing are often subtle yet cumulative. A boy, Silverstein argues, "absorb[s] at an unconscious level that his mother is somehow un-comfortable with him, that she is pulling back from him, that their closeness is problematic" (Silverstein and Rashbaum 31). "Soon," Silverstein contin-ues, "he responds in kind, so that his mother, who wasn't aware that she herself was the original actor in this scenario of withdrawal, eventually assumes that the withdrawal was his not hers" (31). Once the son reaches adolescence, the mother, increasingly concerned about mother–son close-ness and the damage such may inflict on her son's incipient manhood, may abruptly withdraw from her son; an act that the son may experience as abandonment. Confused and hurt by his mother's rejection of him, the son decisively breaks from his mother and forges an identity separate from her modeled upon the masculine values of self-sufficiency and autonomy, par-ticularly as they pertain to emotional identity. Whether the son is fully aware of the mother's distancing, he nonetheless, Silverstein argues, experiences a deep and inexplicable loss that is seldom understood or articulated, a loss that profoundly scars the boy and causes him to grow into a psychologically wounded man. William Pollack, in *Real Boys: Rescuing Our Sons from the Myths of Boyhood*, maintains that the force of such separation is "so hurtful to boys that it can only be called a trauma—an emotional blow of damaging proportions.... [A] relational rupture [that] profoundly affects the psychology of most boys—and of most men—forever" (12, 27).

Demanding that young boys distance and differentiate themselves from their mothers, we require them to deny or repress the so-called feminine dimensions of their personalities. Silverstein argues that sons are deeply betrayed by their mothers' rejection of them and deeply wounded by the loss of the feminine in themselves occasioned by this separation. The result of this, she says, is: "lost boys, lonely men, lousy marriages, and midlife crises," or, as Pollack describes it, "a deep wellspring of grief and sadness that may last throughout [men's] lives" (Silverstein and Rashbaum 12). Over the last decade, and particularly in the last few years, our culture has identified a crisis in masculinity. Though varied and diverse, the majority of commentators on this "crisis in masculinity"—from Robert Bly to feminist journalist Susan Faludi in her recent best-selling book *Stiffed: The Betrayal of the American Man*—agree that masculinity must be redefined, and that such is to be achieved through a reconnection of father and son. In contrast, Silverstein counters this received narrative to argue that: "the real pain in men's lives stems from their estrangement from women" (Silverstein and Rashbaum 225). Similarly, Pollack emphasizes that boys and men: "[are] forever longing to return to [the mother], and to the 'holding' connection she once provided him, a connection he now feels he can never regain. If a boy had been allowed to separate at his own pace, that longing and sadness would not be there" (27). "As a culture we have to," as Silverstein concludes, "face up to the longing [of sons for mothers]—its power, its persistence throughout a man's life, its potential for destruction when unacknowledged" (Silverstein and Rashbaum 225).

Early Anglo-American feminist theorists on mothers and sons believed that motherhood oppressed women, impeded mother–son equality, and fostered both sexism and patriarchal masculinity. This literature consequently downplayed, denied, and at times, disparaged women's maternal identity, viewing as problematic women's responsibility and authority as mothers. A mother must rear her son outside/beyond motherhood, they argued, in order to raise a nonsexist, non-masculine (as it is traditionally defined) boy, and to improve relations between mothers and sons, and men and women generally. In contrast, the "new" Anglo-American feminist theory argues that too little mothering, and, in particular, the absence of mother-son connection, is what engenders both sexism and traditional masculinity in men. Thus a mother must foreground her presence in the life of her son; she must establish and maintain a close and caring connection with her son throughout his life. The mother is, accordingly, afforded agency as a mother, and her maternal responsibility and authority are emphasized and affirmed. This perspective positions mothering as central to feminist politics in its insistence that true and lasting gender equality will occur only when boys are raised as the sons of mothers. As the early feminist script of mother–son connection required the denial of the mother's power and the displacement of her identity as mother, the new perspective affirms the maternal and celebrates mother–son connection. In this, it rewrites the patriarchal and early feminist narrative to give Jocasta and Clytemnestra presence, voice, and a central and definitive role in the lives of their sons.

African-American Feminist Theory on the
Mother and Son Relationship

Most of the writing by African-American women has tended to focus on the mother-daughter relationship; little has been written on the mother-son relationship.[5] The notable exceptions are Joyce Elaine King's and Carolyn Ann Mitchell's *Black Mothers to Sons: Juxtaposing African-American Literature with Social Practice* (1995) and *Saving Our Sons: Raising Black Children in a Turbulent World* (1995) by novelist Marita Golden.[6] In the introduction to their book King and Mitchell, explaining their research interest in mothers and sons, write: "Considering the particular vulnerability of black males in this society and the role that mothers typically play as primary nurturers, this focus on black mother-to-son parenting is long overdue" (2). The initial question King and Mitchell explored in selected African-American fiction and asked of their research participants was: "What have you done to protect your son(s) from society's hostile forces?" (6). In their study of African-American literature they found that protection was the primary aim of black mothering and manifested itself in two diametrically opposed modes of mothering: "mothers who whip their sons brutally 'for their own good' and mothers who love their sons to destruction through self-sacrifice and overindulgence" (9). The first strategy is sustained by the belief that "a black man-child duly 'chastened' or broken at home will pose less of a threat to a society already primed to destroy him" (10), while the latter seeks to shield the child from all that is deemed harsh and upsetting. Each position, they argue, psychologically maims the son; the first by breaking the child's spirit, the latter by thwarting the child's maturation to true selfhood. The conflicting demands of protection and nurturance first identified by Ruddick in *Maternal Thinking* become, in the instance of rearing black sons, an impasse, an irreconcilable contradiction. The women interviewed by King and Mitchell all spoke of this paradox in the mothering of black sons: while sons must go into the world to mature socially, psychologically, and otherwise, this same world threatens their very physical survival. The question black mothers ask in the raising of their sons is, in the authors' words: "How [can they] help sons develop the character, personality, and integrity a black man-child needs to transcend these forces?" (19).

Golden's book also assumes as its central theme the survival of black men, and is dedicated to the black men who have died violently in Washington, D.C., since 1988. Golden wrote this book, as she explains in her epilogue, "because at this moment there is no subject more necessary to confront, more imperative to imagine. Until I wrote about our sons, I could not speak or think or dream of anything else" (185). Homicide, Golden tells us, is the leading cause of death for young black men in America. The violence, drugs, crime, joblessness, and killing of black male youth mark, according to Golden, a new kind of Middle Passage. Her book narrates this crossing as it tells the story of her own son's journey into manhood; in this telling and testifying Golden lists possible causes, drafts solutions, and seeks to imagine what, in her words "we will look like, how will we sound, once we are spewed forth from the terrible hold of THIS ship" (9). As in King's and Mitchell's literary and sociological study, Golden recognizes that for blacks who have the financial means, retreat has become the strategy of choice. In the instance of her own life, Golden withdrew her son from public school in Washington, D.C., and enrolled him in a private boarding school, as she and her husband had purchased a house in the suburbs. However, in saving your son this way, you remove him from the black community, the "sites of resistance"—family, community, history—that have traditionally nurtured and empowered African-Americans by creating black-defined narratives and identities. The women of King and Mitchell's study spoke of the "liberating, healing power of family lore, bloodlines, and family secrets" (37). "Knowing about ancestors," King and Mitchell write, "strengthens identification with family values that can help a son overcome anger and hopelessness. Such family lore can also develop a son's confidence in himself ... it frees black males from the diminished definitions of their humanity and self-worth that society offers them" (38). Golden, too, recognizes that the double consciousness Du Bois eloquently wrote of more than a hundred years ago is, in her words, "draining and sometimes killing our spirits" (14). With integration came the loss of communities, traditions, beliefs, legends, narratives, and rituals, the "sites of resistance" that have long sustained and enriched black American culture. While suburbs and boarding schools may save black sons from the killing fields of the so-called American inner cities, they also result in the further disintegration of black communities, the very thing that holds the promise of salvation for African-Americans.

This again is the impasse of black mothers; one that is etched on the very bodies of black men. As Golden remarks of her own son: "The unscathed openness of Michael's demeanour was proof that he had been a protected, loved child. But this same quality was also suddenly a liability, ones that he has to mask" (95). Nurturing sons to be confident and proud, mothers recognize that these same traits—because they may be misconstrued as insolence, obstinacy, and arrogance by other black youth, police, or whites—put their sons at risk. Golden realizes, as do King and Mitchell, that this paradox of mothering black sons necessitates a new mode of mothering, one fashioned specifically for black male children. And while King, Mitchell, the women of their research group, and Golden have not designed a blueprint for such mothering, they all agree that sons must be taught, in Golden's words, "that the first line of defense against racism is to mold themselves into disciplined, self-respecting refutations of its ability to destroy our souls or ourselves" (186). Or, as James Baldwin wrote in 1971: "It evolves upon the mother to invest the child, her man child, with some kind of interior dignity which will protect him against something he really can't be protected against, unless he has some kind of interior thing within him to meet it" (qtd. in King and Mitchell, 39). Audre Lorde wrote in "Man Child: A Black Lesbian Feminist's Response" that: "for survival, Black children in America must be raised to be warriors. For survival they must also be raised to recognize the enemy's many faces" (75). She goes on to say:

> The strongest lesson I can teach my son is the same lesson I teach my daughter: how to be who he wishes to be for himself. And the best way I can do this is to be who I am and hope that he will learn from this not how to be me, which is not possible, but how to be himself. And this means how to move to that voice from within himself, rather than to those raucous, persuasive, or threatening voices from outside, pressuring him to be what the world wants him to be. (77)

The aim of black mothering is thus to nurture and sustain the "singular soul," "the voice from within," and the "interior thing" of black sons, so that they are able to transcend the maiming of racism and grow into manhood whole and complete. Mothers of black sons, according to these writers, must negotiate between the need to keep their sons physically safe while simultaneously promoting their psychological maturation: this pull between nurturance and protection is at the heart of raising the black male child. This may be contrasted to the challenge and contradiction of feminist mothering according to early Anglo-American feminist thought, which is to redefine loss as gain; boys must learn that in renouncing patriarchal masculinity they achieve humanity. Thus the mothering of sons, according to Anglo-American thought, centers on the taking away of power from sons, while for mothers of black men, it means bringing their sons *to* power; to nurture and sustain that "soul," "voice from within," and "interior thing." For mothers of black sons this is achieved by grounding sons in their culture of origin, the black community. Anglo-American feminist mothering, in contrast, necessitates a challenge to the son's community of identification, the male peer group, or more generally patriarchal culture.

African-American feminist theory, as with the new Anglo-American feminist perspective, emphasizes women's agency, responsibility, and authority as mothers. The presence and involvement of the mother are recognized as crucial and essential to the son's maturation. African-American mothering of sons, however, is specifically racially determined in its emphasis on survival.

"The major challenge ... to a black mother raising sons today," as Claudette Lee and Ethel Williams explain, "[is] survival .... [:] Racism, discrimination, and oppression define the childhood of an African-American male. Mothering for an African-American woman is defined by fear for her male child. Therefore her approach and relationship with her son must be different" (56–7). In its focus on survival— what Ruddick defines "as the central constitutive, invariant aim of maternal practice" (1989: 19)—African-American mothering foregrounds, even more than the new Anglo-American perspective, the importance and centrality of the mother in the sons's life, for it is she who both provides protection and teaches her son how to protect himself, physically and otherwise. African-American feminist thought on mothers and sons, in its emphasis on maternal agency, responsibility, and authority, particularly as they pertain to ensuring the son's survival, recasts Jocasta and Clytemnestra as pivotal characters in the mother–son drama.

Conclusion

Early Anglo-American feminist thought tended to downplay, devalue, and at times disparage motherhood. Arcana asked mothers to abandon traditional motherhood to allow sons to see their mothers in roles other than ones of service and subservience; Forcey championed the "unbinding" of motherhood to free women from the oppressiveness of the responsibility assignment; and Smith argued that only by relating to her son outside of motherhood could a mother hope to secure his respect so as to achieve a relationship based on equality. Sexism and patriarchal masculinity, they contended, are perpetuated and reinforced through maternal practice, by placing women in service to boys (Arcana), by making women responsible for sons (Forcey), and by preventing sons from respecting women (Smith). Maternal responsibility is censored by Forcey and, to a lesser degree, Arcana; maternal authority, in turn, is criticized by Smith. In each, the woman, as *mother* in both definition and act, becomes absent and silent. In contrast, recent Anglo-American feminist thought focuses on maternal presence, arguing that mother–son connection is what makes possible the new non-patriarchal masculinity we desire for our sons, and for all men. The stress on maternal presence and involvement is underscored by an insistence on the significance of maternal responsibility, agency, and authority. Maternal presence and involvement are further emphasized in African-American feminist theory—as is the affirmation of the importance of maternal responsibility, agency, and authority. Presence and participation in the sons' lives are stressed in African-American feminist theory because black boys' lives are at risk. Black mothers must protect their sons to ensure their survival, both physically and psychologically, and teach them how to do the same for themselves.

The above developments in Anglo-American feminist thought on mothers and sons, along with the emergence of a distinct African-American feminist perspective, have recast the roles of mothers and sons. They have rewritten the patriarchal script of mother–son separation/maternal absence as they are enacted in the narratives of Jocasta and Oedipus, Clytemnestra and Orestes. In so doing, they give both voice and presence to the mother and make mother-son connection central to the redesign of both traditional masculinity and the larger patriarchal culture. This new perspective, I want to suggest, allows for real and lasting social change. Feminist positions that depend upon the marginalization of motherhood and a mitigation of maternal authority and agency, I argue, cannot effect change, because they reinscribe, albeit inadvertently, the valorization of the masculine and the degradation of all that is deemed feminine in our culture. The denial and disparagement of the maternal bespeaks a larger unease with, and aversion to, the feminine. The new feminist perspectives—Anglo-American and African-American—in highlighting maternal voice and presence, affirming maternal agency, authority, and responsibility, and foregrounding mother–son connection, have imagined and made possible a truly feminist narrative of mothers and sons.

[1]The disparagement and erasure of the mother that these texts enact may also, as many feminist theorists have argued, be interpreted psychoanalytically as bespeaking both male fear of maternal power, and the need to deny and repress the feminine in order to construct a masculine identity. Nancy Chodorow, in *The Reproduction of Mothering*, argues that the father's absence from the home in the sons' early years necessitates the son defining his masculinity by negation; that which his mother is, he is not. As well, for the infant son, the powers of the mother appear limitless. Our individual flesh-and-blood mother is also identified archetypally with the primordial Great Mother, who held very real life-and-death powers over mortal men. In our individual and collective unconsciousness we remember that time when we lived under the mother's power in the pre-Oedipal and prepatriarchal world. Dorothy Dinnerstein, in *The Mermaid and the Minotaur*, maintains that fear and hatred of women, and of mothers in particular, originate from the infant's experiences of dependency and helplessness, which in turn come to structure adult consciousness.

[2]*Mothers and Sons*, though written by the Australian writer Babette Smith, advances an Anglo-American view on feminism in general and the mother-son relation in particular.

[3]For a critique of sensitive mothering, please see Chapter Four, "'Ain't that Love?': Antiracism and Racial Constructions of Motherhood."

[4]This is examined in Chapter Five, "Across the Divide: Contemporary Anglo-American Feminist Theory on the Mother–Daughter Relationship." See also my article, "Mothers, Daughters and Feminism Today: Empowerment, Agency, Narrative" (O'Reilly 1998) and the introduction to *Mothers and Daughters: Connection, Empowerment, Transformation* (O'Reilly and Abbey).

[5]African-American motherhood has been examined in recent African-American feminist theory. See, in particular, Patricia Hill Collins, *Black Feminist Thought: Knowledge, Consciousness and the Politics of Empowerment* (1990), "The Meaning of Motherhood in Black Culture and Black Mother–Daughter Relationships" (Collins 1993), and "Shifting the Center: Race, Class, and Feminist Theorizing About Motherhood" (Collins 1994). See also my article, "'I Come From a Long Line of Uppity Irate Black Women': African-American Feminist Thought on Motherhood, the Motherline and the Mother–Daughter Relationship" (O'Reilly and Abbey). See also the *Journal of the Association for Research on Mothering* 2 (2) (2000) issue on "Mothering in the African Diaspora."

[6]This chapter will examine book-length studies of African-American mothers and sons as it did with Anglo-American feminist theory. Audre Lorde wrote the classic article, "Man Child: A Black Lesbian Feminist's Response" in *Sister Outsider* (Freedom, CA: The Crossing Press, 1993).

CHAPTER NINE

A MOM AND HER SON

THOUGHTS ON FEMINIST MOTHERING

Over the past year I have been working on an edited volume tentatively entitled *Mothers and Sons: Feminism, Masculinity and the Struggle to Raise Our Sons*. The book is developed from the conference "Mothers and Sons: Challenges and Possibilities" that I coordinated on behalf of the Center for Feminist Research and the Association for Research on Mothering, in the fall of 1998, at York University. As I wrote my chapter for this collection, edited the other submissions and wrote the introduction to the volume, I found myself composing in my head, scribbling along the margins of this book, another mother and son narrative: that of my relationship with my soon-to-be sixteen-year-old son, Jesse O'Reilly-Conlin. As I sorted out the book's thematic sections and sought to clarify a particular feminist theoretical position for my own chapter, I would continuously catch myself in reverie, lost in thought, reflecting upon Jesse and my relationship, and quite oblivious to the urgent scholarly matters that awaited me on the computer screen. More often than not, the bright colours of my screensaver would awaken me from my reverie and call me back to the world of research and theory. I think this personal narrative of mine is a story both of interruption and postponement—while it is a story that demands to be told, it is a story that I have delayed telling.

Feminism, writes Babette Smith in *Mothers and Sons*, "has failed the mothers of sons" (ix). As both a feminist mother of a son and an academic who teaches and researches the mother–son relation, I have often reflected upon this statement by Smith. Have we, in our academic and personal interest in the mother–daughter relationship, as I inquired in my *Mothers and Sons* book, wronged our sons, let them down, or simply forgotten about them? Have we in our negligence or disinterest, academic and otherwise, given our sons up to patriarchy, done to them what we have spent our lives fighting against for ourselves and for our daughters? I know that I have spent far more time this past decade thinking about mothers and daughters than mothers and sons, as I raised my own two girls, Casey (ten) and Erin (thirteen). However, as I wrote my articles, edited my books on mothers and daughters, and designed and taught a course on the topic, and as I sought to raise my girls in a feminist fashion, my son and my concerns for him as a male child in a patriarchal culture were always there; hovering, phantom-like, just beyond full consciousness or articulation. As with other mothers of sons and women who care deeply about boys today, I worried about Jesse and wondered whether he was, would be, okay in a world that seemed destined to harm and maim him emotionally, spiritually, and, increasingly, physically, as he grew into manhood. As time passed, I became more and more disturbed by the feminist silence surrounding mothers and sons, and by my own inability, or perhaps unwillingness, to theorize the mother–son relation and my relationship with Jesse as I had done for mothers and daughters in general, and my two daughters in particular. I initiated the "Mothers and Sons" conference and the book mentioned above in an attempt to make sense out of, at least from an academic point-of-view, the disturbing and puzzling silence surrounding mothers and sons. I wanted to begin a feminist dialogue on what I felt to be an urgent and timely matter. However, as I worked on the book, identifying and investigating the salient issues of this new and emerging field of inquiry, my own story as a feminist mother of a son kept intruding upon and interrupting like some post-modern ellipse, the trajectory of my theoretical ponderings. I realized then that my understanding of the mother–son relation would remain fragmentary and partial until I rememoried—remembered/recollected/relived—to paraphrase Toni Morrison's term, my own narrative. I needed to sort out for myself how feminism has shaped the mothering of my son and how being a mother of a son has redefined my feminism. I realized that in order to understand the bigger picture— feminist theory on mothers and sons—I needed to sketch my own mother and son portrait. To that I now turn.

This narrative is evidently my own; my son has his own story that I hope will be told at another time and place. I am a 39-year old woman of Irish, Scottish, and English ancestry; a professor of women's studies; and a mother of three children—a son (fifteen), two daughters (ten, thirteen)—who, along with my common-law male spouse of eighteen years, has been engaged in what I like to call radical nurturance—a feminist, socialist, anti-racist, nonheterosexist / abilist and learning/education centred parenting.[1] I was raised in a middle-class family by a working-class mother. My class affiliation is thus middle class, though I was mothered more in accordance with working-class styles and values of childrearing; my spouse's class identity, in contrast, is decidedly and proudly working-class. I found myself pregnant with my first child, my son, in the fourth year of my Bachelor of Arts at the age of 22.

In the early months of pregnancy I was horribly ill with unrelenting nausea; in the later months I developed the serious condition of pre-eclampsia, which necessitated the daily monitoring of my blood pressure. I wrote a brilliant paper on the plight of "fallen women" in Victorian literature as my feet swelled and my back ached; the ironies, in retrospect, are splendid. Labour destroyed any remnants of complacency left over from my pre-pregnant self. I hemorrhaged during labour, and I never before had experienced such pain, terror, or aloneness, nor have I since. When my son was finally born, pulled from my body with forceps, my spouse held him as I watched the doctors attempt to repair my ripped and torn self.

I became a mother through the birth of a son. All the while pregnant, as I increasingly identified with the radical feminist celebration of sisterhood, I deeply longed for a daughter. As I marched with my girlfriends on International Women's Day, I believed I marched for and with my unborn daughter Sarah. However, as the days of my pregnancy passed, and as I caressed my swelling belly and talked to my unborn child, I knew with an uncanny certainty that she was a boy. Lesbian author and poet Jess Wells, in her appropriately entitled narrative "Born on Foreign Soil," movingly recounts the displeasure and dismay, fear and panic, she felt upon learning through ultrasound and amniocentesis that her assumed to be girl was in fact a boy "I was profoundly disappointed," writes Wells, "I wept. I sobbed to my friends" (20). Wells wondered, "What did mothers and sons have in common? What could they do together?" and worried, as a "separatist, punk dyke, a radical feminist" that she would be, in her words, "spawn[ing] a member of the oppressing class" (21). As my son was pulled from my body and I was told "it was a boy," there was a disappointment, but as I came to know and love my son, he was no longer a boy, but simply, for better or worse, Jesse.

With my first pregnancy, I lost what I refer to today as my feminist innocence. I discovered that feminism has, at best, an ambivalent relationship to motherhood. When feminist friends and women's studies classmates learned of my unplanned pregnancy, I was greeted with sentiments of pity and concern, and when I spoke with joy and pride about my pregnancy and, later, my children, my colleagues seemed suddenly suspicious of my feminism and made me feel as if I had in some irrevocable and fundamental way failed feminism— sold out, been duped, gone over to the other side, or—in the language of current feminist discourse—fallen prey to the false consciousness of patriarchal ideology. Being a mother of a son made my motherhood identity all that much more problematic. Once at a union meeting shortly after the birth of our son, a woman with whom I had recently developed a friendship, stopped by to chat and upon learning that the baby she cooed at in the carriage was a boy, looked straight at me and said "what a shame and waste it was that a good feminist like me was now going to spend her life raising a man" and with that, turned, and walked away. In March of this year—nearly sixteen years later—

as I discussed the topic of mothers and sons at the Association for Research on Mothering booth at the International Women's Day Fair in Toronto, two women dismissed both me and the topic of sons with a laugh that implied that a feminist would have to be an utter fool to spend her time worrying about boys. While views such as these are no doubt rare, I do believe they bespeak a larger feminist discomfort or disinterest in the topic of mothers and sons. Be that as it may, I can say with complete certainty, after years of teaching and researching the topic of motherhood, that feminists have been far more interested in daughters than in sons, though as of late there has been an emergent feminist interest in sons, due in part to the recent preoccupation with men and masculinity in the popular media. The aim of this article however is not to account for the silence or to chart the emergence of this new field of feminist inquiry. Rather, I am interested in exploring, from a personal viewpoint, how my identity as a feminist influenced the mothering of my son and how, in turn, my identity as a mother of a son shaped my feminism. I turn now to the first question.

My son Jesse would be regarded as a "feminist success story." He and I enjoy a close and intimate relationship; he is as comfortable grabbing my hand or placing his arm over my shoulders as he is debating with me the finer points of feminism or competing with me at the gym. He is sensitive and kind, wise and gentle, witty and affable, empathetic and thoughtful, reliable and generous, hardworking and yet fun-loving; modeling in both his behaviour and demeanour so-called masculine and feminine attributes. He is adamantly anti-racist, anti-elitist/classist, feminist, and, in particular, anti-heterosexist in his politics. Occasionally, I am congratulated on raising such a fine feminist son; more often I am asked, "How did I do it?" This question, each time I am asked it, leaves me feeling baffled, anxious, and strangely off-centre. I don't believe it is possible or desirable to format a blueprint of feminist mothering; mothers don't need yet another normative discourse of the "good mother." Moreover, we know that a whole array of influences—the media, popular culture, genetics, peer groups, schools, extended family, and the like—have as much say, if not more, in how our children "turn out." At the same time, however, I realize that my son's feminine sensibilities and feminist leanings are surely no accident in a patriarchal culture that does its utmost to ensure that boys are anything but feminine and feminist.

Today, standing on my tiptoes to kiss my son good-bye, I saw a young man, wearing his long hair in a ponytail, as he has done since he was nine, sporting his normal attire of a tie-dye t-shirt and blue jeans (and not a name brand in sight), carrying in his hand his *Merchant of Venice*, which we had discussed the night before, debating whether the play is anti-Semitic, as it is often assumed. Jesse, with his straight A grades, basic decency, his love of his immediate and extended family, and so on, would do any mother proud. But what I marvel at is his determination to be himself, his refusal to give in to peer pressure, and his unwillingness to compromise his principles. Given that he has lived in a very conservative, very white, rural community since the age of eight, and attended a school that is often racist, sexist, and consistently homophopic, his conviction and courage are admirable. I remember how he was teased about his long hair, and ridiculed about his odd parents—those leftie, "shacked up," hippies "on the hill." I also recall the many times Jesse came home from school or ball practice deeply upset and troubled by the fag jokes and queer bashing he encountered on the playground. But I also remember a son who, in grade six, wrote and presented a speech about Rosa Parks and won the school speech award. In grade eight, he did a major research report on homophobia; this year he wrote for his history assignment an essay on genital mutilation. No doubt such views are anomalies and aberrations in our very straight (in all senses of the word), conservative "Pleasantville-like" community and no doubt we, his leftie parents, must bear/ take some responsibly or credit (depending on who you are) for our son "turning out this way."

However, to return to the question asked above—the impact of my feminism on the mothering of my son—or the related question, "How did I raise him to be a feminist?"—I still find myself circling, uncertain how to proceed. First, I cannot honestly say that I consciously raised him to be a feminist, nor I am not sure that my son would identify himself as a feminist. With my daughters, my feminist mothering was overt, explicit, and to the point. For example, with my middle girl, an avid reader, I would buy for her, as she began to read independently, only books by women; a justified censorship, I reasoned, given that she will be reading plenty of male-authored books in later life. Over dinner, in the car, I informed them of the injustices of patriarchy and catalogued women's achievements. No topic was taboo: a normal dinner conversation in our household, from the time they could sit up in a highchair, would shift from the witch burnings to suffrage in the time it takes to say "pass the broccoli please." Every film, music video, song, commercial they have seen, has been analyzed "to death"—their misogyny, homophobia, or racism tracked and exposed. I used to change the endings of fairy tales when I read to the children at night, allowing the princess to "live with the prince only after she got her PhD." This year I temporarily pulled my daughter from her school in an act of protest when the principal prohibited her from wearing a particular top, saying it was "distracting to the boys." The mothering of my girls has been actively and adamantly feminist and my daughters unequivocally identify themselves as feminist, though my thirteen-year-old would identify more "third wave grrrl" feminism than the feminism of my generation. With my son, the relationship between my mothering and my feminism has been less direct and perhaps more complicated. Though Jesse has certainly been a part of thousands of conversations about women, feminism, and patriarchy, he has not been schooled and cautioned about patriarchy with the same rigour and thoroughness as my daughters have, nor has his autonomy, emotional, economical, and otherwise, been as emphasized in his upbringing as it was for his sisters. Nonetheless my son, as noted above, has feminine characteristics and feminist political leanings. How did this come to be in a patriarchal culture? The answer, despite the seeming complexity of the question, is, I think, quite simple and straightforward.

My son has a clearly defined feminine dimension to his personality because such was allowed and affirmed in his upbringing. My son, since his birth, has been an exceptionally sensitive child who has needed a great deal of attention and care, emotional, physical and, otherwise. In his first year of life he spent more times in my arms and at my breast than he did in his crib. He could not fall asleep at night without me lying in bed beside him until his early school years. Two and half years after my son was born, I would watch my newborn daughter sitting in her infant chair alone for hours on end contentedly playing with her fingers and toes: I was convinced there was something profoundly wrong with her. At the tender age of one she put herself to bed and has since. She announced to me at the ripe old age of two that "she was the boss of herself" each and every time I asked her to do something. At the same age my son would not leave my side. I remember one day, I suggested to my son (age three), as we walked past the playground, that he should go in and play while I nursed his sister. He looked at me quite terrified and, backing away from the playground gate, proclaimed with feigned stubbornness that he would not go in there. When I, quite baffled by his behaviour, asked him why, he explained: "because children were in there." (We ended up waiting until the daycare kids left before going in for a swing and some sand play.) This image always stands in sharp contrast to the memory of my youngest daughter, also three, running through the same playground in a blur of winter hats and scarves as I waited to pick her up from daycare.

I do not recall these events to prescribe "what a good mother should do" but rather to illustrate that my son, from birth, was "always/already" a child with so-called feminine sensibilities. But it would be dishonest of me to say that raising such a child, boy or girl, was easy. I believe that with every child there is a difficult, or as the parenting books would delicately put it, "challenging" age or stage. With my son, it was, without a doubt, his first five years. He needed so much time, care, and attention that his seemingly endless demands left me exasperated and exhausted, trapped in those bad mother days that Mary Kay Blakely describes so poignantly.[2] However, despite my fatigue, irritability, and anger, I more often than not held/comforted him when he cried, cuddled him at nights, stayed close to him physically/emotionally, and honoured and protected his shy and sensitive personality—not because I was a "good mother," not even because I was a feminist mother wanting to raise a "good" man, but simply and quite honestly because it seemed to be the decent, normal, and only thing to do. When a child (boy or girl) cries, you give comfort; when a child feels lonely, you provide companionship; when a child is afraid you offer reassurance; such was my basic, but looking back now, eminently reasonable, childrearing philosophy at the age of 23 when I first became a mother.

On my son's first day of kindergarten when he asked if I could stay with him, I simply said yes, found a comfortable rocking chair (I had my six-week-old daughter with me), nursed my baby, and spent a morning in kindergarten as I had done a quarter century before. A few years later, when we moved and my son changed schools in December of grade three, I went with him, at his request, to his classroom on his first day and stayed with him. This time my visit was shorter; after ten or fifteen minutes, my son, with tears still falling from his eyes, told me that he would be okay now and that I could go. No doubt we were an odd sight that morning: me, a 30-something mother, sitting in one of those straight back school chairs kindly provided by the teacher, beside my son, in his place in a row of desks, tears streaming down his face with me trying to act as if my heart was not breaking. I am sure that many people thought that, in mothering my child this way, I was spoiling him; or worse, because he was a boy, I was coddling and emasculating him, tying him to my apron strings and turning him into a "Mama's boy." No doubt I worried about that, too. But what I remember most about raising my son is loving him; and that meant making sure he felt loved, protected, and good about himself. My son grew up with the knowledge that it was quite all right to be a sensitive boy and indeed quite normal to need your mother.

Today, when teachers, my friends, and other adults, describe my son, what is mentioned more often than any other aspect of his personally, is a "sense of groundedness," not necessarily self-confidence, but a self-acceptance and assurance in being who he is. I realize now that in my resistance to traditional practices of masculization I was modeling for my son the authentic, radical mothering that Judith Arcana, Adrienne Rich, and Sara Ruddick, among others, argue is necessary for a daughter's empowerment, and, I would add, makes possible a son's self assurance/acceptance in being different.

In allowing my son to be who he was, in affirming this difference and doing so despite social demands to the contrary I raised my son "feminist" or, at the very least, I raised a son comfortable with the so-called feminine dimension of his personality. My son is also, in his political views and personal ways, very feminist. However, I do not think he would identify himself as a feminist. Rather his feminist beliefs are for him simply the normal way to see the world. Jesse and his sisters have been raised with socialist, anti-racist/ heterosexist, and feminist values, which seem to them to be merely sensible. All individuals and, my vegetarian daughter would add, species, are deserving of respect and equality; each entitled to a fair share of the world resources, valued for their differences across race, class, ability, sexuality, and gender, and deserving of a full life of meaningful work, good friendships and loving family.

I, along with my spouse, have sought to model in my day-to-day living and to teach to my children what Carol Gilligan and others have defined as an ethic of care; or more specifically, a world view based on the values of love, respect, fairness, peace, and decency. These values have been fed to them, if you will, since they were babes in arms, served alongside their pablum and later bagels and cream cheese. Feminism for my son is not a politic or an identity but rather a lens through which he views and understands the world. When my children started to encounter sentiments of racism, homophobia, and sexism they were surprised, incredulous, and indeed quite confused. They could not understand why seemingly smart people, in the lingo of the schoolyard, could be "so stupid"; "all people are equal, good, etc.," they reasoned, thus the person saying otherwise must be the fool. Of course, as they grew, they came to realize that what they understood to be the sane and sensible, normal, and natural way to be in the world—good, fair, decent to people regardless of race, class, etc.—was not seen as such by most of the children in our very conservative community. My children now understand that in their community and in the world generally, what seems to them perfectly sensible is, in fact, a particular political stance, and one that is not shared by most. Nonetheless, even today my ten-year-old daughter simply cannot make sense of racism; why would someone dislike a person simply because of their skin colour, birth place, etc? To her that is just "idiotic." Likewise, my son supports feminism not because he is a feminist per se, but because for him that is what any sane and sensible person would do. I could not agree more.

In the conclusion to "Who Are We This Time?" Mary Kay Blakely writes:

> If I've taught [my sons] something about women and justice, my jock sons have taught me something about being a sport. In our ongoing discussions of gender politics, I've looked at the issues as urgently as ever, but through the lens of love and hope rather than anger and despair. (40)

My feminism too has been rethought, reworked, and redefined through the mothering of my son, most significantly in terms of the way I understand gender difference. Prior to my son's birth, I identified with a radical feminist theory of gender difference that positioned "the feminine" (meaning the traits normally associated with the feminine: nurturance, sensitivity, intuition, empathy, relationality, cooperation, etc.) and "the masculine" as more or less fixed and oppositional categories with the former superior to the later. Crudely put, I saw the feminine as good, the masculine as bad; and that women were, more or less, feminine and men masculine as a consequent of patriarchal gender socialization. I defined myself as "feminine" and was quite happy to do so.

However, as my son grew and he seemed far more "feminine" in his disposition than his two sisters, my complacent and simplistic understanding of gender difference was called into question. My son was both feminine and masculine; so too were his sisters. I learned through being a mother of a son that gender is not pure, essential, or stable; as post-modernism teaches us, it is fluid, shifting, and contested. As I came to appreciate the inevitable instability of gender, I continued to define myself as feminine and regarded it as superior, though I now conceded that these preferred traits was available to men as well as women.

As my son grew and I started to spend more time with him, "hanging out," I realized that the two of us were alike in many ways, and that our similarities were to be found in our so-called shared masculine characteristics. This came as quite a surprise as I had never considered myself "masculine" in any sense of the word. However, with Jesse I saw myself in a different light, and came to realize that many of my personality traits are indeed masculine. I am adventurous, assertive, ambitious, more rational than emotional, carefree, usually confident, and often competitive. I pride myself on my independence, resolve, intelligence, and resourcefulness, and attribute the successes I have had in life to my drive, tenacity, stamina, resiliency, self-sufficiency, and willingness to take risks. My friends joke that I am type-A personality personified. I realize now that, while I always knew I had this type of personality, I would not self-identify as such because to do so would mean admitting to being masculine. However, over the last few years, as Jesse has grown into a man, and has begun to demonstrate many of these traits, I have named them in myself and come to see them as good and desirable as long as they are balanced with feminine characteristics. Being the mother of a "good" son I have come to realize that the masculine is not inherently evil and through this realization I have been able to discover and honour dimensions of my personality that were before unknown or shameful to me.

Eight months ago, after much urging from my son, he and I joined the local gym; we now go four to five days a week in the hour between picking him up from school and the time when my daughters' school day ends. Like many women my age, I grew up hating my body. As a teenager I was a compulsive dieter; in my 20s, as I came to both feminism and motherhood, I saw my body as an enemy—an instrument of patriarchal power and control. By my late 30s I had, more or less, forgotten about, given up on my body, and lived, as do many academics, completely in my head. By working out in the gym, I have come to trust, love, respect, challenge, and honour my body as I have my mind. I feel, in an odd way, reborn; as if I have been introduced to a new self, a self more complete and whole, strong and brave. From our time at the gym together, Jesse and I have developed a close bond based on something that is uniquely our own. No doubt many of the young men at the gym, most of whom go to Jesse's highschool, find it odd that a mom and her teenage son would hang out at the gym together. But my son and I delight in each other's company, take pride in each other's accomplishments, and have a great deal of fun doing so.

This week I started horseback riding lessons with my youngest daughter, an activity that I would not have undertaken without this new confidence and trust in my body, particularly because I was thrown from a horse when I was thirteen, never to ride again. After our first lesson, my aching hamstring muscles let me know that I would have to change my workout routine in order to strengthen these muscles. So yesterday at the gym, I tried some machines that I had not used before. At one point I dragged Jesse over to a machine and asked him to explain how it worked. The machine requires that you lie on your back and, with your legs extended, push up and down a press that has weights attached to it. There is a partial and a complete lift. On my back, with Jesse beside me, I did the partial lift and then, at my signal, he released the lever to the full lift. When the weight came down, my weak hamstrings muscles could not push the press up; so there I lay, my thighs almost pressed to my face, unable to move. Jesse and I finally managed to lift the weight and release me. I remember both of us laughing out loud, to the surprise and chagrin of the guy jocks who take working out very seriously. At that moment, as I looked at my son, I thought about this narrative and had one of those rare but profoundly wondrous moments of joy and revelation. It felt right and good to be me, the mother of this man. Reflecting upon this today, I realize that what was revealed to me in that moment was precisely the thesis of this narrative: that my son has made me a better person and hence a better feminist, and my feminism has allowed him to become the good man he was meant to be.

I would like to conclude this narrative by recalling two pivotal turning points in my intellectual travels that led me to this article. The first occurred in the summer of 1995 when I attended a session on "Mothers and Sons" at a women's studies/feminist conference in Scotland. Presented at the session was a preliminary report of interviews the presenters had conducted with feminist mothers of sons. Though the details of their research are evidently important, what was significant to me was their conclusion and the discussion that followed. The feminist mothers of sons interviewed for this study, the presenters concluded, while they had initially been committed to feminist childrearing, had all, more or less, given in up in their attempt to challenge and circumvent their sons' becoming sexist and traditionally masculine. They provided numerous quotations to illustrate the frustration, disillusionment, and resignation felt by these mothers. But all I can remember is the rage and despair I felt when I heard those words. In the question period, I raised my hand and struggled to vocalize the rush of emotions in my heart: "I know that it is hard to go up against patriarchy but we can't give up so quickly and easily. Our sons deserve more … our world deserves more.… The struggle to save our daughters from patriarchy has been equally as tough but we have not given up on them … we can't just give up on our sons." My remonstrances fell largely on deaf ears. Most in the audience agreed with the presenters, some reasoned that our time would be better spent on our daughters, others suggested that perhaps mothers, even feminist ones, secretly take pride in their sons' traditional masculinity and thus don't really want to change things. Still others cautioned that perhaps feminist mothering would turn our sons into misfits, causing them to be miserable.

I left the room shaking, and immediately went to a pay phone to call home and talk to Jesse. My spouse answered the phone and before I could get a word in edgewise he relayed the various newsworthy events of our children's final day of school before summer holidays. The most significant news was that our son, our child who proudly and publicly affirmed his difference every chance he got, had been chosen by his classmates in a year-end ceremony as "the person most liked by others." Politically I find these contests offensive, but at that moment I felt vindicated and wanted to rush back in the room—I think I would have had the session been still on—and say "told you so!" Or more reasonably, I would have tried to explain to them that my feminist mothering had not made my son a freak; in fact it had enabled him to take pride in his difference and become, through his uniqueness and his self-acceptance, the type of person people genuinely like.

The second event is more an image than a story. Last summer, my son, my mother, and I spent two weeks in Norway and then a week in London as part of my conference/research travels. My son, like myself, is an avid traveler; since the age of eight he has accompanied me on numerous research "road trips" throughout the United States. But this was his first time overseas. My mother, likewise, loves to travel, and she and I have travelled a great deal together. However, this was the first time we—a fourteen-year-old-son, thirty-eight-year-old mother, and a sixty-eight-year-old mother/grandmother—would be travelling together. Our trip would include a weekend jaunt to Svalbard, as close as you can get to the North Pole (a two hour flight from northern Norway), a five-day journey down the coast of Norway in a coastal steamer, four days in Tromsö (the location of the conference) and a day in Bergen and Oslo, and finally a week in busy London. (I am still paying off this trip, nearly a year later!). While I eagerly awaited the trip, I wondered whether we were up to each other's company for a full three weeks: bunking together in the same room (on the boat our "room" would be the size of a closet), and all the time moving by boat, train, and airplane. As well, I was concerned that my son, in his youthful exuberance, would wear my mother out the first day and that he would not survive one of her shopping excursions. I need not have worried. Though there were the usual upsets as there always are when people travel together, this journey will remain one of my fondest memories of motherhood. There are hundreds of photos from this trip and even more photos in my mind, each more beautiful than the last, but I would like to conclude this narrative with just one. It is that of my son, my mother, and myself on the top deck of the steamer, as we stood by the railing of the ship, close to breathless in awe of the scenery before us. As we stood there, my son placed one of his arms around me and the other around my mother and, gesturing to the fjords across the water, said, "Isn't it beautiful?" For me the beauty of the moment was less in the fjords than in the three of us together standing arm in arm. While countless circumstances brought us to that moment, I now know, as I conclude this narrative, that what made that moment truly possible was the feminist mothering of my son. That is what I shall write beneath the photograph when it is placed in the photo album.

[1]In this article I refer to "our" children as "my" children and explore raising these children largely in terms of my experience of mothering them. I do this because the article is concerned with Jesse and my relationship as son and mother. However, in practice, my spouse is as committed to the parenting described in the article as I am, and our children are as fully and completely his as they are mine.

[2]"Every one of my friends," writes Blakely, "has a bad day somewhere in her history, she wishes she could forget, but can't afford it. A very bad day changes you forever" (33–34).

CHAPTER TEN

"THIS IS WHAT FEMINISM IS: THE ACTING AND LIVING ... NOT JUST THE TOLD"

MENTORING AND MODELING FEMINISM

The subject of feminist or empowered mothering more generally, as noted in the introduction, has largely been ignored by feminist scholars on motherhood. Only two books have been published solely on the topic of feminist mothering: *Mother Journeys: Feminists Write About Mothering* (Reddy, Roth and Sheldon) and Tuula Gordon's book, *Feminist Mothers*, books now ten-plus years old. In response to the lack of scholarship on empowered mothering I developed two volumes on this subject matter: *From Motherhood to Mothering: The Legacy of Adrienne Rich's Of Woman Born* (2004d) and *Mother Outlaws: Theories and Practices of Empowered Mothering* (2004c). Surprisingly, in the 40-plus chapters included in these two collections only a handful look specifically at the topic of feminist mothering. This omission puzzled me. Feminist mothering is an evident example of empowered mothering and so provides a promising alternative to the oppressive institution of patriarchal motherhood, first theorized by Adrienne Rich and critiqued by subsequent motherhood scholars. So why is the subject of feminist mothering so marginal to feminist scholarship on motherhood, a scholarship committed to imagining and implementing other, less oppressive ways to mother?

While I still remain unsure on the answers, even as I conclude this section on feminist mothering, I believe that this absence is due in part to our inability to define what we mean, or more particularly what we *want or expect to achieve* in, through, and from feminist mothering. Is the concern of feminist mothering anti-sexist childrearing or the empowerment of mothers? Or is it a combination of both? In order to define and develop a theory of feminist mothering we must, I believe, begin with such questions. In this chapter I seek to answer these questions by way of a conversation with my two teen daughters on their perceptions and experiences of being raised by feminist mothering.

From Motherhood to Mothering

Adrienne Rich in *Of Woman Born* defined motherhood as a patriarchal institution that was oppressive to women. She went to argue that this institution must be abolished so that the "*potential* relationship of woman to her powers of reproduction, and to children" could be realized (13, emphasis in original). In other words, while motherhood, as an institution, is a male-defined site of oppression, women's own experiences of mothering could nonetheless be a source of power if they were experienced outside of motherhood. The goal then for feminist mothers was to move from motherhood to mothering or more specifically to mother against motherhood. While Rich's distinction between motherhood and mothering and her call for a feminist mothering apart from patriarchal motherhood have been employed and developed by feminist theorists, what seems to have gone missing in this use of Rich is the radical impetus and implications of her vision.

Feminist mothering, in Rich's view, must first and primarily be concerned with the empowerment of mothers. For Rich the central reason for feminist mothering was to free mothers from patriarchal motherhood. In contrast, the current literature on feminist mothering is concerned with anti-sexist childrearing, or more specifically raising empowered daughters and relational sons with little attention paid to the mother herself or the condition under which she mothers. The focus of this literature is the children and how to make better their socialization with little attention to how motherhood needs to be changed so as to make mothering better for women. While Rich was evidently interested in anti-sexist childrearing, as shown in her two chapters on mothers and daughters and mothers and sons, the overarching purpose of *Of Woman Born* was to abolish patriarchal motherhood so that women could achieve an empowering, or more specifically, a feminist experience of mothering. This mother-centred, and I believe far more radical, vision has become lost in our current preoccupation with anti-sexist childrearing. Moreover, having made the oppression of mothers in patriarchal motherhood tangential to their goal of anti-sexist childrearing, feminist theorists now find themselves in the difficult, nay impossible, situation, of trying to achieve feminist mothering without first having abolished patriarchal motherhood.

Rich's concern was mothers and dismantling patriarchal motherhood so as to make mothering less oppressive for mothers. However, she also realized that the achievement of anti-sexist childrearing also depended upon the abolition of patriarchal motherhood. Mothers can not effect changes in childrearing in an institution in which they have no power as in the case with patriarchal motherhood. Anti-sexist childrearing depends upon motherhood itself being changed; it must become, to use Rich's terminology, mothering. In other words, only when mothering becoming a site, role, and identity of power for women is feminist childrearing made possible. In dismantling patriarchal motherhood you invest mothers with the needed agency and authority to affect the desired feminist childrearing. Only then does anti-sexist childrearing become possible.

A challenge to traditional gender socialization is, of course, integral to any theory and practice of feminist mothering. However, I argue, as Rich did 30 years ago, that the empowerment of mother must be the primary aim of feminist mothering if it is to function as a truly transformative theory and practice. To fully and completely liberate children from traditional childrearing, mothers must first seek to liberate themselves from traditional motherhood; they must, to use Rich's terminology, mother against motherhood. By way of a conversation with my two daughters—Erin (18) and Casey (15)—this chapter will explore the interface between the empowerment of mothers and anti-sexist childrearing and Rich's argument that the later depends on the former. More specifically I will argue that, in order for mothers to mentor feminism for their daughters, they must model it in themselves.

Mother and Daughters: "As Daughters We Need Mothers Who Want Their Own Freedom and Ours"

The early literature on mothers and daughters, notably the writings of Adrienne Rich, Judith Arcana (1979), Jesse Bernard, recognized this connection between mentoring and modeling. These writers argue that that mother–daughter connection empowers daughter *if and only if* the mother with whom the daughter is identifying is herself empowered. "What do we mean by the nurture of daughters? What is it we wish we had, or could have, as daughters; could give as mothers," asks Rich:

> Deeply and primally we need trust and tenderness; surely this will always be true of every human being, but women growing into a world so hostile to us need a very profound kind of loving in order to learn to love ourselves. But this loving is not simply the old, institutionalized, sacrificial, "mother-love" which men have demanded; we want courageous mothering. The most notable fact that culture imprints on women is the sense of our limits. The most important thing one woman can do for another is to illuminate and expand her sense of actual possibilities. For a mother, this means more than contending with reductive images of females in children's books, movies, television, the schoolroom. It means that the mother herself is trying to expand the limits of her life. To *refuse to be a victim*: and then to go on from there. (246, emphasis in original)

Similarly, Sociologist Jesse Bernard wrote to her daughter: "For your sake as well as mine, I must not allow you to absorb me completely. I must learn to live my own life independently in order to be a better mother to you" (272). Judith Arcana, in her book on mothers and daughters wrote, "We must live as if our dreams have been realized. We cannot simply prepare other, younger daughters for strength, pride, courage, beauty. It is worse than useless to tell young women and girls that we have done and been wrong, that we have chosen ill, that we hope they will be more lucky" (1979: 33). What daughters need, therefore, in Rich's words:

> [are] mothers who want their own freedom and ours.... The quality of the mother's life—however, embattled and unprotected—is her primary bequest to her daughter, because a woman who can believe in herself, who is a fighter, and who continues to struggle to create livable space around her, is demonstrating to her daughter that these possibilities exist. (247)

Whether it is termed courageous mothering, as Rich describes it, or empowered or feminist mothering, this practice of mothering calls for the empowerment of daughters *and* mothers, and recognizes that the former is only possible with the later. As Arcana concludes: "If we want girls to grow into free women, brave and strong, we must be those women ourselves" (1979: 33).

As a mother of two feminist daughters, now 19 and 16, I read all the feminist literature on mothers and daughters and increasingly became intrigued by the connection made in the scholarship between modeling and mentoring feminism. I had my children quite young, between the ages of 23-28, when I was an undergraduate and later a graduate student. I write this chapter as a 44-year-old heterosexual woman of Irish/ Scottish/English descent who has been in a common-law relationship with the children's father for 23 years. While I was raised middle-class, my partner and I raised the children as broke, full-time students, and now, as a tenured professor and my partner an adjunct professor, we are upper-middle class (though still paying off our own student loans and funding the education of two children who live away from home).

I am a mother, a feminist, and a feminist mother. My daughters Erin and Casey are radical "out" third wave feminists: Erin has been so forever and Casey in the last two to three years. I am a feminist mother and my daughters are feminist. The question that brings my to this chapter is how did my daughters become feminists, or more specifically what is the relationship between my feminist mothering and their becoming feminists? The feminist mothering of my son is not explored in the chapter, not because I do not think such is important; rather because I believe that the feminist mothering of a son *is* different to that of a daughter and the space allowed to me in this chapter does not permit to examine both well.[1] What I am interested in exploring in this article is not my feminist mothering per say but my *daughters' perceptions and experiences of being raised by feminist mothering*. In particular, I want to examine in the context of our lived lives as a feminist mother and feminist daughters the argument made by Rich and other early writers that feminist mothering must first be concerned with the abolition of patriarchal motherhood so as empower mothers. Only then is feminist childrearing made possible. In other words, how did my identity as a feminist and my work of feminist mothering give rise to the feminism of my daughters? How did they become feminist: was it through anti-sexist childrearing, i.e., raising empowered daughters, as is the focus of more contemporary writers? Or was it through me being a feminist, or more specifically me being a mother who sought to mother against the institution of patriarchal motherhood and practice feminist mothering? Was it my challenge to patriarchal motherhood that afforded me the agency and authority to impart my feminism to my daughters, practice anti-sexist childrearing? I will return to these questions after a summary of my daughters' observations.

Feminism: "A Saturated Reality"

The comments of Erin and Casey discussed below are drawn from an 80-minute taped discussion. The discussion took place as we sat on the floor of Casey's bedroom and was informally structured. I asked a general question and then asked them to take turns in answering the question asked. I instructed them to answer the questions honestly. And while I do agree that an interview between a parent and child can never be fully candid, I believe that our interview was as honest as one could be as my daughters and I enjoy a intimate and very open relationship.

I opened the interview with a general question: How would you define a feminist mother; what does she do or not do, what is feminist mothering? Erin commented:

> *A feminist mother quietly incorporates feminism into your life And it is not like feminism is a separate thing, it is the make up of the world that you live in because everything that you do is textured by feminism and the entire way that you grow to see the world is being shaped for you through a feminist perspective … so things like absence of teen magazines lying around the house or books written by women piling up in front of you that you could read at your leisure. I would say a feminist mother makes feminism something that is a normal part of your life.*

Rocking the Cradle

Casey commented:

> *I remember when I was in grade eight this girl came up to me and said your mom is a feminist, eh? She was so confused and concerned as to why my mom was a feminist or what feminism even was. But in some way or another every mother incorporates feminism as basic survival because girls need feminism, whether it is called feminism or not, to survive. It is absolutely essential to the survival of girls.*

When they were asked for specific examples of feminist mothering from their own childhood, Erin and Casey mentioned examples of anti-sexist childrearing. Casey remembers in grade three not listening to the Spice Girls or playing with Barbies as her friends did and wearing track pants and being made fun of because of this by her fashion-conscious friends. Erin also remembered when she was in grade five and received a Barbie doll and "understanding in some vague way that it was a symbol of patriarchy." Both commented upon how all their friends received plastic make-up sets in elementary school while they did not. Erin also talked about while she did play with girl toys as she grew up, there was, she explained, "more variety; the toys were more geared to my personality and not my gender, for example I collected coins....that is a dorky thing for a girl to do." Casey remembers not knowing how to put on make-up or nail polish like the other girls who were taught this: "I remember not knowing how to do this…. I never got those lectures on [beauty and hygiene]. I didn't start wearing makeup until grade eight. I am now glad that I [never learned like the other girls] because now I can do whatever the fuck I want with it." When I mentioned to them that I did wear make-up and wore fashionable clothing, Erin remarked: "You were a femme feminist, but you didn't force it on us. Being a girl didn't mean that … it could mean what we wanted it to mean." "Other mothers," Erin went on to say, "want their daughters to exist successfully in patriarchy, so the daughter has to be feminine. You had different hopes for us, different than that." As well, Erin noted further, that while I might have worn fashionable clothing, "then you walked off to work and talked about issues to me…. What I noticed about you was not that you were or were not fashionable … but that you were constantly expressing your mind."

These examples of anti-sexist childrearing show that my daughters learned feminism by way of it being modeled to them. When I asked them about their earliest memory of being raised by a feminist mother, Erin said: "You worked. Work was a normal part of your life, the same as Dad's if not more so. It didn't seem weird that you went out to work. When kids of stay-at-home moms came to our house they saw not a fresh batch of muffins but a brand new batch of graded essays." Casey, too, remarked that she was proud that her mom worked though she was teased by others because of this. Wanting to understand more on modeling feminism I asked them about how they perceived the relationship of me and their father growing up. They both agreed that in some ways our relationship was traditional. When they were young the discipline was done by their father but they both emphasized that they were still not like other families. "You both cooked dinner ... and he was always the one doing the dishes." Also "dad had really long hair. That was weird among my friends. I have seen dad cry, most people don't." Speaking on how opposite-sex relationships are structured by traditional gender roles, Erin commented that while that was there, "you never took it ... you were always a bitch ... and would fight back. [The idea] that he was the 'man' would only go so far ... you would scream and yell and say 'excuse me I don't think so.' We saw it [traditional roles] happen but we also saw that if it does happen the woman can say no.... I will do it my way."

When asked how the general feminist belief that patriarchy was wrong and the women should be equal to men was conveyed to them, Erin commented: "It was in everything we did and around us. I was a girl and I knew that boys would think they were better than me and I knew they weren't." The message, Erin continued,

> was that it was great to be a girl. A lot of girl pride given to me. Books. Goddess worship was a big thing. You always said thank the Goddess. Just the idea that a woman could be worshiped like that. Around the house there were goddesses everywhere. You also talked about being a mother.... This sense of pride of being a woman was in the things you said, things that were up on the wall, subtle ways, in book, comments. It saturated our existence.

Casey agreed: "It was constantly everywhere. Saturated feminism as you say. When I was little I ignored it as I wanted to be a 'normal' girl." Yet Casey goes on to say that when she was kindergarten and a boy wouldn't stop bothering her she warned him to stop or she would cut open his finger. He said that "you won't fight back because you are a girl" and "as I said, wanna bet ... so I did."

Speaking of their own experience of coming to feminism, Erin said:

> I was always a freak. I couldn't avoid it because it was so saturated. I didn't realize that I was doing feminist things, it was just the way I acted. I was a loud girl. If I had something to say I said it. Feminism did make it harder for me growing up because it made me different but it was so worth it in the end. I came out the other side of all that. I am my own person. The girls I

grew up with are still playing all those games. Still trapped in that world ... still don't say what they think.

Casey commented:

I feel the same way. Worth it in the end though going it through was hard particularly in elementary school. I was always a freak. I couldn't be pretty. I just failed. I didn't know how to dress "normally." As you grow older you come to appreciate it more. I live in this world without being swallowed up.

Central to their understanding of feminist mothering was "being allowed to express myself" and being supported in this. Erin talked about how when she stopped shaving her armpits, "mom was okay with it. Other girls are told it is disgusting and unclean and their mother wouldn't let them." Both Erin and Casey emphasized the development of critical thinking. Casey remarked: "I always had arguments with dad on music and movies. I never sat and accepted things that are supposed to be accepted. They gave us access to information to make our own opinions. Just because you have strong opinions doesn't mean that I would have your own opinions ... because we grew up in this household where that was possible." Erin explained that the difference was that they were "treated like people instead of being treated like children. Other parents just say no and while we got that to a degree, I would argue, argue. Say what I wanted to say; not told to shut up just because you are a kid." Erin commented further:

People think if you are raised in a feminist setting ideas are put in your head. In our family we were encouraged to think for ourselves ... that was the big thing ... encouraged to think about things. Even if you disagreed we would argue it to end. We were encouraged to think for ourselves ... critically to come up with our own opinions despite the fact that world is trying to shove other ideas down your throat.

At the conclusion of the interview I explained the research questions of this chapter and asked them to speak directly to two sets of questions. The first: How is feminism learned: is it modeled or taught? I explained to them Rich's argument that more important than feminist childrearing, is the mother seeking to achieve in her own life what she wishes for her daughters. In response to this, Erin commented:

That is what I mean when I said our reality was totally saturated with it. It was shown, not just told (though we were told as well). I agree with you, definitely 100 percent. If it had just been talked about, it would not have been the reality that it was. Feminism was the world I lived in because the fact that you were a feminist in what you did and acted. I mean I remember you going out with your friends ... and me saying "I want you to stay home and be a good mother and baby me" and you saying mothers need to go out too. This is what feminism is: the acting and living ... not just the told. Feminism was expressed to us in the way you lived your life. And the way you set things up...we saw it everywhere. That is how it became our reality. Instead of something we talked about, it was what everything was.

Casey remarked: "When I was young I was resentful that my mom wasn't home making me cookies. I am now glad you worked and was not home baking cookies." On the related topic that there is the assumption that a feminist mother is selfish while a "good" mother is selfless and that former puts her career first and the latter her kids, Erin said: "Anybody who said you put your career first would be a liar.... No way in hell you put your career first. You were an involved mother ... and you had a career. What is so amazing is that you were so involved with kids and did a career." She added:

When I was little there were times that I said come play with me and you said I have to do this.... It was not a big deal. Around enough ... times that you weren't, I never felt neglected. I never ever felt that way. I think it is a demonizing idea that they put out against women who work and decide to be a mother. It is completely possible to do it ... you did both very well.

I also asked them to reflect upon another common assumption in some feminist writings on the mother-daughter relationship: namely, the mother represents to the daughter patriarchal oppression and hence the daughter must turn against the mother to become a "free" woman. Adrienne Rich termed this sentiment matrophobia: "The fear not of one's mother or motherhood but of becoming one's mother" (235). In response, Erin said:

Never felt your life was inhibited ... you got what you wanted ... had three kids still managed to suck fun out of life.... In this you were a role model to me, you have your cake and eat it too. [The belief] is that a woman is not allowed to be a mother and get a Ph.D. ... and you always did it all ... that is inspiring to me. I knew that I could have it all ... which I do.

Speaking specifically on what impact, if any, being raised by a feminist mother has made on whether they plan to be a mother, Erin concluded: "You definitely made motherhood something I want to do ... I know it is a lot of work but you have shown that it is possible to be a mother and have your own life.

Thoughts

From the above commentary it is evident that my daughters perceived and experienced their upbringing as anti-sexist childrearing and that my daughters understood their childhood in this way. They both mentioned several times that we didn't 'girl' them in their upbringing (Casey spoke of how fishing, playing with frogs, and getting dirty in the mud was a normal part of her childhood) As well they commented on how they did not experience the "normal" sexist feminization of daughters (they didn't play with Barbies, wear make up or listen to the Spice Girls.) As well, both of them emphasized the importance of being offered alternative—empowered—examples and images of womanhood (feminist books/music, Goddess figures, etc). But equally my daughters spoke about how they learned feminism directly from the way I lived my life. This came up far more than I had anticipated. What they remember about me is "working, standing up to traditional gender roles, and always talking about issues." They saw me living a life outside of motherhood. As Erin remarked: "You had a long relationship with dad, work, friends, partying. You did everything: you never had a shitty non-life." My daughters, in watching me live my life, learned that feminism was possible, do-able, and normal. And, as importantly, they learned that motherhood does not, should not, shut down other dimensions of a woman's life: work, sexuality, friendship, activism, leisure, and so forth. Listening over and over again to my daughters' voices as I transcribed the interview, I finally "got" Rich's insight at a deeply personal level. To paraphrase Rich: The quality of my life—however, embattled and unprotected it may have been—was my primary bequest to my daughters, because in believing in myself, in fighting, in struggling to create liveable space around me, I demonstrated to Erin and Casey that these possibilities exist. Feminist mothering of girls is not about choosing blue over pink, or trucks over dolls, but about *living,* to use the title of Marilyn Waring's work, *as if women counted.* And more specifically, in the context of motherhood, feminist mothering demonstrates to our daughters that women have a selfhood outside of motherhood and have power within motherhood.

Conclusion

This story is evidently that of myself and my two daughters. What I learned in interviewing my daughters is not generalizable to all women. Moreover, the routes by which daughters come to feminism are varied: feminist mothering is just one of many. However, what I take from this narrative and what I believe may be of use to others who likewise seek to imagine and achieve feminist mothering, is that the future we wish for our daughters must be struggled for today in our *own daily lives*. We must be the changes that we seek. Would my daughters have become feminists in patriarchal motherhood? The interview findings suggest that such would not have possible or not to the degree that I, as a feminist mother, would wish. In patriarchal motherhood, feminism would not have become the "the saturated reality" of my daughters' upbringing. I certainly could not have lived and modeled a feminist life in patriarchal motherhood; nor would I have had the agency and authority to impart feminist childrearing to my daughters. I believe that what our daughters need most from us is not self-sacrifice or selflessness, as preached in patriarchal motherhood, but selfhood and, yes, a healthy dose of *selfishness*. For a mother who insists upon "a life of her own" tutors her daughter that she too is deserving of the same. Or to conclude with Erin's words: "What you have shown us is that it is possible to be a mother and have your own life." That is the lesson we, as mothers, must impart to our daughters by living it ourselves.

[1]Please see Chapter Nine, "A Mom and her Son: Thoughts on Feminist Mothering," and my edited volume, *Mothers and Sons: Feminism, Masculinity and the Struggle to Raise our Sons* (2001).

BIBLIOGRAPHY

Allen, Paula Gunn. *Spider Woman's Granddaughters: Traditional Tales and Contemporary Writing by Native American Women*. New York: Ballantine Books, 1990.

Althusser, Louis. "Ideology and Ideological State Apparatuses." B. Brewster, trans. *Lenin and Philosophy and Other Essays*, New York: Monthly Review Press, 1971.

American Association of University Professors. *Statement of Principles on Family Responsibilities and Academic Work*. Online: http://www.aaup.org/ statements/REPORTS/re01fam.htm. September 2004.

Arcana, Judith. *Every Mother's Son: The Role of Mothers in the Making of Men*. New York: Anchor Press/Doubleday, 1983.

Arcana, Judith. *Our Mother's Daughters*. Berkeley, CA: Shameless Hussy Press, 1979.

Arden, Jann. "Good Mother," *Living Under June*, CD 31454 0789 2 (1994, A & M Records, a division of PolyGramGroup Canada Inc.).

Association for Research on Mothering and The Journal of the Association for Research on Mothering. Website: www.yorku.ca/crm.

Ballingsley, Andrew. *Black Families in White America*. Englewood Cliffs, New Jersey: Prentice Hall, 1968.

Ballingsley, Andrew, ed. *Climbing Jacob's Ladder: The Enduring Legacy of African American Families*. New York: Simon & Schuster, 1992.

Barthes, Roland. *Mythologies*. Trans. Annette Lavers. London: Paladin Grafton Books, 1972.

Bell-Scott, Patricia, Beverly Guy-Sheftall, Jaqueline Jones Roysler, Janet Sims-Wood, Miriam De Costa-Willis, and Lucie Fultz, eds. *Double Stitch: Black Women Write About Mothers and Daughters*. Boston: Beacon, 1991.

Bernard, Jesse. "Letter to her Daughter." *Between Ourselves: Letters Between Mothers and Daughters*. Ed. Karen Payne. Boston: Houghton Mifflin Company, 1983: 271-72.

Bernard, Wanda Thomas, and Candace Bernard. "Passing the Torch: A Mother and Daughter Reflect on their Experiences Across Generations." *Canadian Woman Studies/les cahiers de la femme* 18 (2,3) (Summer/Fall 1998): 46-50.

Berry, Cecelie. "Home is Where the Revolution Is." Online: www.Salon.com. September 1999; accessed January 20, 2006.

Blakely, Mary Kay. "Who Are We This Time?" *Mothers and Sons: Feminism, Masculinity and the Struggle to Raise Our Sons.* Ed. Andrea O'Reilly. New York: Routledge, 2001. 25-46.

Bly, Robert. *Iron John.* New York: Vintage, 1990.

Brown, Lyn Mikel, and Carol Gilligan. *Meeting at the Crossroads: Women's Psychology and Girls' Development.* Cambridge, MA: Harvard University Press, 1992.

Büskens, Petra. "The Impossibility of 'Natural Parenting' for Modern Mothers: On Social Structure and the Formation of Habit." *Journal of the Association for Research on Mothering* 3 (1) (Spring/Summer 2001): 75-86.

Caplan, Paula. *Don't Blame Mother: Mending the Mother–Daughter Relationship.* New York: Harper and Row, 1989.

Chase, Susan, and M. Rogers. *Mothers and Children: Feminist Analyses and Personal Narratives.* New Brunswick, New Jersey: Rutgers University Press, 2001.

Chodorow, Nancy. *Feminism and Psychoanalytic Theory.* New Haven: Yale University Press, 1989.

Chodorow, Nancy. *The Reproduction of Mothering: Psychoanalysis and the Sociology of Gender.* Berkeley: University of California Press, 1978.

Cixous, Helene and Catherine Clement. *The Newly Born Woman.* Betsy Wing, trans. Minneapolis: University of Minnesota Press, 1986.

Collins, Patricia Hill. "Shifting the Center: Race, Class and Feminist Theorizing About Motherhood." *Mothering: Ideology, Experience, and Agency.* Eds. Evelyn Nakano Glenn, Grace Chang, and Linda Rennie Forcey. New York: Routledge, 1994. 45-65.

_____ . "The Meaning of Motherhood in Black Culture and Black Mother–Daughter Relationships." *Double Stitch: Black Women Write About Mothers and Daughters.* Eds. Patricia Bell-Scott and Beverly Guy-Sheftall. New York: HarperPerennial, 1993. 42-60.

_____ . *Black Feminist Thought: Knowledge, Consciousness and the Politics of Empowerment.* New York: Unwin Hyman/Routledge, 1990.

Cooper, Baba. "The Radical Potential in Lesbian Mothering of Daughters." *Politics of the Heart: A Lesbian Parenting Anthology.* Eds. Sandra Pollack and Jeanne Vaughan. Ithaca, NY: Firebrand Books, 1987. 233-40.

Council of Ontario Universities. *Employment Equity for Women: A University*

Handbook. Toronto: Council of Ontario Universities, March 1988.

Crittenden, Ann. *The Price of Motherhood: Why the Most Important Job in the World is Still the Least Valued*. New York: Henry Holt, 2001.

Dagg, Anne Innis, and Patricia J. Thompson. *MisEducation: Women &Canadian Universities*. Toronto: OISE Press, 1988.

Daly, Brenda O. and Maureen T. Reddy, eds. *Narrating Mothers, Theorizing Maternal Subjectivities*. Knoxville: The University of Tennessee Press, 1991.

Dally, Ann. *Inventing Motherhood: The Consequences of an Ideal*. London: The Hutchinson Publishing Group, 1982.

Davies, Carole Boyce. "Mother Right/Write Revisited: *Beloved* and *Dessa Rose* and the Construction of Motherhood in Black Women's Fiction." *Narrating Mothers Theorizing Maternal Subjectivities*. Eds. Brenda O. Daly and Maureen T. Reddy. Knoxville: University of Tennessee Press, 1991. 44-51.

Debold, Elizabeth, Marie Wilson, and Idelisse Malavé. *Mother Daughter Revolution: From Good Girls to Great Women*. New York: Bantam Books, 1994.

Delancy, Dayle. "Motherlove Is a Killer." *Sage* 8 (Fall 1990): 15-18.

de Lauretis, Teresa. *Technologies of Gender: Essays on Theory, Film and Fiction*. Bloomington: Indiana University Press, 1987.

de Waal, Mieke. "Teenage Daughters on their Mothers." *Daughtering and Mothering*. Eds. Janneke van Mens-Verhulst, Karlein Schreurs, and Liesbeth Woertman. New York: Routledge, 1993. 35-43.

Dinnerstein, Dorothy. *The Mermaid and the Minotaur: Sexual Arrangements and the Human Malaise*. New York: Harper Colophon, 1976.

Dixon, Penelope. *Mothers and Mothering: An Annotated Bibliography*. New York: Garland Publishing, 1991.

Dooley, Cate and Nikki Fedele. "Raising Relational Boys." *Mother Outlaws: Theories and Practices of Empowered Mothering*. Ed. Andrea O'Reilly. Toronto: Women's Press, 2004. 357-385.

Douglas, Susan J and Meredith Micheals. *The Mommy Myth: The Idealization of Motherhood and How it Has Undermined Women*. New York: New York: Fress Press, 2004.

Edelman, Hope. *Motherless Daughters: The Legacy of Loss*. New York: Bantam Doubleday Dell Publishing Group, Inc., 1994.

Edwards, Arlene. "Community Mothering: The Relationship Between Mothering and the Community Work of Black Women" *Journal of The Association for Research on Mothering* 2 (2) (Fall/Winter 2000): 66-84.

Emecheta, Buchi. *The Joys of Motherhood*. London: Heinemann, 1988.

Faludi, Susan. *Stiffed: The Betrayal of the American Man*. New York: W. Morrow and Co., 1999.

Forcey, Linda Rennie. *Mothers of Sons: Toward an Understanding of Responsi-*

bility. New York: Praeger, 1987.

Fothergill, Alice and Kathryn Felty. "'I've Worked Very Hard and Slept Very Little': Mothers on the Tenure Track in Academia." *Journal of the Association for Research on Mothering* 5 (2)(Fall/Winter 2003): 7-19.

Friday, Nancy. *My Mother/My Self: The Daughter's Search for Identity.* New York: DelacortePress, 1977.

Gibson, Priscilla. "Developmental Mothering in an African American Community: From Grandmothers to New Mothers Again." *Journal of The Association for Research on Mothering* 2 (2) (Fall/Winter 2000): 31-41.

Gilligan, Carol. *In a Different Voice: Psychological Theory and Women's Development.* Cambridge, MA: Harvard University Press, 1982.

Glickman, Rose. *Daughters of Feminists: Young Women with Feminist Mothers Talk about Their Lives.* New York: St. Martin's Press, 1993.

Allen, Paula Gunn . *Spider Woman's Granddaughters: Traditional Tales and Contemporary Writing by Native American Women.* New York: Ballantine Books, 1990.

Golden, Marita. *Saving Our Sons: Raising Black Children in a Turbulent World.* New York: AnchorBooks/Doubleday, 1995.

Gordon, Tuula. *Feminist Mothers.* New York: New York University Press, 1990.

Gore, Ariel and Bee Lavender. Eds. *Breeder: Real-Life Stories from the New Generation of Mothers.* Seattle W.A.: Seal Press, 2001

Green, Fiona. "Feminist Mothers: Sucessfully Negoiating the Tensions Between Motherhood and Mothering." *Mothering Against Motherhood. The Legacy of Of Woman Born.* Ed. Andrea O'Reilly. Albany, NY: SUNY Press, 2004. 125-136.

Gutman, Herbert. *The Black Family in Slavery and Freedom: 1750-1925.* New York: Vintage, 1976.

Hall, Pamela Courtney. "Mothering Mythology in the Late Twentieth Century: Science, Gender Lore, and Celebratory Narrative." *Canadian Woman Studies/les cahiers de la femme* 18 (1,2) (Summer/Fall 1998): 59-63.

Hamilton, Sylvia. "African Nova Scotian Women: Mothering Across the Generations." *Redefining Motherhood: Patterns and Identities.* Eds. Sharon Abbey and Andrea O'Reilly. Toronto: Second Story Press, 1998. 244-256.

Hamilton, Sylvia. *Black Mother, Black Daughter* (videorecording). National Film Board of Canada, 1989.

Harman, Lesley D. and Petra Remy. "When Life Gets in the Way of Life: Work/Family Conflicts Among Academic Women and Men." *Women in the Canadian Academic Tundra: Challenging the Chill.* Eds: Elena Hannah, Linda Paul, Swani Vethamany-Clobus, Montreal: McGill-Queen's University Press, 2002. 104-111.

Harris, Trudier. *From Mammies to Militants: Domestics in Black American*

Literature. Philadelphia: Temple University Press, 1982.

Hays, Sharon. *The Cultural Contradictions of Motherhood*. New Haven: Yale University Press, 1996.

Heilbrun, Carolyn. *Writing a Woman's Lfe*. New York: Ballantine, 1988.

Hewett, Heather. "Third-Wave Era Feminism and the Emerging Mothers Movement." *Journal of the Association for Research on Mothering* 8 (1,2) (Forthcoming, Summer 2006).

Hile-Bassett, Rachel. Ed. *Parenting and Professing: Balancing Family Work with An Academic Career*. Nashville Tenessee: Vanderbilt University Press, 2006.

Hirsch, Marianne. *The Mother/Daughter Plot: Narrative, Psychoanalysis, Feminism*. Bloomington: Indiana University Press, 1989.

Hite, Shere. *The Hite Report on the Family*. New York: Grove Press, 1994.

Holloway, Karla and Stephanie Demetrakopoulos. *New Dimensions in Spirituality: A Biracial and Bicultural Reading of the Novels of Toni Morrison*. New York: Greenwood, 1987.

hooks, bell. "Homeplace: A Site of Resistance." *Yearning: Race, Gender, and Cultural Politics*. Boston: South End, 1990. 41-49.

hooks, bell. "Revolutionary Parenting." *Feminist Theory: From Margin to Center*. Boston: South End Press, 1984. 133-46.

Horwitz, Erika. "Mothers' Resistance to the Western Dominant Discourse on Mothering." Unpublished Ph.D. dissertation. Simon Fraser University, 2003.

Horwitz, Erika "Resistance as a Site of Empowerment: The Journey Away from Maternal Sacrifice." *Mother Outlaws: Theories and Practices of Empowered Mothering*. Eds. Andrea O'Reilly, Toronto: Women's Press, 2004. 43-58.

Ingman, Marrit. *Inconsolable: How I Threw My Mental Health Out with the Diapers*. Seattle Washington, Seal Press, 2005.

Irigaray, Luce. *The Sex Which is Not One*. Catherine Porter, trans. Ithaca: Cornell University Press, 1985.

Jackson, Marni. *The Mother Zone: Love, Sex, and Laundry in the Modern Family*. Toronto: Macfarlane Walter and Ross, 1992.

James, Stanlie M. "Mothering: A Possible Black Feminist Link to Social Transformation." *Theorizing Black Feminism: The Visionary Pragmatism of Black Women*. Eds. Stanlie James and A. P. Busia, Routledge, 1999. 44-54.

Jenkins, Nina Lyon. "Black Women and the Meaning of Motherhood." *Redefining Motherhood: Patterns and Identities*. Eds. Sharon Abbey and Andrea O'Reilly. Toronto: Second Story Press, 1998. 201-213.

Jeremiah, Emily. "Murderous Mothers: Adrienne Rich's *Of Woman Born* and Toni Morrison's *Beloved*." *From Mothering to Motherhood: The Legacy of Adrienne Rich's Of Woman Born*. Ed. Andrea O'Reilly. Albany, NY: Suny,

2004.

Johnson, Miriam. *Strong Mothers, Weak Wives*. Berkeley: University of California Press, 1988.

Joseph, Gloria I., and Jill Lewis, eds. *Common Differences: Conflicts in Black and White Feminist Perspectives*. Boston: South End, 1981.

Journal of the Association on Mothering issue on "Mothering in the Academy." 5 (2) (Fall/Winter 2003).

Kaplan, Elaine Bell. *Not Our Kind of Girl: Unraveling the Myths of Black Teenage Motherhood*. Berkeley: University of California Press, 1997.

King, Joyce Elaine, and Carolyn Ann Mitchell. *Black Mothers to Sons: Juxtaposing African-American Literature with Social Practice*. New York: Peter Lang, 1995.

Kristeva, Julia. *The Kristeva Reader*. Ed. Toril Moi. New York: Columbia University Press, 1986.

Kristeva, Julia. *Revolution in Poetic Language*. Margaret Walker, trans. New York: Columbia University Press, 1984.

Kuwabong, Dannabang. "Reading the Gospel of Bakes: Daughters' Representations of Mothers in the Poetry of Claire Harris and Lorna Goodison." *Canadian Woman Studies/les cahiers de la femme* 19 (2,3) (Summer/Fall 1998): 132-138.

Ladner, Joyce. *Tomorrow's Tomorrow: The Black Woman*. New York: Doubleday, 1971.

Ladd-Taylor, Molly and Lauri Umansky. *Bad Mothers: The Politics of Mother Blame in Twentieth Century America*. New York: New York University Press, 1998.

Lawson, Erica. "Black Women's Mothering in a Historical and Contemporary Perspective: Understanding the Past, Forging the Future" *Journal of The Association for Research on Mothering* 2 (2) (Fall/Winter 2000): 21-30.

Lee, Claudette, and Ethel Hill Williams. "Masculinity, Matriarchy and Myth: A Black Feminist Perspective." *Mothers and Sons: Feminism, Masculinity and the Struggle to Raise Our Sons*. Ed. Andrea O'Reilly. New York: Routledge, 2001. 56-70.

Lorde, Audre. *Sister Outsider*. New York: Quality Paper Back Club, Triangle Classics, 1993.

Lorde, Audre. "Man Child: A Black Lesbian Feminist's Response." Eds. Sandra Pollack and Jeanne Vaughan. Ithaca, NY: Firebrand Books, 1987. 220-226.

Lowinsky, Naomi Ruth. *The Motherline: Every Woman's Journey to Find Her Female Roots*. (Formerly titled, Stories *from the Motherline: Reclaiming the Mother-Daughter Bond, Finding Our Feminine Souls*.) Los Angeles: Jeremy P. Tarcher, 1992.

Luxton, Meg. *More Than a Labour of Love*. Toronto: The Women's Press, 1980.

Mann, Judy. *The Difference: Growing Up Female in America*. New York: Time Warner, 1994.

Martin, Emily. *The Woman in the Body: A Cultural Analysis of Reproduction*. Boston: Beacon Press, 1987.

Mason, Theodore O., Jr. "The Novelist as Conservator: Stories and Comprehension in Toni Morrison's *Song of Solomon*." *Toni Morrison*. Ed. Harold Bloom. New York: Chelsea, 1990. 564-81.

Maushart, Susan. *The Masks of Motherhood: How Becoming a Mother Changes Everything and Why We Pretend it Doesn't*. New York: The New Press, 1999.

McAdoo, Harriette Pipes, ed. *Black Families*. Beverly Hills, CA: Sage, 1981.

McAdoo, Harriette Pipes, *Family Ethnicity Strength in Diversity*. Beverly Hills, CA: Sage Publications, 1993.

McClaurin, Irma. "The Power of Names." *Double Stitch: Black Women Write About Mothers and Daughters*. Eds. Patricia Bell-Scott *et al*. Boston: Beacon, 1993. 148.

Middleton, Amy "Mothering Under Duress: Examining the Inclusiveness of Feminist Theory." Paper presented at the Eighth Annual Conference of the *Association for Research on Mothering*, on "Motherhood and Feminism," York University, October, 2004.

Mogadime, Dolana. "A Daughter's Praise Poem for her Mother: Historicizing Community Activism and Racial Uplift Among South African Women." *Canadian Woman Studies/les cahiers de la femme* 18 (2,3) (Summer/Fall 1998): 86-91.

Morrison, Toni. *Love*. New York: Alfred A. Knopf, 2003.

_____. *Paradise*. New York: Alfred A. Knopf, 1998.

_____. *Jazz*. New York: Alfred A. Knopf, 1992.

_____. *Beloved*. New York: Plume, 1987.

_____. *Tar Baby*. New York: Plume, 1986

_____. "Rootedness: The Ancestor as Foundation." *Black Women Writers (1950-1980)*. Ed. Mari Evans. New York: Doubleday, 1984. 339-45.

_____. *Sula*. New York: New American Library, 1973.

_____. *The Bluest Eye*. New York: Washington Square, 1970.

_____. *Song of Soloman*. New York: New American Library, 1977.

Morton, Patricia. *Disfigured Images: The Historical Assault on Afro-American Women*. Westport, Connecticut: Greenwood Press, 1991.

Moynihan, Daniel P. *The Negro Family: The Case for National Action*. Washington, D.C.: U.S. Department of Labor, Office of Policy Planning and Research, 1965.

Naylor, Gloria. "A Conversation: Gloria Naylor and Toni Morrison." *Conversations with Toni Morrison*. Ed. Danille Taylor-Guthrie. Jackson: University Press of Mississippi, 1994.

O'Brien, Mary. *The Politics of Reproduction*. Boston: Routledge & Kegan Paul, 1981.

O'Reilly, Andrea. *Feminist Mothering*. New York: SUNY, forthcoming.

_____. "Between the Baby and the Bathwater: Towards a Mother-Centred Feminist Theory of Mothering." *Journal of the Association for Research on Mothering* 8 (1,2) (forthcoming, Summer 2006).

_____. "Forward." *Parenting and Professing: Balancing Family Work with An Academic Career*. Ed. Rachel Hile-Bassett. Nashville, Tennessee: Vanderbilt University Press, 2005. xiii-xvii.

_____. *Mother Matters: Motherhood as Discourse and Practice*. Toronto: ARM Press, 2004a.

_____. *Toni Morrison and Motherhood: Politics of the Heart*. New York: SUNY, 2004b.

_____. *Mother Outlaws: Theories and Practices of Empowered Mothering*. Toronto: Women's Press, 2004c.

_____. *From Motherhood to Mothering: The Legacy of Adrienne Rich's Of Woman Born*. Albany, NY: Suny, 2004d.

_____, ed. *Mothers and Sons: Feminism, Masculinity and the Struggle to Raise Our Sons*. New York: Routledge, 2001.

_____. "'I Come From a Long Line of Uppity Irate Black Women': African-American Feminist Theory on Motherhood, the Motherline and the Mother–Daughter Relation." *Mothers and Daughters: Connection, Empowerment and Transformation*. Eds. Andrea O'Reilly and Sharon Abbey. New York: Rowman and Littlefield, 2000. 143-159.

_____. "Mothers, Daughters and Feminism Today: Empowerment, Agency, Narrative." *Canadian Woman Studies/les cahiers de la femme* 18 (2,3) (Summer/Fall 1998): 16–21.

_____. "'In Search of My Mother's Garden, I Found My Own': Motherlove, Healing and Identity in Toni Morrison's *Jazz*." *African American Review* 30 (3) (1996): 367-379.

_____ and Sharon Abbey, eds. *Mothers and Daughters: Connection, Empowerment, and Transformation*. New York: Rowman and Littlefield, 2000.

_____ and Silvia Caporale-Bizzini. *MotherSelf: Theorizing and Representing Maternal Subjectivities*. Forthcoming, 2007.

_____ and Judith Stadtman Tucker. *Mothering a Movement: Activist Mothers Speak Out on Why We Need to Change the World and How To Do It*. Forthcoming, 2007.

_____, Marie Porter and Patricia Short. *Motherhood: Power and Oppression*. Toronto: Women's Press, 2005.

_____, and Sharon Abbey, eds. *Redefining Motherhood: Changing Identities and Patterns*. Toronto: Second Story Press, 1998.

Park, Christine and Caroline Heaton, Eds. *Close Company: Stories of Mothers and Daughters*. London: Virago Press, 1987.

Pipher, Mary. *Reviving Ophelia: Saving the Selves of Adolescent Girls*. New York: Grosset/Putnam, 1994. Maureen Reddy, Martha Roth, Amy Sheldon, eds. *Mother Journeys: Feminists Write about Mothering*. Minneapolis: Spinsters Ink, 1994.

Pollack, Sandra and Jeanne Vaughan. *Politics of the Heart: A Lesbian Parenting Anthology*. Ithaca, NY: Firebrand, 1987.

Pollack, William. *Real Boys: Rescuing Our Sons from the Myths of Boyhood*. New York: RandomHouse, 1998.

Rainwater, Lee, and William L. Yancey, eds. *The Moynihan Report and the Politics of Controversy*. Cambridge: M.I.T., 1967.

Rich, Adrienne. *Of Woman Born: Motherhood as Experience and Institution*. New York: W.W. Norton, 1986.

Reddy, Maureen, Martha Roth, Amy Sheldon, eds. *Mother Journeys: Feminists Write About Mothering*. Minneapolis: Spinsters Ink, 1994.

Reyes, Angelita. "Ancient Properties in the New World: The Paradox of the 'Other' in Toni Morrison's *Tar Baby*." *Black Scholar* 17 (1986): 19-25.

Rigney, Barbara Hill. *Voices of Toni Morrison*. Colombus: Ohio State University Press, 1991.

Rophie, Anne. *Fruitful: A Real Mother in a Modern World*. Boston: Houghton Mifflin Co., 1996.

Ross, Val. "Giving a human face to 'chaos'." *Globe and Mail* 5 May 1995: C1.

Rothman, Barbara Katz. *Recreating Motherhood: Ideology and Technology in Patriarchal Society*. New York: Norton & Co., 1989.

Ruddick, Sara. *Maternal Thinking: Toward a Politics of Peace*. New York: Ballantine Books, 1989.

Russell, Sandi. "It's OK to Say OK: An Interview Essay." *Critical Essays on Toni Morrison*. Ed. Nellie McKay. Boston: G. K. Hall, 1988. 43-47.

Sanchez, Sonia. "Dear Mama." *Double Stitch: Black Women Write About Mothers and Daughters*. Eds. Patricia Bell-Scott *et al*. Boston: Beacon, 1993. 24-26.

Scales-Trent, Judy. "On That Dark and Moon-Less Night." *Double Stitch: Black Women Write About Mothers and Daughters*. Eds. Eds. Patricia Bell-Scott *et al*. Boston: Beacon, 1993. 213.

Shelley, Mary. *Frankenstein*. New York: Oxford University Press, 1990.

Silverstein, Olga, and Beth Rashbaum. *The Courage to Raise Good Men*. Viking: New York, 1994.

Simeone, Angela. *Academic Women: Work Towards Equality*. South Hadley, MA.: Bergine & Garvey, 1987.

Smith, Babette. *Mothers and Sons: The Truth About Mother–Son Relationships*.

Sydney: Allen and Unwin, 1995.

Smith, Janna Malumud. *A Potent Spell: Mother Love and the Power of Fear.* Boston: Houghton Mifflin, 2003.

Stack, Carol B. *All Our Kin: Strategies for Survival in a Black Community.* New York: Harper & Row, 1974.

Staples, Robert and Leanor Boulin. *Black Families at the Crossroads: Challenges and Prospects.* San Francisco: Jossey-Bass, 1993.

Steady, Filomina Chioma, ed. *The Black Woman Cross-Culturally.* Rochester, VT: Schenkman Books, 1981.Smith, Janna Malamud. *A Potent Spell: Mother Love and the Power of Fear.* New York: Houghton Mifflin Company, 2003

Steele, Cassie Premo. "Drawing Strengths from Our Other Mothers: Tapping the Roots of Black History." *Journal of The Association for Research on Mothering* 2 (2) (Fall/Winter 2000): 7-17.

Taylor-Guthrie, Danielle. Ed. *Conversations with Toni Morrison.* Jackson: University Press of Mississippi, 1994.

Thomas, Audrey. *Mrs. Blood.* Vancouver, BC: Talonbooks, 1975. First published 1970.

Thurer, Shari. *The Myths of Motherhood: How Culture Reinvents the Good Mother.* New York: Penguin, 1994.

Trebilcot, Joyce. *Mothering: Essays in Feminist Theory.* Totowa, NJ: Rouman and Allanheld, 1984.

Treichler, Paula A. "Feminism, Medicine and the Meaning of Childbirth." *Body/Politics, Women and the Discourses of Science.* Eds. Mary Jocobus, Evelyn Fox Keller, and Sally Shuttleworth. New York and London: Routledge, 1990.

Turnage, Barbara. "The Global Self-Esteem of an African-American Adolescent Female and Her Relationship with Her Mother." *Mothers and Daughters: Connection, Empowerment and Transformation.* Eds. Andrea O'Reilly and Sharon Abbey. Lanham, Maryland: Rowman and Littlefield, 2000. 175-187.

Umansky, Laurie. *Motherhood Reconceived: Feminism and the Legacy of the Sixties.* New York: New York University Press, 1996.

Urban Dictionary. http://www.urbandictionary.com/.

Wachtel, Eleanor. "Interview with Toni Morrison." CBC FM Radio, 18 July 1993.

Wade-Gayles, Gloria. *Pushed Back to Strength: A Black Woman's Journey Home.* Boston: Beacon, 1993.

Walker, Alice. "In Search of Our Mothers' Gardens." *In Search of Our Mothers' Gardens.* San Diego: Harcourt Brace Jovanovich, 1983.

Walker, Margaret. "Lineage." *Double Stitch: Black Women Write About Mothers and Daughters*. Eds. Patricia Bell-Scott *et al*. Boston: Beacon, 1993. 178.

Walkerdine, Valerie and Helen Lucey. *Democracy in the Kitchen: Regulating Mothers and Socializing Daughters*. London: Virago Press, 1989.

Wallace, Michele. *Black Macho and the Myth of the Superwoman*. New York: Verso, 1990 [1979].

Wane, Njoki Nathani. "Reflections on the Mutuality of Mothering: Women, Children and Othermothering" *Journal of The Association for Research on Mothering* 2 (2) (Fall/Winter 2000): 105-116.

Waring, Marilyn. *If Women Counted: A New Feminist Economics*. San Francisco: Harper & Row, 1988.

Washington, Mary Helen. "I Sign My Mother's Name: Alice Walker, Dorothy West, Paule Marshall." *Mothering the Mind: Twelve Studies of Writers and Their Silent Partners*, Eds. Ruth Perry and Martine Watson Brownley. New York: Holmes and Meier, 1984.

Washington, Valerie. "The Black Mother in the United States: History, Theory, Research, and Issues." *The Different Faces of Motherhood*. Eds. Beverly Birns and Dale F. Hay. New York: Plenum Press, 1988. 185-213.

Weems, Renita. "Hush, Mama's Gotta Go Bye-Bye." *Double Stitch: Black Women Write About Mothers and Daughters*. Eds. Eds. Patricia Bell-Scott *et al*. Boston: Beacon, 1993. 123-130..

Weldon, Fay. *Down Among the Women*. London: Heinemann, 1971.

Wells, Jess. "Lesbians Raising Sons." *Mothers and Sons: Feminism, Masculinity and the Struggle to Raise Our Sons*. Ed. Andrea O'Reilly. New York: Routledge, 2001. 16-21.

Westkott, Marcia. "Mothers and Daughters in the World of the Father." *Frontiers* 3 (2) (1978): 16-21.

Woertman, Liesbeth. "Mothering in Context: Female Subjectives and Intervening Practices." *Daughtering and Mothering*. Eds. Janneke van Mens-Verhulst, Karlein Schreurs, and Liesbeth Woertman. New York: Routledge, 1993. 57-61.

Wolf, Naomi. *The Beauty Myth*. New York: Anchor Books, 1991.

Woolf, Virginia. *A Room of One's Own*. New York: Granada, 1977 [1929].

Wylie, Philip. *A Generation of Vipers*. New York: Rinehart & Company, 1942.

PERMISSIONS

Thank you to the following publishers and editors for generously permitting the following pieces to be reprinted in *Rocking the Cradle: Thoughts on Motherhood, Feminism and the Possibility of Empowered Mothering.*

Chapter One: O'Reilly, Andrea. "Labour Signs: The Semiotics of Birthing." *Journal of the Association for Research on Mothering* Vol. 3.1., Toronto: ARM Press. (Spring/Summer 2001). 216-223.

Chapter Two: O'Reilly, Andrea. "Talking Back in Mother Tongue: A Feminist Course on Mothering-Motherhood." *Feminism and Education: A Canadian Perspective*, Vol. 2, Eds. Paula Bourne, Philinda Masters, Nuzhat Amin, Marnina Gonick and Lisa Gribowski. Toronto: OISE Press, 1994. 221-241.

Chapter Three: O'Reilly, Andrea. "What's a Girl Like You Doing in a Nice Place Like This?: Mothering in the Academe." *Women in the Canadian Academic Tundra: Trials and Tribulations*. Ed. Elena Hannah. Montreal: McGill-Queens University Press, 2002. 183-188.

Chapter Four: O'Reilly, Andrea. "'Ain't That Love?': Antiracism and Racial Constructions of Motherhood." *Everyday Acts Against Racism: Raising Children in a Multiracial World*. Ed. Maureen Reddy. Washington: Seal Press, 1996. 88-99.

Chapter Five: O'Reilly, Andrea. "Across the Divide: Contemporary Anglo-American Feminist Theory on the Mother–Daughter Relationship." *Redefining Motherhood: Changing Identities and Patterns*. Eds. Andrea O'Reilly and Sharon Abbey. Toronto: Second Story Press, 1998. 69-91.

Chapter Six: O'Reilly, Andrea. "'A Politics of the Heart': African-American Womanist Thought on Mothering." *Mother Outlaws: Theories and Practices of Empowered Mothering*. Ed. Andrea O'Reilly. Toronto: Women's Press, 2004. 171-191.

Chapter Seven: O'Reilly, Andrea. "A Politics of the Heart: Toni Morrison's Theory of Motherhood as a Site of Power and Motherwork as Concerned with the Empowerment of Children." *Toni Morrison and Motherhood: A Politics of the Heart*. Andrea O'Reilly. New York: SUNY Press, 2004. 26-47.

Chapter Eight: O'Reilly, Andrea, "In Black and White: Anglo- American and African-American Feminist Perspectives on Mothers and Sons." *Mothers and Sons: Feminism, Masculinity and the Struggle to Raise Our Sons*. Ed. Andrea O'Reilly, New York: Routledge, 2001. 91-119.

Chapter Nine: O'Reilly, Andrea. "A Mom and Her Son: Thoughts on Feminist Mothering." *Journal of the Association for Research on Mothering* 2 (1) Toronto: ARM Press (Spring/Summer 2000): 179-193.

Chapter Ten: O'Reilly, Andrea. "'This is What Feminism Is : The Acting and Living ... Not Just the Told': Mentoring and Modeling Feminism." *Feminist Mothering* New York: SUNY Press, forthcoming 2006.

MEMBER OF SCABRINI GROUP

Québec, Canada
2006